Knights of the Razor

Knights of the Razor

Black Barbers in Slavery and Freedom

DOUGLAS WALTER BRISTOL, JR.

Johns Hopkins University Press
Baltimore

Printed in the United States of America on acid-free paper
2 4 6 8 9 7 5 3 1

Johns Hopkins Paperback edition, 2015

Johns Hopkins University Press
2715 North Charles Street
Baltimore, Maryland 21218-4363
www.press.jhu.edu

The Library of Congress has cataloged the hardcover edition of this book as follows:

Bristol, Douglas Walter, 1965–
Knights of the razor : black barbers in slavery and freedom /
Douglas Walter Bristol, Jr.
p. cm.
Includes bibliographical references and index.
ISBN-13: 978-0-8018-9283-7 (hbk. : alk. paper)
ISBN-10: 0-8018-9283-X (hbk. : alk. paper)
1. African American barbers—History. 2. Free African Americans—History. 3. African American businesspeople—History. 4. African American business enterprises—History. 5. United States—Race relations—History. I. Title.
HD8039.B32U6195 2009
646.7'2408996073—dc22 2008052303

A catalog record for this book is available from the British Library.

ISBN-13: 978-1-4214-1839-1
ISBN-10: 1-4214-1839-8

Special discounts are available for bulk purchases of this book. For more information, please contact Special Sales at 410-516-6936 or specialsales@press.jhu.edu.

Johns Hopkins University Press uses environmentally friendly book materials, including recycled text paper that is composed of at least 30 percent post-consumer waste, whenever possible.

Contents

Acknowledgments

As I reflect on the many debts I have incurred while writing this book, my mind wanders to the movie *Barbershop*, a comedy about one Saturday at a black-owned shop on Chicago's South Side. Calvin, who recently inherited the shop from his father, has become frustrated with the challenges and limited financial prospects of operating a small inner-city business. Early in the movie, he glances up at a large Ernie Barnes–style mural depicting his father and says, "I don't know how you did it—stuck it out all these years." Calvin, having impulsively mortgaged the shop to finance several disastrous get-rich-quick schemes, faces foreclosure and sells the business to a loan shark. When he tells Eddie, the oldest barber in the shop, what he has done, his father's old friend delivers a homily on the barbershop. After berating the younger generation for its lack of values, Eddie holds up Calvin's father as a model of rectitude. "Now your father—he had integrity, he believed in somethin'." That something turns out to be concern for his fellow man: "He believed that a little ol' hair cut could change how a man was feelin' that day." Calvin objects, noting that his father died with little money to show for his efforts. "Boy," Eddie replies, "he might not 'a' had money, but he was rich with advice, encouragement. He was so rich he invested in people. You think I was the only one he ever gave a job to? The man gave every knucklehead in Chicago a job, a chance to be somebody—a licensed professional barber."[1] After hearing this speech, Calvin finally understands his father and why he enjoyed owning this barbershop. A series of madcap plot developments leads to Calvin's winning back his shop and paying off his debts, so the movie has a happy ending.

When I began this book, I was like Calvin in many ways. I was frustrated with the challenges of writing a dissertation and the limited prospects of the academic job market. I was dazzled by academic fads and saw little profit in old-fashioned social history. I wondered at the fortitude of my mentors, knowing they had toiled for years to produce their books. Although there was no one person who led me to an epiphany through an impassioned speech like Eddie's, many people helped me learn what really mattered. The late Marie Perinbaum instilled in me the belief that I had something important to say; she did this by spending countless hours with me in her office, demanding that I articulate my ideas forcefully. The students in my African American history courses at Coppin State College in Baltimore's inner-city taught me that being a historian is about helping people draw strength and wisdom from their past. My dissertation advisor, Ira Berlin, a man rich in advice and encouragement, invested heavily in me, giving a knucklehead the chance to become a professional historian through a meticulous tutorial in how to write history and his support when I looked for a job. Finally, the black barbers who are the subject of this book inspired me as well. While I searched for barbers in hundreds of reels of microfilmed census returns, I first thought that I was looking for needles in a haystack; but over time, I realized that panning for gold would be a better metaphor, given the charm, force of personality, and sheer grit that it took for these men to succeed. Every historian should be so lucky as to find such a story.

Taking the next step, producing a finished book, required the help of many individuals and institutions. I am fond of bragging that I had the best dissertation committee at the University of Maryland. In addition to Ira Berlin, they were James Gilbert, Alfred Moss, Carla Peterson, and David Sicilia, and they labored to save me from error and to broaden my horizons. I am particularly grateful to David for introducing me to business history and getting me involved professionally in the field. While at Maryland, I received generous financial support to begin my research from the History Department and from the Committee on Africa and the Americas. I also learned much from my fellow graduate students, especially Harvey Cohen, Susan Malka, Rennie Scott-Childress, Rebecca Shurberg, and Jon Shurberg. While at Coppin State College, my colleagues Bettye Gardner, Larry Martin, Pat May, and Cynthia Neverdon-Morton took an unusual interest in a visiting professor's work, sharing citations and methodological tips along with giving me the chance to present my work. The leaders in the study of black business history, Juliet E. K. Walker and Robert Weems, have served as friends and mentors for a decade, and they chaired or commented on numerous conference panels that allowed me to refine my ideas. Throughout this time, the man who led me to the study of African American history, my Master's thesis advisor, Loren Schweninger, and his wife Pat became good friends to whom I could always look for encouragement. At the Johns Hopkins University Press, Bob Brugger tirelessly championed my work and patiently waited when setbacks in the aftermath of Hurricane Katrina slowed my progress on the manuscript; then Anne Whitmore helped turn that manuscript into a book.

My past and present colleagues in the History Department at the University of Southern Mississippi have supported this project with advice, encouragement, and help. I sharpened my ideas through valuable conversations with Doug Chambers, Eric Nelson, and Pat Smith. Louis Kyriakoudes and Andy Wiest helped me navigate the process of finishing a first book. Both my former chair, Chuck Bolton, and my current chair, Phyllis Jestice, gave me course releases at critical moments, and Phyllis generously volunteered to proofread the entire manuscript. I am also indebted to Associate Provost Pat Joachim for providing me with a new laptop when I really needed one and to the interlibrary loan staff of Cox Library.

I was able to make the leap from dissertation to book manuscript during my time as a summer postdoctoral fellow at the Smithsonian Institution's National Museum of American History. I am indebted to the helpful staff there for making me aware of entirely new types of research materials and for the feedback they provided during the two times that I presented my research at the museum's colloquium. In addition, I benefited from fascinating conversations with Pete Daniel and Faith Ruffin at the Smithsonian. I had similar experiences when I was a John Hope Franklin Fellow at the Special Collections Division of Perkins Library at Duke University.

Archives and historical repositories were key to completing this book. I am grateful to the staff at the following institutions. In Mobile: the City Archives, the Mitchell Archives at the Historic Mobile Preservation Society, the Local History and Genealogy Division of the Mobile Public Library, and the University of South Alabama Archives. In Philadelphia: the City Archives and the Historical Society of Pennsylvania. In Washington, D.C.: the George Meany Labor Center, the Library of Congress, the Moorland-Spingarn Research Center at Howard University, the National Archives, the McKeldin Library and the Samuel Gompers Project at the University of Maryland, and the Wirtz Library at the U.S. Department of Labor.

Friends and family have been a source of strength while I finished this book. The example of my mother and father, both academics, inspired me to go to graduate school in the first place, and they sustained me with their love while I was there. I could always count on my brother, David, for encouragement and unflagging interest in my work. The same is true of my extended family, particularly Ann, Dolly, Jim, John, and Trish. As I finished the book, I appreciated the respite of good company with my friends Jane Alford, Ted and Margene Dawson, Sandra Farve, Pat Robinson, Christine Spears, Kathy and Roy Troendle, and yes, even you, Bradley. Last and most importantly, my long-term partner Dwight Isaacs supported me from the inception of this project through both the good times and the rocky patches. He had greater faith in me than I did in myself and never grew tired of my borrowing his ear to try out an idea. I could not have done it without him.

Knights of the Razor

Introduction

With a flick of the wrist, nineteenth-century black barbers could have slit the throats of the white men they shaved. The ritual of white men being shaved by black barbers, commonplace throughout the United States before the twentieth century, illustrated the tensions at the heart of race relations. As the observation of one astonished English visitor made clear, the potential menace of the black man's razor held a distinctive appeal to white American men. He wrote, "Nothing struck me more forcibly than an American under the razor. . . . Shrinking usually from the touch of a nigger as from the venomed tooth of a serpent, he here is seen . . . placing his throat at his mercy." While no record exists of a black barber behaving like Sweeney Todd, stories circulated that reminded white customers of the threat. In one such account, from New Bern, North Carolina, a local physician, Hugh Jones, entered a barbershop, sat in the barber's chair, placed his revolver on the counter, and told Brister, the slave barber, that, if Brister were to cut him, he would be shot. Brister calmly shaved the man without a nick. Afterward, another customer asked Brister if his hand had trembled while he served Dr. Jones. The barber replied that, quite the opposite, he had remained calm because he "had made his mind up to save his own life by cutting the throat of Dr. Jones, if it became necessary."[1] By expressing a readiness to protect his own life, Brister contradicted the stereotype of the fawning slave. This scene offers a new vantage point for examining race relations. From barbershops where white men relaxed while black men stropped their razors to a finely honed edge comes an unparalleled wealth of historical detail that helps clarify the meaning of race in the nineteenth century.

A black barber shaving a white customer in his Richmond shop. Note the proximity of the barber's razor to his customer's jugular vein. (By Eyre Crowe, from the *Illustrated London News*, March 9, 1861, vol. 38, p. 207; courtesy of Special Collections, University of Virginia Library, Charlottesville.)

Black barbers accomplished far more than challenging stereotypes; they used their trade to navigate the forbidding terrain of a racist country. In colonial and revolutionary America, slave barbers parlayed close ties to masters and a familiarity with highbrow culture into opportunities to gain their freedom and to own barbershops. They consolidated their hold over the trade in the early Republic by exploiting the stigma that white men increasingly associated with personal service. And, as was true for their counterparts in maritime work, their trade made them relatively fortunate for black men of the time.[2] They worked in pleasant indoor environments at a time when most black men could find only sporadic employment in physically demanding, outdoor jobs. In spite of restrictive laws and white discrimination, they operated increasingly lavish barbershops on Main Streets throughout the nation, prospering in Boston and San Francisco as well as in Baltimore and Charleston.

Black barbers came to occupy a unique place in American society. Even though other skilled trades excluded black men during the antebellum period, black barbers competed against white barbers for white customers, and they won, dominating the upscale tonsorial market serving affluent white men. They formed close, if unequal, personal relationships with their customers that gave them unparalleled access to the white elite. Although sectional tensions in the late 1850s and the subsequent Civil War threatened to unravel their achievements, black barbers recovered quickly, moving into the forefront of Reconstruction politics, where they served as emissaries between the races. They continued in this role even as the nation's commitment to racial equality faded during the Gilded Age. Meanwhile, they took their first-class barbershops to new heights of opulence that placed their businesses at the apex of black enterprise. As race relations deteriorated at the end of the nineteenth century, they reinvented their traditions to serve the growing black population emerging in the cities, establishing major corporations and creating the modern-day black barbershop. Barbering, in short, allowed black men to transform themselves from slaves into businessmen and leaders.

The history of black barbers also sheds light on the daily experience of living with prejudice. As James Baldwin observed, the stereotypes that white men and women created obscured the identity of the black people serving them. Baldwin contended that this suited African Americans, who remained enigmatic deliberately. Speaking of these black servants from the perspective of white people, he wrote, "they had a life—their own, perhaps a better life than ours—and they would never tell us what it was." Many prominent black barbers, however, expressed their innermost thoughts in books, diaries, letters, newspaper articles, and speeches. These sources provide a rare opportunity to peer behind this veil and gain insight into the question that Baldwin raised about their dual lives, namely, "What depths of contempt, what heights of indifference, what prodigies of resilience, what untamable superiority allowed them so vividly to endure, neither perishing nor rising up in a body to wipe us from the earth." When black barbers were in personal service to white men, they had to project a cheerful subservience and repress any anger they felt over how they were treated. The close contact, necessitating scrupulous attention to the conventions of racial etiquette that all African Americans found humiliating, magnified their experience of racism. Consequently, they possessed to an acute degree what W. E. B. DuBois labeled "double consciousness," "always looking at one's self through the eyes of others, . . . measuring one's soul by the tape of a world that looks on in amused contempt and pity."[3]

Black barbers dealt with white contempt by developing an empowering group identity based on their trade. In their own view, they were knights of the razor, gallants with a rapier wit that saw American society through jaundiced eyes. Barbering grew out of the courts of European aristocracy, lending the trade positive connotations that black men appropriated for their own purposes. Rather than seeing themselves as despised menials occupying a marginal economic niche, black barbers conceived of themselves as heirs to a tradition that made them men of the world. The self-esteem gained from being knights of the razor partially liberated them from the snare of double consciousness by allowing them to grasp its corollary, which one scholar has described as "a unique insight into the vulnerable and unfulfilled soul" of white men. Black barbers peered into the eyes of white customers and gained an awareness of white insecurities that prevented them from being snarled in the measuring tape that white men used to judge African Americans.[4] Their self-esteem also gave black barbers the confidence to set their own course and navigate the many pitfalls that racism created for ambitious black men. Their achievements in business, however, represented only a means to an end, for they sought to establish a basis for a black middle-class identity.

Nineteenth-century black barbers developed a conception of respectability based on economic independence and the virtues associated with small businessmen. Unlike most of the black elite, black barbers met objective economic standards for middle-class status, if only as members of the petite bourgeoisie of artisans and shopkeepers. As long as affluent white men kept coming to their shops, they could afford to let their wives remain at home, educate their children, and serve as deacons of their churches—in short, they could enjoy the trappings of middle-class respectability.[5] Like other small businessmen, white as well as black, they had conservative goals. They wanted to maintain their independence, provide decent jobs for other African Americans, and pass something on to their children. They also had conservative views about race relations insofar as their pessimism led them not to expect much. Based on their experience in the workplace, they did not believe that racial integration was at hand, so they promoted separatism and self-help. This did not mean that they relinquished their claim on the American Dream.

With their good reputation, thrift, and work ethic they were conspicuously upstanding members of society, or at least of their own community. This status, along with their relative wealth, made them prominent in the African American community. They sought and achieved this higher status and the rights that came with it. As successful entrepreneurs, they had the leisure and the money to pursue leadership positions within a host of organizations, including churches, fraternal orders, and the mutual aid societies established by black barbers. Just as many black leaders stepped out from behind the barber's chair as down from the pulpit or away from the editor's desk.

Their leadership exhibited the common touch that came from working with one's hands. No matter how many employees they had, black barbershop owners attended to their best customers personally, and they worked alongside their employees. They took pride in their manual labor, celebrating their skill with a razor. They also disputed the menial character of service work by celebrating their knack for handling temperamental white customers. Within their own ranks, the knights of the razor took little notice of differences of wealth and skin color, attesting to a brotherhood forged out of a shared work culture. Their social network, moreover, expanded from their homes and shops to include a broad circle of family, friends, and neighbors. Within these communities they demonstrated a leadership that balanced a sympathetic understanding of life's travails against a relentless drive for self-improvement. Despite all of the compromises black barbers had to make, the African American community welcomed their guidance, which can still be seen in their legacy, the modern black barbershop.

Time and place, however, decisively shaped what type of leadership black barbers could offer. When they were slaves, they often served as a plantation lieutenant for their master, enforcing his discipline over other slaves even as they thwarted their master's authority. The circumstances of black barbers diverged after the American Revolution. By 1820, slavery had died out in the North and the Cotton Kingdom had expanded into the Old Southwest. Depending on whether a black barber called the North, the upper South, or the lower South home, he enjoyed different freedoms and pursued different strategies. As an expanding slave society in the lower South threatened the independence of free African Americans, black barbers from the region embraced the planter ideal. Their northern counterparts, in sharp contrast, plunged first into the colonization movement and then into the abolition movement. Over time, civil rights activism supplanted barbering as the touchstone of their identity. Black barbers in the upper South avoided this division of loyalties between their trade and larger racial issues; instead, they struggled to reconcile their work with their roles at home and in their local community, making their trade brotherhood into a fraternal order that nurtured young men and forged strong bonds within their ranks.

After the Civil War, regional differences continued to shape the experience of black barbers. Black barbers in the lower and upper South maintained their ties to the white elite at the same time that their northern counterparts increasingly refused to serve white customers. Those who served white customers acquired new ones wherever they moved in the United States. Black barbers in the upper

South continued to identify with and hold leadership roles in their African American communities. As leaders, they vigorously advocated separatism and self-help. This stance legitimated the segregation they maintained in their shops, but it also expressed a conviction that spending money where one lived and exercising strong moral values would make African Americans more independent.

Regardless of region, black barbers' status raises some troubling questions. Although a sympathetic examination of the African American community and its culture has focused on resistance to oppression, the search for agency of that resistance may have gone too far. Scholars looking for evidence of cultural autonomy and individual resilience have often emphasized black gestures of defiance without considering the extent to which those gestures alleviated the plight of African Americans; they have underestimated the difficulty of challenging racism.[6] Throughout the nineteenth century, black and white people interacted on profoundly unequal terms. African Americans lived in a democracy that refused to acknowledge them as citizens, while their government worked actively to subordinate them to white Americans, who consequently received license to treat black men and women largely as they saw fit. Much worse, white Americans tended to view African Americans through the lens of dehumanizing stereotypes that denied them the compassion that would have come from seeing them as real people. Some white Americans, projecting their fantasies and fears onto their black countrymen, attempted to cast the blame for their own sins onto African Americans. The resulting situation left black Americans little room to maneuver and threatened terrible consequences for missteps. Hence, although the knights of the razor possessed an occupational identity that provided a buffer against some of the tribulations of racism, the stark realities of their lives required making compromises that they regretted but saw as unavoidable.

These compromises explain why nineteenth-century black barbers have not received their due from historians.[7] When viewed outside their historical context, black barbers seem to have accepted and accommodated racial inequality. With the exception of a small group of northern black men, they legitimated segregation by refusing to serve black customers in their shops. They reinforced the association of African Americans with servitude by applying their entrepreneurial talents to personal service. Worst of all, they seemed to validate the racial stereotypes of white customers by playing demeaning roles in their barbershops. These behaviors made it appear that, like Esau, they had sold their birthright for a mess of pottage. Yet, to judge them harshly ignores how limited their choices were. Although a barber's apprenticeship included learning the three Rs, most had no formal education, and no prominent nineteenth-century black barber saw the inside of a college as a student. Racial discrimination closed most other trades to them, and a lack of capital precluded other lines of business for all but a handful. Faced with poverty so grinding that the modern concept of the underclass is inadequate to describe it, a group of black men embraced barbering as a good opportunity and made the most of it.

The reluctance of historians to address this lack of alternatives, to understand what went into making the sausage, deserves some reflection. Quite understandably, scholars have favored uncompromising black leaders such as Frederick Douglass and Ida B. Wells because their lives compellingly demonstrated the triumph of character and principle over adversity. Moreover, as the better scholarship has persuasively shown, they claimed virtues such as individualism and respectability in a bid to turn the tables on white Americans by grounding their appeal for justice in the ideologies of Victorian America. Yet white Americans, by and large, failed to view African Americans in a new light, no matter what incentive black leaders provided. Elite black activists who advocated diminishing the stigma of race by observing the social norms of the middle class ended up with a Sisyphean task: they had to uplift their race without having the power to overcome the barriers that discrimination placed in front of their goal.[8]

The history of black barbers sheds new light on African American life during slavery and segregation. In particular, the lives of black barbers reveal an ongoing negotiation with their white customers over race relations. These men catered to white vanity in order to wrest from a repressive society a significant degree of control over their own lives. They made these sacrifices at work in order to achieve gains at home. Forced to display a public identity for the white man to see while safeguarding a private identity for themselves, they adopted a model of separate spheres to rationalize their lives.[9] Whether this strategy made black barbers accomplices in their own oppression is for the reader to decide. Either way, they went through life with their eyes wide open, striving to negotiate the best deal they could with white men and offering few apologies for it. They projected a confident self-image that allowed them to cross lines of color and class to achieve remarkable success in businesses far removed from black neighborhoods. Dominating the upscale end of their trade, their barbershops prospered and, more importantly, persisted. Their traditions survived into the twentieth century, when the opportunity to serve black customers lifted from their shoulders the burden of negotiating race relations. Their twenty-first-century heirs remain central figures in the African American community. By successfully navigating a unique course across the dangerous terrain of nineteenth-century-American racial history, black barbers exemplified grit and ingenuity.

CHAPTER ONE

The Origins of Black Barbers

On August 15, 1743, Benjamin Catton led an African boy into the courthouse of York County, Virginia, complying with a law that required slave owners to establish the age of imported slaves for the purposes of taxation. The justices decided that the boy was ten years old, and a clerk recorded the boy's age along with the name his owner had given him, Caesar. As it had been only two months since the boy had climbed out of the hold of a slave ship from West Africa, he probably did not understand the conversation between the white men in the courthouse that day, much less that his legal identity had just been established by them. His name, a trifling joke on Catton's part, denied his African heritage; the legal transaction marked him as human property. Thirty-six years later, in 1779, another group of white officials, legislators in the Virginia Assembly, gave the now middle-aged slave from Africa a new name, this time one of his own choice. The legislators enacted a bill granting his freedom and establishing his new legal name, from that day forward, as John Hope. Richly symbolic, the name he chose expressed both his desire to break with his slave past and his optimism for the future. Hope lived to the ripe old age of sixty-seven, and having accumulated a small amount of property, he left a will. In that document, he referred to himself as Caesar Hope, a hybrid name combining the two parts of his identity. While his wife and children knew him as John Hope, the influential white people who had given him his freedom and provided his livelihood called him Barber Caesar.[1]

The evolution of Caesar Hope's name reflects the changing experience of slaves in the colonial and revolutionary periods. Unlike the first two or three generations of bondsmen in mainland North America, whose anglicized names and surnames showed that they had been incorporated into colonial life, their successors bore names more appropriate for livestock than people, an expression of the contempt their masters felt for them. The evolution of slave names attests to a fundamental shift in power with the arrival of the plantation regime. Around the Chesapeake Bay and in the South Carolina Lowcountry, second and third generation slave owners amassed great estates. These men, born to mastery, expected unquestioning obedience from their dependents, whether they were sons and daughters or slaves. In a largely successful effort to maintain their authority, they remained aloof from all but a handful of their slaves. The black men and women favored with their master's attention had a chance to enjoy privileges if they could endure intensely claustrophobic relationships with their patriarchal owners.[2] By embracing an identity as Barber Caesar, the ambitious freedman distinguished himself in the eyes of white colonists from the largely anonymous mass of slaves.

The American War of Independence shifted the balance of power among the residents of the colonies, giving slaves new choices. While between five and six thousand slaves residing in Virginia fled across British lines early in the war, Caesar remained with his owner. His decision proved wise. In appreciation for the slave's fidelity, his widowed mistress freed Caesar, and he chose the name, John Hope. Yet, he had to relocate before he could begin living as a free man. He did not begin using his new name in official records until he moved to Richmond and established his own household, which suggests that he realized his aspiration for greater independence only after he established a separate family life. To sustain this new life, the free black barber relied on the courts to recognize the freedom of the family members he had purchased and emancipated, an illustration of the limits on the gains that African Americans made during the revolutionary era.[3] The compromise he made by referring to himself as Caesar Hope in his last will and testament is exemplary of how he had reconciled the demands of white society with his own aspirations. Successful black barbers like John Caesar Hope had developed an effective strategy for straddling two worlds and prospering.

As they moved from slavery and poverty to freedom and modest prosperity, black barbers formed an identity that allowed slave barbers to take advantage of their masters' own social aspirations and establish a privileged status not unlike that occupied by European barbers in the early modern era. This process of acculturation involved becoming fluent in English and acquiring a working knowledge of Anglo-American customs and society, in order to interact confidently with members of the dominant race. The type of work a slave performed largely determined how much opportunity he or she had to become versed in European culture. A slave barber, generally called a "waiting man" in colonial America, served his master personally, and the slave's immersion in the master's affairs provided a wide-ranging education in the ways of the colonial elite. In the rapidly changing new world of colonial North America, the masters were also engaged in forming an identity, laying claim to a social status within the British Empire commensurate with their economic and political influence. Merchants and planters asserted that they formed a colonial aristocracy by demonstrating their gentility, an ideology that naturalized social distinction through displays of refinement.[4] As essential ancillaries to gentlemen, personal servants exercised considerable leverage over their masters, a circumstance that was magnified in the households of upwardly mobile slave owners. The genteel code represented an external standard of behavior, one beyond the master's control. Dependent on their slaves to uphold their social pretensions according to rules not of their making, masters had no choice but to recognize that they were beholden to their slave barbers.

The American Revolution fundamentally challenged the genteel social order, with mixed results for slave barbers. By setting into motion forces that soon created a substantial free black population, the Revolution provided circumstances that allowed slave barbers to become free men. The wave of egalitarianism receded quickly, in large part due to the founding of the Cotton Kingdom, which spread inexorably across the Old Southwest, the slave states acquired through the Louisiana Purchase and Indian removal. Paradoxically, the expansion of slavery created a demand for skilled slaves in the South that bolstered the position of black barbers. The ideology of the American Revolution, republicanism, had the same effect. Because material independence was made a prerequisite for citizenship, white men avoided labor that contained the least trace of dependence; and occupations such as barbering which were associated with servants quickly became anathema for white citizens. These republican scruples created a lucrative occupational niche for black barbers even as republican ideology frustrated their quest for equality. Despite their having earned a degree of status based on their knowledge of gentility, the ideology that guaranteed them work branded them as degraded. Substituting race for rank, supporters of the Revolution elevated all white males by subordinating all black males.[5] Moreover, the stigma attached to personal service stayed with black barbers, who continued to serve whites long after Emancipation, tainting their accomplishments in the eyes of many African Americans, who questioned their credibility as leaders. Hence, their success came at the expense of humiliating compromises necessitated by the overwhelming power of white America.

In no facet of black barbering was the influence of white men greater than in their privilege of choosing which slaves would have the opportunity to learn the barbering trade. Because masters typically assigned recently enslaved Africans to agricultural labor on remote plantations, where they could more easily be controlled, Caesar Hope had a lucky escape from a life of drudgery when Benjamin Catton decided to purchase him. The needs of Catton's growing business ventures partially explain his willingness to take on an unskilled young slave. Already the operator of a tavern in Yorktown, Virginia, Catton expanded into the hair trade two years after he bought Caesar. In an advertisement informing readers of the *Virginia Gazette* that he had recruited three of the most accomplished wigmakers in London to work in his shop, Catton promised that, in addition to finding a selection of wigs at his establishment, "Ladies and Gentlemen may have their hair cut in the most fashionable manner." Catton had acquired the services of an indentured servant, but the Irish teenager had run off in 1746, underscoring the merits of purchasing a slave for life. Other considerations, such as appearance and deportment, may have influenced Catton to look favorably on Caesar. These were important considerations in house or personal servants. For example, when George Washington was preparing to retire from the presidency and return to Mount Vernon, he wrote his steward a letter evaluating which of his slaves would be appropriate for employment as personal servants. Although he considered the children of one of his female slaves "among the best disposed negros I have," he expressed concern whether any of them would look the part. Whatever Catton's reasons were for selecting Caesar, he ensured that his slave learned how to use a razor and scissors well, as evidenced by the high price paid for Barber Caesar when, following the death of his master, he was sold.[6]

Over the next thirty years of working as a slave barber, Caesar had the opportunity to learn about the white society in which he had landed. Jobs such as barbering allowed slaves a rare chance to interact with a cross-section of the white community, giving them a chance to understand Anglo-American culture and the white psyche. At work, over meals, at leisure, Caesar came to know the ways of the Virginians, British immigrants, and household slaves who lived in Catton's household, while the simple fact of living in an urban environment dramatically increased his exposure to the wider world. Since his master owned a business, Caesar ran errands that took him to all corners of town. Barbering, however, provided the finest school for learning the ins and outs of colonial Virginia. The proximity of Yorktown to Williamsburg, the colonial capital, meant that Barber Caesar became acquainted with local notables such as Thomas Jefferson, who recorded paying nine pence to Caesar for a shave in 1769.[7] Given this kind of clientele, during the growing crisis with Britain, Caesar undoubtedly overheard heated political discussions, especially since many pivotal events transpired within a few miles of his shop. Royal Governor Lord Dunmore, who sought to intimidate the patriots into submission by offering to free any slave that would take up arms in his service, took refuge on a ship anchored near Yorktown and sailed past the community when he fled Virginia in 1775. Through working in this environment, Caesar gained an understanding of the white colonists that led directly to his manumission and the establishment of his own barbershop in Richmond.

The typical path to barbering and freedom for enslaved men began in their masters' household, where work as a personal servant exposed them to the changing Anglo-American culture. By the 1690s, wealthy American colonists had begun adapting the cultural practices of the European aristocracy to the circumstances of the New World, importing genteel culture in pursuit of higher status. Whether they erected brick mansions or, as in the case of Ben Franklin, merely ate their porridge out of a china bowl with a silver spoon, America's great merchants and planters brought with them or began to acquire the trappings of genteel living. In some cases, people who could never have aspired to a higher social position in Europe, by learning new manners and adopting different styles of presentation, transformed themselves from rude provincials into cosmopolitan members of "polite society." Their emulation of aristocrats, notwithstanding the lack of court society, ensured the transmission of genteel traditions to North America. When young George Washington laboriously copied out 110 "Rules of Civility," he was acquainting himself with precepts for behavior that dated back to the Renaissance.[8]

At the core of genteel values lay a conviction that outward behavior and appearance reflected the inner self. A spiritual divide was thought to exist between genteel people and common folk, with the former reputed to possess finer sensibilities and a more refined taste for beauty while the latter, supposedly lacking well-developed intellectual or emotional faculties, stood lower on the scale of human development. These distinctions justified inequality by presenting class differences as the natural order of things. To be acknowledged by others as genteel, therefore, validated one's claim to membership in the ruling class. Hair assumed a prominent role in displays of gentility. European monarchs established the link between hair and hierarchy, when members of royal courts emulated the way their sovereign had his locks and whiskers trimmed. By the eighteenth century, hair fashions had grown sophisticated enough to allow for variety, but a devotion to hierarchy asserted itself through the identification of certain hairstyles with certain professions. In 1782, James Stewart wrote, "We hear of the clerical, the physical, and the tie peruke [type of wig] for the man of the law, the brigadier or major for the army or navy. The merchant, the man of business and of letters were distinguished by the grave full-bottom or more moderate tie, neatly curled, the tradesman by the snug bob or natty scratch, the country gentleman by the natural fly and hunting peruke."[9] The American definition of rank and status through hairstyles reflected how Europeans adapted to social relations in the New World by embracing the values of Old World gentility. Barbers obviously played an important role in helping the socially ambitious maintain a genteel appearance. One seventeenth-century English critic of this fact opined, "May I not truly say of too many . . . that the barber is their chaplain; his shop, their chapel; the looking-glass, their Bible; and their hair . . . their God?"[10]

Polite society also embraced barbers for their reputation as witty, literate *bons vivants*, which flowed out of their need to entertain customers. Authors as far back as Plutarch commented on the pleasant nature of beard trimmers. Yet, this demeanor resulted, to a large extent, from the barbers' ability to create an atmosphere in which courtiers and the upper classes felt at home. Drawn by the opportunity to relax and exchange ideas, poets, merchants, and intellectuals joined the crowd, leading one barber to boast that the barbershop was "a place almost within the precincts of the Temple of Learning." The literary talents of several famous tonsorial artists burnished this reputation.[11]

Nonetheless, because they served others, barbers were excluded from the ranks of the genteel, which made their customers often treat them with contempt. This was a sore spot for barbers. In popular lore by and about barbers, expressions of self-pity and disappointment abound. One poem, for instance, laments that "shaving is a helpless trade." The dissatisfaction of barbers stemmed, in part, from their trade's low status; the barbers' guild in London was classed with those of executioners, gravediggers, dog catchers, musicians, and actors.[12] In a series of three plays written on the eve of the French Revolution, Pierre Augustin Caron de Beaumarchais captured these tensions with his central character, Figaro, the barber of Seville. Beaumarchais had one character describe Figaro in a manner that reveals similarities between the stereotypes about European barbers and those about American waiting men: "Never angry, always in a sunny mood, devoting himself to the joy of the moment, worrying about the future as little as he sorrows about the past. Dashing."[13] The last characteristic attributed to Figaro—dashing—suggests a quality frequently overlooked in discussions about servants, whether black or white.

Figaro's appeal lies in his combination of refinement and rudeness. Possessing knowledge of social etiquette and genteel living, Figaro is a commoner who moves in the best society. His awareness of transgressing social boundaries leads him to hubris, which irritates his superiors and creates an excuse for abusing him. Even though he retaliates against his aristocratic tormentors with a sharp wit and a glib tongue, it sometimes fails to salve his wounded pride. Figaro sums up his resentment against the ruling class in a soliloquy bemoaning his employer's attempts to seduce Figaro's fiancée. "Nobility, fortune, rank, influence," he declares, "they all make a man so proud! What have you ever done to earn such wealth? You took the trouble to be born. . . . Whereas me, my God! Lost in the obscurity of the herd, I needed more skill and know-how even to exist than it has taken to govern the Spanish Empire for the last hundred years."[14] The bond between Figaro and the count whom he serves—fraught with tension, lightened by humor and grudging respect, cemented by mutual dependence—sums up the social relations of European barbering during the seventeenth and eighteenth centuries.

Slaves who were waiting men performed the role of a barber, ensuring that their master looked his genteel best by polishing his boots, shaving his beard, and cutting his hair. Slave owners valued this last skill especially highly. Edward M'Crady praised his seventeen-year-old waiting man for being "an exceeding good hair dresser," while another Charleston slave owner boasted that his slave Cuffy could "shave and dress wigs very well." Robert Darnall praised the skills of his waiting man by explicitly comparing him to tonsorial professionals, claiming that he could "shave and dress a Wig as well as most Barbers." In addition to grooming their masters, waiting men also served variously as doctors, traveling companions, and general plantation lieutenants. The descriptions that slave owners left of their waiting men, moreover, reveal that these men had a penchant for acquiring a wide variety of skills. Consider this account by William Roane of Virginia of his waiting man Joe: "[He] understands house business, as well as the management of horses. He is a good shoemaker, and can do many other things, can read and write tolerably well." Once they had earned the trust of their master, waiting men also ran errands, allowing them to become familiar with the people and places in their neighborhood or even farther afield. One Virginia master said that his waiting man was "well acquainted with the lower Parts of the Country, having constantly rode with me for some years past"; that master frequently sent his man "upon Business" to Williamsburg on his own. From their extensive interaction with white colonists, waiting men acquired such a command of English that it often drew comment from their masters. James Mercer commented that his waiting man Christmas was "very fluent of Speech" and spoke "with great Propriety." Similarly, Hamilton Ballantine noted that his waiting man spoke "good English," and Charles Yates said that his man was "very fluent in speech."[15]

Such accomplishments in a waiting man, however useful they might have been to plantation management, had to be accompanied by a degree of polish, because planters considered themselves to be aristocrats in need of a retinue. According to several planters, their waiting men took to high style so adroitly that they earned the right to be called genteel. Nineteen-year-old George, described as "genteel and well made" and "as complete a waiting boy as perhaps any on the continent," attired himself in fine clothes and routinely carried a pair of pistols. Similarly, Bacchus wore "plush blue breeches," a "fine cloth pompadour waistcoat, a clean white shirt," shoes adorned with silver buckles, and a "fine hat cocked in the Macaroni Figure." One planter even reported that, by the age of eighteen, his waiting man had accompanied him to England. As this example suggests, masters often encouraged sophistication in their waiting men. Henry Laurens, the president of the Continental Congress, parted with his waiting man Shrews-Berry so that the slave could tend to Laurens's son John while the latter served in the Continental Army, then stationed at Valley Forge. Apparently, Laurens feared that camp life might be making it difficult for his waiting man to be properly attired, for he told his son to ask "my old friend Shrews-Berry" whether a linen coat, waistcoat, and breeches would "be acceptable." If Shrews-Berry approved, his old master promised to send him the material and then the slave should "consult his Taylor."[16]

This familiarity between master and slave resulted from shared pastimes as well as from the services that waiting men provided. Philip Fithian, engaged as a tutor by a leading planter in colonial Virginia, grew exasperated with one of his young students, whose "genius" appeared to be betting on cockfights, "much in Company with the waiting Boys."[17] Because planters engaged in leisure activities such as cockfighting, horseracing, and hunting to distinguish themselves from small farmers and establish status within their ranks, the role that their waiting men played in these activities was vital to their masters and served to incorporate the servants further into the world of the colonial gentry. This knowledge of social etiquette and genteel fashion made waiting men the most completely acculturated slaves in the colonial period.

The ability to interact comfortably with powerful whites established distinctions between slaves. Scipio, a servant turned waterman, bragged that he could "go before gentlemen, for he had waited before his master in Council Chamber and was used to it." Because one of his crew members "did not know how to talk before white people," Scipio declared the man "a fool." Acculturation proved to be such a valuable asset that waiting men sometimes took great pains to display their refinement. In addition to wearing fine clothing in the European style, many waiting men styled and powdered their hair so it would resemble their owners' wigs. A Maryland waiting man named Jem wore "his own black Hair . . . tied in a Cue behind, or platted, and [arranged in] curls on each Side of his Face." An even more fashionable waiting man in South Carolina named Frank "dress[ed] the wool of his hair in a macaroni taste," imitating the exaggerated pompadours then stylish among English dandies. It is noteworthy that Frank alternated

Waiting man wearing his hair with a queue. Acculturated slaves, particularly waiting men, often displayed their cosmopolitanism by styling their hair in the latest genteel fashion. (Illustration by Benjamin Latrobe; courtesy of the Maryland Historical Society, Baltimore.)

between this hairstyle and wrapping his head in a handkerchief—the distinctive African headgear. There was much cultural diversity within colonial society, and waiting men grew fluent in multiple cultures; they did not simply assimilate Anglo-American culture. But Anglo-American society itself was in flux, changing rapidly.[18] Enslaved barbers and waiting men consequently found themselves in the unusual situation of learning about gentility even as their masters did.

Acculturation of black personal servants reduced the cultural differences between masters and slaves, fostering unusually close bonds. This process is particularly well documented in the diaries of one Virginia planter from 1752 to 1778. To Landon Carter, master of Sabine Hall, his waiting man Nassau not only served as his barber and boon companion, but Carter also delegated significant responsibilities to his slave. Nassau functioned as Carter's majordomo, counting and branding livestock and inspecting crops. That Carter esteemed the slave's judgment became apparent in a journal entry in which he wrote, "Dr. Nassau says he had seen much tobacco, and never saw any stand better." The honorific "Dr." reflected another of Nassau's valuable services. Describing Nassau as "the best bleeder about," the planter not only had his waiting man tend to his sick slaves but also had him treat, on occasion, his own children. At one point, Carter hired a white apothecary to help Nassau in his medical activities. Nassau evidently thought that his knowledge and position gave him a distinct place in the social hierarchy, which he demonstrated when he once refused to bleed one of Carter's overseers.[19]

According to Carter's detailed journal, Nassau also thought that his status gave him the right to defy his master. Slave owners confronted a paradox in their waiting men. While they wanted slaves to become acculturated in order to perform their job well, the process produced wily African American men capable of and willing to challenge their masters' authority. Knowing their master better than he would ever know them, waiting men and other domestic servants were well prepared to act stealthily. Nassau demonstrated his power by disguising the nature of a slave's illness so that he could treat the individual himself rather than have Carter prescribe a dose of one of his notorious purgatives. When one of Carter's slave overseers caught a runaway slave lying out in the woods near the plantation, he captured him after a brief struggle and, revealing the position Nassau occupied, turned over the other slave to Nassau. The waiting man attempted to cover up the runaway's altercation with the overseer, instead making it appear that the slave had returned voluntarily, in order to diminish his punishment, a fundamental subversion of Carter's mastery over his slaves.[20] By intervening on behalf of fellow slaves, Nassau also demonstrated that his status in the big house did not prevent him from identifying with the field hands living in the slave quarters. There was more to Nassau than met his master's eye.

The slaves who accommodated themselves the most thoroughly to the cultural norms of their masters received more autonomy,[21] but masters paid a price for this compliance. In the process of learning gentility, waiting men—like the fictional Figaro—helped themselves to some of their owner's power. Nassau demonstrated this ability in ways reminiscent of the animal tricksters featured in tales that came to America aboard the slave ships, stories in which the weak made use of the strong. Once, Nassau went for an unauthorized coach ride with his son, Nat. On an early spring day in 1770, Nat had driven Carter and his daughter to a nearby plantation for a celebration. Because Carter would have to leave earlier than his daughter, Nassau was instructed to bring Carter's horse to him at an appointed time. As Carter recorded the outcome in his diary, "I came home but without Nassau or Nat." Nassau, according to Carter, "mired my horse up to his saddle in crossing a marsh that none but a blind drunkard would ever venture upon and Mr. Nat [was] so engaged with boon companions as never to get my chariot." With no one to help him, an infuriated Carter extricated the horse from the mud himself and rode home. Several hours later the coach rolled up at Sabine Hall "with the drunken father and Son" inside, occupying the position that belonged to their master.[22]

Over years of making a show of conforming to his master's identity, or more accurately, serving as his alter ego, Nassau appeared to take Carter into his confidence, which explains why the experienced slave owner grew so outraged when his waiting man disobeyed him. Scholars have described a "culture of dissemblance" that created in black domestic servants "the appearance of disclosure, or openness about themselves and their feelings, while [they were] actually remaining an enigma to whites." Carter could determine what waiting men looked like and what skills they possessed, but he could not dictate the meaning of a slave's collaboration with him. As the old slave song put it:

> Got one mind for the white folks to see,
> 'Nother for what I know is me,
> He don't know, he don't know my mind.

Mastering gentility, in a certain sense, even reversed the balance of power between master and slave. Although historians of slavery have long appreciated that acculturation promoted resistance to white authority, none have considered specifically the impact of slaves' becoming versed in gentility, the ideology that naturalized their masters' class position. This gentrification, as it were, of slaves raises issues analogous to the ways in which slaves exploited their masters' patriarchy.[23] Since having a genteel waiting man validated Carter's credentials for gentility, he had a strong personal incentive to overlook Nassau's faults. However, Nassau's misbehavior called into question Carter's own self-image as a country squire presiding over contented villagers on his estate.

The centrality of a waiting man to his master's self-image explains why the fault that Carter found unforgivable in Nassau was not his sometimes flagrant disobedience but his prodigious drinking habit. At one point, Carter recorded in his journal that his waiting man had "not been sensibly sober one evening since this day fortnight." He also recorded the spectacle of Nassau crawling about the room one night. Rather than simply punishing Nassau for his nocturnal imbibing, Carter made reforming his slave into a personal crusade. He wrote, "I have threatened him, begged him, Prayed him, and told him the consequences if he neglected the care of one of the sick people; that their deaths through such want of care must be an evidence against him at the great and terrible day, talked a great deal to him in most religious and affectionate way." Contemplating his failure to change Nassau's ways prompted Carter to do a little soul-searching of his own. "I confess I have faults myself to be forgiven," he admitted. Yet Carter ultimately realized that Nassau seemed "resolved to drink in spight of me, and I believe in order to spight me." The battle over Nassau's drinking became a struggle for power.[24]

Nassau apparently thought that his accomplishments merited a fundamental change in his relationship to Carter, but Carter would not surrender his prerogatives as master. In 1768, Carter, having decided to sell his recalcitrant slave because he could no longer be "trusted," advertised for a replacement, only to change his mind. The bond linking the two men by then ran so deep—perhaps because, out of all of the people on Carter's plantation, only Nassau shared his vision of establishing a refined country house—that the eminent planter could not bear to part with him. Two years later, Carter recorded how torn he was by the struggle, writing in his journal, "I have been learning to do without [Nassau] though it has been but very badly yet I can bear it and I will." Yet, in the next sentence he wrote, Carter once again expressed hopes for Nassau's reformation: "And then perhaps by a course of punishment I may do the rascal some good."[25] But he did not, and their conflicts escalated.

Their most dramatic clash revealed that Carter and Nassau held fundamentally different worldviews. In September 1775, many slaves on Carter's plantation had taken ill, leaving him short-handed and ill-tempered. "I have hardly a servant to wait on me," he complained, "and the only [one] to assist my endeavours after humanity is drunken Nassau. Receiving word that an overseer required medical attention, he sent Nassau to care for his employee, but the waiting man failed to return. Carter raised the alarm, but "nobody could find him." After a while, someone found Nassau sleeping on the ground, "dead drunk." Carter's patience at an end, he "offered to give him a box on the ear." Nassau snapped and, according to Carter, "fairly forced himself against me. However I tumbled him into the Sellar and there had him tied Neck and heels all night." The next morning, Carter confronted Nassau with another servant prepared to beat him, "a fellow with an uplifted arm." Openly weeping, Nassau begged forgiveness and "called on God to record his solemn Vow that he never more would touch liquor." Carter then assumed the role of inquisitor: "I expostulated with him on his and his father's blasphemy of denying the wholly word of God in boldly asserting that there was neither a hell [n]or a devil." After talking about the promise for believers and the "eternal torments" for disbelievers, Carter forgave Nassau and released him, explaining his clemency as an expression of hope that he had saved a soul.[26]

Carter's forgiveness sprang from his understanding of patriarchy. Just as the planter submitted to God in hopes of receiving divine mercy, Carter believed that his slaves should offer him deference and obedience in return for his care and protection. Thus, the hierarchy on his plantation mirrored the divine order. Nassau paid lip service to his master's theology by invoking God in his vow to stop drinking. Yet, by openly questioning whether God judged people's souls after they died, the slave threatened to uproot his master's authority. Acculturation had provided Nassau with a weapon that Carter's roughly five hundred other slaves lacked; he knew enough about his master's culture to be profane as well as genteel. Although Carter had few equals for influence and wealth in Virginia, his enslaved waiting man had the power to spark an existential crisis within his master. The slave owner put himself into that position when he began relying on Nassau to help him realize his vision of himself as a benevolent, genteel patriarch. To appreciate the degree to which Carter was beholden to Nassau, one should consider that the slave owner wrote about him more than fifty times in his diary, a document in which he rarely mentioned slaves by name. Most of these entries concerned the slave's drinking, conveying a sense of despair over the loss of a disciple. The entries continued despite Nassau's vow, leading to further quarrels and to Nassau's running away at least twice in 1777, before he returned or was captured. During the next year, he ran away again, only to wind up back on Carter's plantation, where his up-and-down relationship with his master continued until Carter's death. One day Nassau reassured Carter that the heavy rain would not ruin his corn, while the next day he would get so drunk that he would "contradict . . . boldly" everything that Carter said.[27]

Another sign of the effect on waiting men of their acculturation and the special relationship they had with their masters was the frequency with which they attempted escape and their masters' responses to this behavior. Although waiting men constituted only a tiny portion of the slave population, they accounted for a disproportionate number of the skilled fugitives listed in runaway slave advertisements in South Carolina and Virginia between 1736 and 1801. The notices for them described slaves much like Nassau. Advertising for the return of "my Man Christmas," James Mercer acknowledged that he not only was "lusty, well made, and genteel" and shaved "extremely well" but also communicated in such an "artful" way that he could "invent a plausible Tale at a Moment's Warning." The skills of waiting men gave them many of the abilities needed for independence. Noting that Christmas had "lived a little short of [freedom] with me," James Mercer blamed himself for his slave's propensity for disobedience in terms reminiscent of Landon Carter's relationship with Nassau: "Having been too much indulged, and being very idle during my present Indisposition, he has grown wanton in Licentiousness, and several gross Acts of Behavior this Week past, are now completed by an Elopement last Monday night." The parallel to Nassau included drinking as the main issue of contention between Christmas and Mercer. At wit's end with his alcoholic slave, Mercer finally resolved to sell Christmas but still considered his waiting man entitled to privileges, such as being allowed to pick his new master. Wellins Calcott also expressed a propensity to indulge his runaway waiting man Bob. When Calcott placed a notice in a Charleston newspaper for Bob's return, he sent a message to his slave, saying, "As he went away for a small Fault, if he returns he may depend on being forgiven." Another runaway waiting man, named Romeo, bore striking similarities to Nassau as well. In addition to working as a slave doctor, Romeo had strong ties to the slave community and had forged passes and certificates of manumission for runaways.[28]

Romeo's master noted of his waiting man that "his upper lip turns up when he speaks or when he is alarmed, and shews his teeth." Far from being unusual, this kind of nervous tick was common in runaway waiting men. Half of all advertisements for runaway slave men in Virginia newspapers from 1736 to 1801 described slaves with a speech defect, and of those with skills in this group, more than half were either sailors or waiting men, the two groups of slaves who constantly dealt with a variety of whites in multiple environments. A waiting man went from being a plantation lieutenant directing other slaves one moment to blacking his master's shoes the next and moved between the closed world of the plantation and the diverse society in town. The tensions generated by the disparity between having to be adroit and confident and then having to display the self-effacement demanded by their masters found an outlet in drinking, speech defects, and running away.[29]

Fleeing the site of their enslavement was an active way for waiting men to cope with their dilemma. Unlike field hands, who typically stayed near their plantation when they ran away, waiting for their master's temper to cool, waiting men and other skilled slaves tended to seek out urban areas, where they could blend into the free black population. They often received indirect assistance from non-slave-owning whites, who employed them without asking too many questions. Virginia planter Alexander Strachan, in his advertisement for the fugitive slave, wrote that, since his runaway slave Matt's mode of speech was "very clever as a waiting-man, he may probably endeavour to hire himself to some Gentleman." Another runaway's owner guessed that his slave would "pretend to be free; and as he is well qualified for it, may attempt at a Distance to hire himself as a Waiting-Man, the station in which he has always been employed."[30]

Yet, although they were highly valued slaves whose masters actively sought their recovery, waiting men remained too proud of their gentility to abandon its trappings. Bacchus, Gabriel Jones's waiting man, was an especially pronounced example of this decision. Jones attested to his slave's ambition with the speculation that Bacchus, traveling under the name John Christian, would attempt to pass himself off as a free man, travel to Great Britain, and seek his freedom in the courts there, following the recent Somerset case, which had set a precedent of permitting slaves to sue for their emancipation. Given the wardrobe that he stole away with, Bacchus also apparently planned to make a splash in British society. Jones's advertisement detailed that Bacchus had packed up "two white Russian Drill Coats, one turned up in blue, the other quite plain and new, with white figured Metal Buttons, blue Plush Breeches, a fine Cloth Pompadour Waistcoat, two or three thin or Summer Jackets, sundry Pairs of white Thread Stockings, five or six white Shirts, two of them pretty fine, neat Shoes, Silver Buckles . . . a double-milled Drab Great Coat, and sundry other Wearing Apparel."[31] At a time when most white men possessed only a few homespun garments, the luggage alone required for this wardrobe would have been enough to attract suspicion, much less the spectacle of a black man wearing such finery, even if the garments were well-worn hand-me-downs from his master. However risky such display was, many waiting men followed the same course; practically all of the descriptions that survive of how waiting men dressed come from runaway slave advertisements. Their acculturation, while it did not end their identification with other slaves, did give waiting men a different set of ambitions and a distinctive strategy for achieving them.

Waiting men, for all of their unique qualities, never developed a group identity. Their small numbers partially explain this. Before the middle of the eighteenth century, most slave owners went without a personal servant, preferring to have all of their slaves working in the field. Robert "King" Carter, despite owning more than seven hundred slaves in 1732, did not employ a personal servant and had only one slave domestic working in his house. With the growth of a native-born slave population who acculturated more readily, and as the colonial elite grew more economically stable, it became socially mandatory for gentlemen to have slave personal servants attending them when they appeared in public. One of King Carter's grandsons exemplified this evolution of slave ownership; in 1791 he kept three housemaids, a cook, a waiter, and two coachmen among his slaves. While the quest for genteel status led to increases in the number of slaves working as personal servants, still only a small number of elite households could afford this extravagance. In Virginia, a third of all the personal servants working in the 1780s had been trained in the households of just forty planters. In South Carolina during the same decade, waiting men constituted only one percent of the entire slave work force in representative slave inventories for lowcountry plantations.[32] The lack of a strong occupational identity for waiting men made genteel ways all the more valuable to them, both as an asset in dealing with whites and as a symbol of their accomplishments as individuals. Yet, the gentility of waiting men remained bound to the context in which they served their master as his representative to the world, as an extension of his identity, unless they managed to run away successfully or entered a skilled trade.

Being reassigned to different jobs also prevented waiting men from developing an esprit de corps. At worst, an incorrigible waiting man might get sold to work on sugar plantations in the West Indies, while lesser miscreants would receive a demotion within the plantation hierarchy. One waiting man's proclivity for theft, according to his master Charles Yates, "induced me lately to put him to labour in the field," quite a change for a slave "brought up from his infancy [as] a house servant." The slave, an eighteen-year-old named Bob, "having never been used to hard work, or to go without shoes," apparently found being barefoot, dirty, and working with a hoe disagreeable, for he ran away. The death of a master and subsequent sale of his slaves could also force waiting men to learn new jobs, as in the case of Sam, whose new master employed him as a porter. For the most promising, however, waiting on the master often served as a youthful prelude to working as a skilled tradesman. Hercules, who "formerly used to wait on his Master in

Charlestown," after a move to the countryside began working as a plantation cooper. Such changes of occupation did not erase the impact of years as a waiting man. Adam had, by his master's account, become "a fine Shoemaker by Trade" but retained a high standard of dress. His owner's description of Adam's attire—a brown Holland coat, a check stuff jacket, and a pair of Russian drill breeches—shows that even in a workshop, Adam remained genteel in his appearance. Given the relative independence of slave artisans, the work was preferable to serving as a waiting man. Slave artisans received more lenient treatment from their masters because learning a skill and practicing it expertly could not be imposed by force. In order to earn money for their master, they traveled widely to find white customers, thereby escaping the close supervision that waiting men found so exasperating.[33]

Perhaps the most independent artisans were the barbers. They were also in the best position to observe the effect on slavery of the War of Independence. By 1775, the Revolution had come to Yorktown, Virginia, along with its potential to unravel slavery, and white colonists were dividing into opposing camps. That summer Caesar Hope probably heard excited conversations in his barbershop about Thomas Cox, a white man arrested on suspicion of fomenting a slave insurrection. Perhaps Hope watched Royal Governor Dunmore's ship as it sailed down the York River to the Chesapeake that fall to issue a proclamation, in November, freeing those slaves who would fight for the king. Local slave owners grew so alarmed that the *Virginia Gazette* took the unprecedented step of publishing a letter addressed directly to slaves, warning them of British treachery. Over the month of November, more than eight hundred slaves accepted Dunmore's offer and fled from their masters. By early December, the editor of the *Gazette* grew so desperate to stem the flow of runaways that he turned directly to the slave population for comment. The editor asked "an honest negro" what he thought of Dunmore's offer of liberty and quoted the slave as replying "that he did not know anyone foolish enough to believe [Dunmore], for if he intended" that slaves should be freed, "he ought to set his own free." The editor identified the commentator as "Caesar, the famous barber of York."[34] By virtue of his privileged position serving revolutionary leaders in his barbershop, Hope entered the historical record, not through an advertisement for a runaway, but as a respected pundit. His skill at his trade had made him a slave worthy of note.

Hope's skepticism about Dunmore's intentions reflected a conservative strategy for advancement within his occupation as a barber. In his early forties, which at the time was regarded as the end of one's laboring years, and with at least one child, Hope probably contemplated a sedate old age. His inclination to remain faithful to his master had served him well in the past, for he had managed to keep working on his own under three successive masters for more than twenty years. Not long after the Dunmore episode, his pragmatism was rewarded. The death of his master in 1779 prompted his widowed mistress, Susanna Riddell, to petition the Virginia House of Delegates for his freedom. It was an unusual request; the revolutionary legislature had freed only one other slave before Riddell sought permission to manumit Hope; yet thirty-two men in Yorktown endorsed the petition, including some of the most prominent residents in the community. The rationale offered in the petition demonstrated that conforming to white expectations paid benefits. In addition to the formulaic assertion of his "uniform good behavior," the petitioners recommended granting Hope freedom based on his "extraordinary skill . . . Industry, Sobriety, and Honesty." Hope had therefore capitalized on his public identity as a barber by exemplifying the qualities of a hard-working tradesman, which the petitioners stressed by saying that "in every instance [he] set so good an example to others, as to render himself worthy of the public regard."[35] Since almost all of the free black barbers who achieved some measure of prominence following the War of Independence had gained their freedom through the agency of their masters, Hope's strategy of finding an accommodation with the role created by white Americans documents the beginnings of a tradition of black barbering.

While black barbers such as Hope found fertile ground during the colonial and revolutionary period in that barbering had a limited appeal to white tradesmen, barbers of the period labored under the burdens of a small market for their services and condemnation for trafficking in "artifice." Gentility, and the consequent need for barbers, only flourished where sufficient numbers of refined people lived to make possible the formal dinners, balls, and tea parties that occupied the leisure time of polite society. In the eighteenth and early nineteenth centuries, only larger towns and great plantations met this criterion. In small towns and the countryside, Americans embraced gentility only in a limited way. One barber's ledger from eastern Pennsylvania, for example, showed that, on average, customers came for a shave once every three months—hardly a lucrative clientele. Even in those places capable of supporting genteel life, more homespun Americans objected to barbering and hairdressing as frivolous extravagances. One critic, in an essay questioning the utility of educating young women in the genteel arts, wondered how adopting hairstyles requiring five hours of a barber's labor would prepare a girl to run a household. Similarly, John Trumbull, one of "the Connecticut Wits," bemoaned, in his poem on the "Life and Character of Dick Hairbrain," how the barber, the dancing master, and the tailor produced a "Clockwork-Gentleman," camouflaging the "dull eye and clumsy face" behind powdered curls, bows, and lace.[36]

Lighthearted satires about barbers and their customers gave way to denunciations of genteel hairstyles as republican ideology spread during the political controversy with Britain, making colonists anxious about indulging in luxury. Many American leaders grew alarmed over the increase in luxurious living, especially after the Seven Years War (1756-1763). According to one leading historian of republican ideology, a fear that self-indulgence would corrupt Americans provided an important stimulus to the revolt against the British. Revolutionary leaders who examined the history of republics concluded that the United States would survive only if its citizens were willing to sacrifice their private interests for the public good; accordingly, it would be the character of Americans that would form the mainstay of the republic. If seduced by a love of refinement and a craving for distinction, they predicted, the people would be left unfit and unwilling to serve their country. The republican critique of luxury also furnished an ideological response to changes in colonial society that had increased the gap between the rich and the poor. Viewing British oppression through the lens of republican ideas, American clergy lamented the plight of colonial Americans as God's punishment for vanity, greed, and envy. Southern planters, especially in Virginia, saw republican values as an antidote to a growing ostentation and indebtedness among some of the colonial elite that had called into question their ability to lead. For example, George Washington's praise for a boycott of English goods highlighted a desire among planters to demonstrate their moral fitness. In a letter to George Mason, Washington commended the 1769 nonimportation proposal for giving planters a "pretext to live within bounds" and save their credit. He also thought that curbing extravagance would help win over the "poor and needy man" to the revolutionary cause.[37]

Republican ideas provided support for the movement away from ostentatious male fashion and toward a more understated appearance, and colonial leaders demonstrated their patriotism by throwing away their wigs. Dubbed the "great masculine renunciation" by fashion historians, American men thought they no longer needed to display their authority through their outward appearance, as in the past, since the citizens of a republic were inherently virtuous. Most famous among revolutionary leaders who symbolized their commitment to republicanism with an unpretentious appearance was Ben Franklin, who appeared at the French court "very plainly dressed, wearing my thin, gray straight hair that peeps out under my only coiffure, a fine fur cap." Franklin flouted convention with his unstyled hair, amusing himself greatly in the process. "Think," he exclaimed, "how this must appear among the powdered heads of Europe!" At least one resident of Versailles was struck by Franklin's "hair-style without trappings or powder," concluding that the contrast between the simplicity of the American representative and the elegance of the French made the latter culture seem "weak and servile."[38]

Although Franklin meant to subvert the iconography of gentility with his thinning, gray hair and to create an enduring image of republican virtue, many of his countrymen proved reluctant to follow his lead. As soon as the Revolution ended, a powdered head regained its status. Abigail Adams, writing to Thomas Jefferson in 1787, expressed concern that "vanity was becoming a more powerful principle than patriotism." Likewise, a writer for the *Philadelphia Aurora* observed, "Those in the high life ape the fashions and manners of the English, French, and other nations; the middle class, those higher or more affluent . . . and the poor copy the example of the class above them." Republican stalwarts took aim at the ostentation around them by hurling barbs at the genteel and their barbers. Employing satires and jeremiads, writers made the postwar fop into a symbol of the decadence they condemned. Whether they depicted "the powdered beau rolling in his carriage" or walking with mincing steps in his dog-skin shoes, the writers equated the fop's powered hair with an "empty head." Timothy Dwight, in a poem contrasting republican simplicity with European splendor, dismissed the refined world of the would-be aristocrats as shallow and their splendor as nothing more than "fashion" and "frippery" in a world of barbers, milliners, tailors, and dressmakers. The use of feminine imagery to describe genteel excess also implied that men who frequented barbershops lacked the manly independence required for citizenship in a republic. Moreover, in some of the anti-luxury writings, xenophobic authors cast barbers in a sinister light by associating them with French hairdressers, who, they argued, spread vanity and lust. One mock newspaper advertisement from the 1780s promised "Gentlemen, who of French fashions are fond," that barbers could make "all without seem fair—tho' polluted within." Even the former ambassador to France, Thomas Jefferson, warned readers in his *Notes on the State of Virginia* that French émigrés would corrupt Americans.[39]

These social crosscurrents notwithstanding, barbers emerged from the Revolution with their popularity renewed, even though their image had become tarnished. Americans established an uneasy truce between gentility and republicanism. In general, denunciations of *luxury* resolved the contradiction between genteel and republican values, allowing for an uneasy coexistence. Exaggerated criticism of luxury defined what sorts of behavior and fashion were unacceptable in a republic and established the parameters within which gentility could flourish. These distinctions were necessary, because refinement served important functions for the young nation. As John Adams pointed out to a correspondent alarmed by the resurgence of luxury, Americans had never been Spartans, and he hoped they never would be, for it would make them "lazy drones." In other words, the *quest* for distinction spurred consumption and bolstered the national economy. In addition, Americans lacked indigenous rituals and customs to dignify their accomplishments, so to provide distinction they imported the pomp and genteel splendor of aristocratic Europe. Americans also resented European charges that they were vulgar, even as they expressed fears, like that voiced by one newspaper editor, that "the age of ultimate refinement in America is yet to arrive." So, Americans continued to seek a balance. Emulation of aristocratic ways brought into existence a decorum that had been lacking, particularly in the conduct of government officials,[40] yet pursuing distinction too avidly evoked charges that one had succumbed to corruption.

In the end, barbers and others whose labors made refinement possible suffered the most from the ambivalence that Americans felt regarding the persistence of genteel customs in a democratic nation. The combination of republican ideology and new forms of social relations made white Americans shun the trade, fearing that by working as servants they risked losing their independence. In the minds of revolutionary leaders, self-sufficiency was a prerequisite for civic virtue. Individuals dependent on others for their livelihood could not be trusted to act selflessly, because they were vulnerable to being intimidated or bribed to do their employer's bidding. Since these views had great currency among Americans, the transition to wage labor in the decades following the Revolution caused anxiety among workers. The incorporation of rural households into a market economy, the development of transportation networks, and the growth of manufacturing drew an increasing number of formerly independent Americans into wage work. In the long run, wage earners reassured themselves of their independence by accepting the idea that a worker's labor was a commodity to be sold in the marketplace. In the meanwhile, they were haunted, as Alexis de Tocqueville put it, by a "confused and imperfect phantom of equality," which promised parity but also reminded them that some Americans were more equal than others. One English traveler reflected on the situation of American servants and concluded, "Disguise it as we may, under all specious forms of reasoning, there is something in the mind of every man which tells him he is humiliated in doing personal service to another."[41]

As a result, the barbering trade became associated with the dependence of indentured servants and slaves and the degraded status of free blacks. Americans had recent memories of indentured servants working as barbers. Between 1773 and 1776, all but one of the 119 British immigrants coming to Maryland who worked in service trades arrived with indentures; and even among those immigrants bound for the same trades in New York, four out of ten had indentures. Apprenticeships and indentured servitude for white men, however, declined rapidly in the early nineteenth century, displaced by a contractual relationship between employers and employees in which they had no obligations to each other beyond the exchange of labor for wages. By contrast, the overwhelming majority of African Americans remained unfree, whether in the South, where cotton had revived the institution of slavery, or in the North, where gradual emancipation laws trapped many in restrictive apprenticeships and many more remained enslaved until reaching the age dictated by law. The prevalence of enslaved and marginal barbers reinforced the republican conviction that barbering was unsuitable work for citizens. Even when servants felt no ambivalence about their work, fellow Americans often shamed them, as happened to one young barber attending a dance in Boston. Despite being a "fine looking fellow" who dressed well and wore a diamond ring, the young white man lost a comely dance partner the moment she learned he was a barber.[42] This incident highlights the contempt barbers endured despite their many accomplishments.

The memoirs of John Todd, a white barber in antebellum Portland, Maine, document the pitfalls of working as a barber in the United States. He boasted about his considerable distinction, as befitted the custodian of gentility in a small town. "Quite a dude" by his own admission, donning a tall silk hat and kid gloves for his Sunday walks, Todd parlayed his knowledge of style and his good humor into popularity with the town's leading men, who made his barbershop into a gathering spot. He also burnished his reputation by cultivating a literary bent. According to Todd, he read for five to six hours a day in his barbershop and conversed with "many of the best men in the country." His enthusiastic admiration for Thomas Paine, moreover, showed that his gentility did not preclude a commitment to republican ideals. Yet, his work imposed humiliating limitations on his behavior and status. He forthrightly acknowledged his lifelong habit of deference to the rich, who had provided him with a comfortable living for over half a century. Todd's pride at associating with people of renown, however, did not blind him to their condescension toward him, which led him to question their superiority. "They may have great reputations," he declared bitterly, "but is that always character?" Such flashes of resentment, reminiscent of the tensions between Figaro and his count, exposed the class conflicts beneath the surface of Todd's relationships with his customers. Whereas John Todd accepted the subservience and low status of barbering as the price of a secure livelihood, fewer and fewer white American men made the same choice. The American economy, booming at unprecedented levels after the War of 1812, furnished young white men with opportunities to enter more respectable trades.[43]

Barbering fit well, however, with the new circumstances of African Americans following the Revolution. In the North and the upper South, economic and ideological developments combined to emancipate tens of thousands of slaves. The diminishing centrality of slave labor in these two regions reduced opposition to a wave of manumissions and emancipation laws that drew inspiration from the egalitarian ideology of the Revolution and the evangelical fervor of the Second Great Awakening. Even in the lower South, where cotton and sugar cultivation revived slavery, a distinctive free black population emerged. Slave owners there engaged in a more selective process of manumission, freeing slaves for whom they cared personally, typically their mistresses and children. At the same time, the influx of free people of color fleeing the slave uprising in Saint Dominique during the 1790s augmented this small group of free blacks.[44] Once they became free, black barbers could fulfill the promise of their trade, enjoying greater autonomy and self-esteem.

The service sector quickly became the mainstay of free blacks in urban areas throughout the nation. Whites already saw freed blacks as degraded through their association with slavery, so it appeared natural for the former bondsmen to perform the menial occupations that white workers shunned. Menial they may have been, but they were of great consequence for African Americans. Catering food, cleaning chimneys, driving teams of horses, maintaining stables, as well as cutting hair and providing shaves gave free black men the chance to operate their own business.[45] With the money they earned, black barbers could make their freedom meaningful by establishing their families on a secure basis. They purchased the freedom of their wives and children, who could then come to live with them in their own households.

The relationship of free black barbers to their white customers went beyond pecuniary considerations, for the men who sat in their chairs also stood up for them in court to guarantee their rights. Emancipation and manumission had severed their ties to their master's self-interest, but lacking the rights of citizens themselves, they needed white allies. Yet, they confronted a paradox when seeking white patrons and had to execute a delicate balancing act. The degradation associated with their race had helped create their occupational niche, but it also cast doubt on their ability to function as custodians of gentility and to confer status on their customers. They owed their genteel credentials to their association with masters who occupied the front ranks of the colonial elite. As free African Americans, they were no man's man and hence lacked the social credentials to help the socially ambitious establish themselves in polite society. Hence, black barbers, unsurprisingly, often maintained ties to their former masters in order to preserve their social cachet.

These relationships between freed black barbers and their former masters typify the next stage in the evolution of black barbers as African Americans who derived their public identity from a trade and occupied a distinct social position. During the colonial period, masters had rewarded with a promotion slaves who proved adept at learning the behavior and skills appropriate to working in a genteel household. These waiting men, through the process of acculturation, gained a limited measure of power over their masters by virtue of their uncommon abilities and the role they played in establishing their master's social position. Between the Revolution and the 1820s, free black barbers cultivated former masters as patrons. The greater autonomy of black barbers as free men made the relationship less trying for them than it had been in slavery. For the masters, the unquestioning deference being shown by the black barbers looking for patronage compensated for the loss of authority, which had often been illusory anyway. The roles played by former masters and former slaves became more formal over time and served as the basis on which black barbers could recruit patrons more generally from the white elite.

In the decades immediately following the Revolution, the difference between the experience of slave and free barbers could be quite small. Sam Harrison had grown close to his master, Virginia planter Robert Carter, by serving as his waiting man. When Carter manumitted Harrison in 1792 along with the rest of his five hundred slaves, he permitted him to rent a house on the plantation. Carter demanded in return that Harrison continue to provide him services for free, but in the course of attending to his former master, the black barber retained access to Carter's extended household of residents and visitors, who became his paying customers. Harrison's conduct suggests that he still considered himself a member of the household. One morning the plantation's tutor recorded in his diary, "I was waked by Sam the barber thumping at my door."[46] Although the white tutor thought that Harrison made undue claims for rights, the black barber had managed to demonstrate that he was no slave, even though he remained a member of his former master's household.

Caesar Hope also remained under the roof of his former owner after receiving his freedom, but he found a way to move beyond its confines. Hope's life as a free man began and ended with the aid of white patrons. Shortly after freeing Hope,

Susanna Riddell fled war-torn Yorktown, and Hope lived with his former mistress at her new home in Williamsburg, working as a barber and saving enough money to purchase the freedom of his son Aberdeen in the summer of 1783. The Williamsburg tax list from the following spring shows that he had established his own household. The population growth in Richmond after the state capital was moved there in 1780 prompted Hope to move again. The Richmond tax collector listed Hope as the head of a household of six African Americans in 1787, parenthetically noting that he worked as a barber. After beginning another family with a slave woman named Tenah, who was thirty-three years younger than he, Hope managed to save enough money to purchase his wife's freedom before old age caught up with him. He could not afford to free any more of his children. At age sixty-two, his taxes were delinquent, which suggests that advanced age prevented him from working. When he drew up his last will and testament, Hope must have worried about his family's future. He turned once again to the role that had given him a career and independence. By listing himself as Caesar Hope rather than John Hope, he signaled in his will that he accepted the identity forged through his collaboration with whites. His allegiance, as before, found a reward, because Edmund Randolph, a former Virginia governor, U.S. attorney general, and U.S. secretary of state, agreed to serve as his executor. Although his fortunes had waned by the time he died in 1810 at the age of sixty-seven, his widow managed to purchase the freedom of their child Judith.[47] The legacy of his life as a barber appears to have ensured that his family received the gift of freedom.

Attracted by the relative independence that poor whites, free blacks, and slaves had carved out in Richmond's burgeoning waterfront neighborhoods, other black barbers sought work there. Between 1782 and 1810, Richmond's population grew tenfold, reaching ten thousand. The construction of a canal as well as the need for men to sail and unload barges created a large demand for hired slaves. Already in 1782, residents of Richmond and the surrounding Henrico County had petitioned the legislature to prevent slave owners from letting their slaves hire themselves out, which attests to how common the practice had become. The possibility of self-hire created economic incentives that prompted slave owners to let their slave barbers relocate to the city. When given permission, slave barbers lived in town and found their own work, then sent their masters a portion of their earnings. The opportunity to live independently of their master appealed to these men. One sixteen-year-old slave barber named Lewis made this type of agreement with his owner in the 1790s so that he could move from his rural home in King and Queen County to Richmond. The movement of slave barbers occurred in other urban areas as well, and they came to dominate the trade, which made it more likely that they would have a chance to purchase their freedom. By 1792, barber John Kennedy had earned enough money to buy not only his own freedom but also that of another family member.[48] These barbers understood that by serving the interests of their masters, they could carve out a limited autonomy for themselves.

When slave barbers had white fathers, they often enjoyed a special status. Ties of blood and personal concern led masters to help their slaves become established as free men, and the freed slaves were more likely to affirm their connection to the family. Barbering provided a way to achieve a considerable measure of independence that did not challenge the racial order. John Stanly, the child of an Ebo woman and the white merchant-shipper who owned the ship that had brought her to America, was born a slave in 1774 in New Bern, North Carolina. Despite bearing the name of his father and his white half-brother, he belonged to Alexander Stewart, a good friend and neighbor of John Stanly, Senior, who had captained the ship in question. Stewart taught the bright child how to read and write before hiring him out as an apprentice barber. While only a teenager and still in bondage, Stanly established his own barbershop, which prospered in the busy port town. Stewart and his wife, Lydia, appear to have been pleased with their slave's character and success, for when he turned twenty-one they petitioned the Craven County court for his freedom. Three years later, Stanly himself petitioned the General Assembly to pass a law confirming his freedom, stating his case in a way that revealed his understanding of what made him acceptable to white society. He identified himself as a "man of mixed blood," presumably to underscore his kinship to white members of the community. More central to his rationale was his conformity to the values of the merchant-planter elite; "by honest & preserving industry," he declared, he had acquired "a considerable real and personal estate." The willingness of the General Assembly to pass special legislation on his behalf suggests that the youthful Stanly had learned, as had other black artisans, that deferential free black businessmen could win the respect of whites. Known popularly as the "Barber of the town of New Bern," Stanly had embraced an occupational identity that allowed him to achieve remarkable financial success—he became one of the wealthiest free black men in the South—while remaining unthreatening because he remained in a service trade, personally grooming the leading citizens in the area.[49]

Even as Stanly asserted his right to independent standing as a free black man, he refused to sever the ties of birth and affection that linked him to the Stanlys and Stewarts. He indicated his understanding of the connection between his independence and preserving his connection to his white families when he purchased the freedom of his children, a fundamental prerequisite of being his own man, and legally named two of his sons John Stewart Stanly and Alexander Stewart Stanly. In another symbolic act linking himself to the Stewarts, he gratefully accepted Lydia Stewart's help in arranging for him to buy two pews for his family at the New Bern First Presbyterian Church, where he demonstrated his fealty to his former mistress every Sunday morning. One longtime resident recalled that, until her death in 1822, Mrs. Stewart "could be seen on the streets of Newbern . . . hanging on her old servant John for support." He also maintained close ties with his white half-brother, with whom he shared his first as well as surname and his year of birth. Suggesting what advantages social position might have given the barber but for his race, the white John Stanly, Jr., rose to prominence as a congressman, as the Speaker of the North Carolina House of Commons, and as president of the Bank of New Bern. Their relationship extended to the black barber's abetting his white brother's penchant for speculative investments. After the white John Stanly had overextended the bank's credit, the black John Stanly came to his aid by cosigning a security note for $14,962, which he had to pay when his brother was forced to resign as the bank's president. The debt ultimately ruined him, and he had to close the barbershop that had provided his start in business.[50] Herein lay the pitfall of his strategy: what connection to one member of his white family had given him, his link to another took away.

Following the American Revolution, black barbers arrived from the Caribbean in greater numbers, and the contrast between their lives and those of black barbers already in the United States illustrates how the imperatives of barbering shaped the experience of the former, making it similar to their American counterparts. The Haitian Revolution of 1793 began a mass exodus of French colonists and their slaves to the United States; hundreds ended up in Boston, New York, and Philadelphia. Free black men John Cord and John Quaid settled in Philadelphia, where they worked as barbers and became two of the wealthiest African Americans in the city.[51] Another one of their countrymen, Pierre Toussaint, rivaled their success by becoming the Vidal Sassoon of his day in New York City.

The history of Haitian slaves in New York City is tumultuous. Inspired, no doubt, by the successful revolution in their homeland, slaves from Saint Domingue (present-day Haiti) demonstrated a penchant for rebelliousness. They constituted a disproportionate number of the city's runaways, played a role in a spate of arsons in 1796 in New York, and fought in a major riot there in 1801. Others never reconciled themselves to exile and committed suicide.[52] Pierre Toussaint avoided such extremes, but he did make a statement in the name he chose after becoming a free man. The surname of his former master, whom he had regarded highly, was Berard, but he adopted a different name as a free man. He combined Pierre, the name chosen his French owners, with Toussaint. Given his Haitian origins, he probably adopted the latter in honor of Toussaint L'Ouverture, the leader of the slave revolt on the island, taking it less as a sign of contempt for white authority than as a way to assert his independence. Since his white biographer, who described herself as one of his closest friends, failed to note the symbolism of his name, he may have cloaked his reasons behind a deferential façade. Like Caesar Hope of Virginia, Pierre Toussaint used his name to express the merger of two identities, one that reflected white expectations and one that reflected his personal aspirations.

Toussaint won scores of admirers, particularly among the white socialites whom he served as a hairdresser. In their stories of Toussaint, the characteristics that endeared him to them stand out. A large part of his appeal came from his West Indian heritage. In *The Echoes of a Belle*, a novel purportedly written by a southern lady, Toussaint makes a cameo appearance as the ideal combination of the exotic and the domestic, his gold earrings juxtaposed against "a snowy apron." Much of what is known about his life, however, comes from a biography penned by another society woman, Hannah Sawyer Lee, whose romanticized portrait of Toussaint idealized his deference and gentility. More recently, in 1968 New York's Cardinal Terence Cooke nominated him for sainthood for his selfless acts of charity, and in 1990 Cardinal John O'Connor had his remains moved into the crypt of St. Patrick's Cathedral.[53] Although Toussaint has attracted public notice for many admirable qualities, his success at transcending racist stereotypes in Federalist New York relates directly to the experience of black barbers during the early national period. It exemplifies how black barbers expanded their appeal beyond the narrow confines of plantation districts and proceeded to take control of the trade nationally.

Black barbers started this journey to freedom and a secure economic niche by getting off the plantation. The age of revolutions in many cases gave black barbers the chance to relocate to an urban environment, where they could hire themselves out and earn the money to purchase their freedom. Just as the American Revolution had brought Caesar Hope to Richmond, the Haitian Revolution brought Toussaint to New York City along with four other household servants of Jean Berard and his young bride, including Pierre's sister. Financial setbacks experienced during these wars made slave owners look favorably on hiring out their slaves. Because Toussaint's master lost his entire estate, the prospect of gaining extra income from hiring out a skilled slave must have been welcome, so he apprenticed his twenty-one-year-old slave to a French hairdresser. His decision was timely, as he died shortly afterwards in Haiti while attempting to reclaim his property. Ultimately, Toussaint became the sole means of support for his master's wife and family when the New York firm managing the Berard's remaining money failed during a financial panic. This reversal of fortune allowed Toussaint complete freedom to pursue his career as a barber and hairdresser.[54] (Since men also powdered their hair and wore wigs, their barbers had to dress their hair, blurring the distinction between hairdressing and barbering.)

Toussaint's apprenticeship in a trade and the right to hire his own time facilitated his acculturation, the process that figured so largely in the success of colonial black barbers. Had he remained occupied entirely within a French-speaking household, he might never have learned English, much less the peculiar ways of New Yorkers. Paying daily visits to the homes of society women exposed him to Anglo-American gentility. Toussaint's ability to internalize genteel customs, those learned in his youth and those encountered in New York, seems to have counted for more than his language skills. "Though he labored under the disadvantage of speaking the language imperfectly, it being late before he became familiarized with English," wrote one biographer, "he seemed always to say just what was proper." Toussaint's limited command of English did not prevent him from expressing his thoughts, such as his philosophical attitude toward the parade of new styles in hair: "Fashion keep change, change."[55] His acculturation paved the way for Toussaint to enter a lucrative trade and win freedom for his family as well as for himself.

Toussaint and his clients had a relationship similar to that between planters and waiting men, which demonstrates that black barbers formed ties to powerful white people outside of the institution of slavery. The barbers validated the genteel credentials of polite society by helping socialites conform to standards of beauty that originated in European courts. When Toussaint began working as a hairdresser, the elaborate wig, with architectural elements perched in it after the manner of Marie Antoinette, remained in vogue. One reason these ladies turned to barbers was that they needed their heads shaved to ensure a proper fit for these large wigs.[56] While Toussaint needed a gracious manner and skill with a razor to serve his elite customers, he also functioned as an authority on genteel culture, in much the way a fashion designer does for members of the jet set today. The powdered heads of New York society represented a collaboration between hairdressers and their clients. Together, they enabled the port on the Hudson River to achieve a cachet similar to that of London or Paris. Toussaint appeared to take pride in his work and in the prominence of his acquaintances, but he also sought to advance his own interests through the distinct position that his trade afforded him.

In order to serve the white elite, barbers and hairdressers needed a reputation for gentility. Toussaint's gentility derived from his association with the Berards. He had been born in the great house of the sugar plantation on Saint Domingue and spent his early years as a playmate to the Berard children. His grandmother, Zenobe Julien, had cemented the ties between the white and black families when she escorted first the Berard's son and then their two daughters to Paris for their education, a service for which she received her freedom from the grateful Berards. Toussaint's mother, Ursula, served as Madame Berard's waiting maid, and his sister, Rosalie, also worked as a house servant.[57] As the third generation in personal service to an elite French family, Toussaint had a deep exposure to gentility.

By remaining connected to his genteel owners, Toussaint also set himself apart from the largely destitute population of former slaves in New York in the late eighteenth century. He did not follow the example of northern slaves who bartered with their masters for their immediate freedom or simply ran away, since the gradual emancipation provision of the law ending slavery promised freedom anyway. Instead, he chose to remain with Madame Berard to help preserve her social status and his own as well. Soon after Toussaint had arrive in New York, a group of free blacks and Quakers urged him to run away and become a free man. Allegedly he replied that his freedom belonged "to my mistress." For the rest of her short life, he was devoted to her, using his own savings to pay her debts, and, at one point, redeeming her pawned family jewels. Beyond providing for the young widow's necessities, he carried invitations to her friends for evening visits, waited on the company when they arrived, and purchased genteel luxuries for the table, such as ice cream. Toussaint made it possible for Madame Berard to continue presiding over a fashionable salon, one in which he played an important supporting role. As a New York friend of the Berards recalled, Toussaint cut quite a figure, "dressed in a red jacket, full of spirits and very fond of dancing and music, and always devoted to his mistress, who was young, gay, and planning future enjoyment."[58] In the company of his mistress, he could be a fashionable *bon vivant* rather than, as an independent free black man, the object of white contempt.

Based on Toussaint's story, it appears that elite black men and women had to make a public display of their loyalty to their former masters. White associates of Toussaint, for instance, remarked on his very public devotion to his mistress. Hannah Lee recalls his saying, "I remember her . . . she was very pale; her health was always delicate, but she looked so lovely, and we were all so happy!" Toussaint painted an idyllic portrait of his situation, in which his days were filled with efforts to cheer his ailing mistress. Along with providing evidence that he bore no ill will against the people who had held him in slavery, his stories emphasize sumptuous details that invoke the grandeur of the French colony at the height of its prosperity. "Rosalie and I," he recalled, "would stand at opposite corners of the room and pull the strings of a magnificent fan of peacock's feathers, swaying it to and fro" in order to ease the suffering of his mistress until her untimely death. Perhaps Toussaint sought to reassure clients in post-Emancipation New York City that they could enjoy his stories about aristocratic plantations without feeling qualms about his enslavement.[59]

Toussaint quickly built up a distinguished clientele "of the highest class in rank, cultivation, and wealth," people who quite naturally appreciated his genteel ways. One of his customers, a "highly cultivated and elegant woman" according to his biographer, explained his appeal: "Some of the most pleasant hours I pass are in conversing with Toussaint while he is dressing my hair. I anticipate it as daily recreation." Following the custom of self-hire, his master's widow allowed him to keep a portion of his earnings, which he used to purchase the freedom of his sister, his wife, and his daughter. His own emancipation came as a gift from his dying mistress, who praised Toussaint for his hard work and devotion.[60] Once he had used his earnings to deliver his family from slavery, Toussaint's own freedom became meaningful, yet he paused before taking the next logical step and establishing his own household.

So great was his determination to preserve the bonds that gave him status that Toussaint and his wife remained in the home of Madame Berard's second husband, Monsieur Nicholas, even after she had freed Toussaint and died. Another impoverished émigré from Saint Dominique, Nicholas eked out a living as a musician, performing in theater orchestras and giving lessons, which perpetuated the household's genteel reputation. Only when Nicholas left New York for the South four years after his wife's death did Toussaint and his wife, Juliette, establish their own household. Their home on Franklin Street, described as "pleasant and commodious" displayed Toussaint's prosperity, but importantly, it also "was arranged with an air of neatness, and even gentility." To ensure that the right people knew of his home's refinement, Toussaint and Juliette invited white "acquaintances," American as well as French, to their home for tea parties. Juliette waited on her guests, serving them delicacies such as French chocolate, "of which she did not herself partake." Toussaint would only join the company after they had finished eating and moved to the adjoining room. According to his biographer, his absence during the repast demonstrated "his sense of propriety. . . . He never mingled the two races."[61] Thus the couple perpetuated their roles as genteel servants within their own home, incorporating his clientele into rituals that linked the Toussaints to the aristocratic French émigrés who had brought them to New York City.

The racial and social hierarchies that Toussaint reproduced in his own home provide a context for understanding his experience as well as that of other black barbers. From the perspective of former slaves, his life had improved dramatically. The fact that the Toussaints lived in their own household symbolized freedom. If they had to bow before polite society in order to achieve a stable family life, they did it. This voluntary subordination, however distasteful, probably to them seemed necessary in a nation that withheld key rights from African Americans. It also had unexpected benefits. When Toussaint was summoned to the City Hotel to serve a visiting French woman who spoke no English, he learned of the fate of Aurora Berard, his former master's daughter. From that point, the former slave and the former mistress corresponded faithfully until his death. In part, he acted out of a sense of duty, because the woman was his godmother. Members of slave-owning families in Haiti and elsewhere throughout the Caribbean served as godparents to slaves, who could expect their godparents to intercede on their behalf with other whites. Yet, in their new lives away from the island, their roles had been reversed. The young Frenchwoman, now living in Paris, had not married and faced dire straits, so Toussaint sent her gifts and money. Although Toussaint consigned himself to occupying a lower rank in a hierarchical society, he was nevertheless helping support his white godmother.[62]

Toussaint and other black barbers had taken advantage of the circumstances of their slavery to form a genteel identity that allowed them to transcend many of the liabilities of their race without forfeiting an autonomous self-consciousness. Their strategy forged the beginnings of an African American tradition of barbering. Their symbiotic relationship with powerful members of the white elite helped them gain their freedom and become self-employed. The American Revolution facilitated this transformation. By making barbering odious to white workers, republican ideology created a lucrative occupational niche for black men. At the same time, the revolutions in America and the Caribbean created situations that allowed black men to learn barbering, relocate to urban areas, and lay the groundwork for their freedom by hiring out. Freedom, if it came, was never complete. Since the young nation upheld racial inequality, black barbers understood that they had to make outward displays of accepting their place in the new society. As a reward, elite white patrons gave them steady business, which allowed black barbers and hairdressers to establish their own households. The surnames that Caesar Hope and Pierre Toussaint chose as free men, however, suggest that black barbers derived a sense of empowerment from their accomplishments that owed nothing to the opinions of white men.

The self-esteem and success of men like Caesar Hope and Pierre Toussaint came to form the basis for establishing a collective identity as Knights of the Razor during the antebellum period. This fraternal order transmitted knowledge and self-esteem from generation to generation through apprenticeships and trade associations. The invention of the first-class barbershop played an integral role in sustaining the trade. By incorporating elements of aristocratic parlors into their shops, black barbers created an institutional embodiment of their gentility. Henceforth, the prestige associated with black barbers came from their workplace and traditions rather than their connections to specific members of the white elite. The financial success of these businesses, in turn, gave them the means to sustain a respectable lifestyle, which in turn formed the basis for their claim to high status and equal rights.

CHAPTER TWO

Becoming Knights of the Razor

A central issue for antebellum black barbers was how to distinguish themselves from the rest of the African American population in the eyes of whites after they had lost their close ties to genteel masters. Even as free black businessmen, they needed white guardians to protect their fragile independence. They also needed to retain a genteel cachet if they wished to continue serving affluent white men. Two innovations allowed black barbers to retain their valuable ties to the white elite. The first generation of free black barbers distilled their experience into a coherent tradition of African American barbering by which they transmitted their skills and social wiles to younger men. To a large extent, family and community ties nurtured this tradition as it grew into a fraternity based on artisanal customs. Black barbers also invented the first-class barbershop. Combinations of upscale decor and masculine conviviality, these establishments quickly became a favorite destination for white men, a place where they stopped by to debate politics and swap tales as well as to get a shave.

Black barbers struck a bargain with white customers. The barbers assured white men that a barbershop friendship did not imply racial equality, and white men granted black barbers the right to pursue respectability without harassment. The barbers may have conceded too much. They certainly wrestled with the consequences of their decision. Nevertheless, antebellum black barbers established ties to the white elite that would persist throughout the rest of the nineteenth century. The race relations of the barbershop hinged on black barbers' serving as reference points for their white customers. The barbers validated white privilege through elaborate rituals of deference, and, as the hosts of upscale businesses, they offered white customers an appropriate setting for demonstrating their own respectability. The barbers' ability to be all things to white men let them become comfortably ensconced on Main Streets throughout the antebellum United States. As black barbers and their barbershops became established and important parts of the society, black barbers transformed from genteel servants to respected knights of the razor.

The earliest free black barbers relied on family members and white friends to retain their independence. Sally Thomas, an enslaved black woman living independently, had been hiring out her own time as a washerwoman for several years when her master died. Sally feared that her new master intended to sell her son James, then seven years old. She pleaded for assistance from a longtime white acquaintance, Ephraim Foster, a prominent Tennessee attorney, planter, and politician, who had inquired about buying James's freedom. He discovered that, although she had painstakingly saved $350 from her meager wages, her new master was demanding $400 for the boy. Foster agreed to lend Sally the extra $50. However, a slave could not legally own property—which she would have done had she bought her son—so Foster purchased young James on Sally's behalf. She later repaid Foster's loan and received freedom papers for her son. Because Tennessee law required that emancipated blacks leave the state, Foster kept up the pretense of owning James Thomas. Only after the young man had learned the barbering trade and opened his own shop was it safe for James, with the help of this white family friend, to secure a legal manumission and permission to remain in Tennessee.[1]

James Thomas enjoyed a far less certain relationship to white patrons than had his colonial predecessors had. Reflecting on the antebellum period when he wrote his autobiography, Thomas made it clear that he had no illusions that white men felt a sense of obligation toward free African Americans like himself. He dwelled at length on how the slave trade had broken up families, as his own had almost been; and he was especially bitter about the callousness of white fathers who sold their slave children. "How many hundreds of thousands of mixed bloods in the country were auctioned off while their fathers were fighting wordy battles for the oppressed and downtrodden of some far off people?" His comments seem to have been inspired by his own white father, John Catron, a prominent Nashville attorney who later served on the United States Supreme Court. Thomas recalled, "He had no time to give me a thought. He did give me twenty-five cents once. If I was correctly informed that was all he ever did for me." Even a white man as sympathetic to African Americans as Ephraim Foster, who ensured that Thomas could grow up with his mother and who also helped several other slaves in Nashville purchase their freedom, could impose upon his black clients. Years earlier, when he learned that Sally Thomas had given birth to a son, Foster told her to name the boy after his political hero, Andrew Jackson. When she replied that she had already named her son after James the Apostle, Foster then told the woman he called Aunt Sally that she could call him James Andrew Jackson Thomas, which she did.[2]

James Thomas's upbringing exemplifies the circumstances of many antebellum black barbers; although many had white fathers who provided little help, they and their families were adept at cultivating white patrons. Mothers such as Sally Thomas often played an especially crucial role in winning barbers' freedom and imparting strategies for survival. For example, Thomas's half-brother John Rapier also received his freedom through one of his mother's white patrons. The young boy lived with Sally in Nashville until she arranged for Richard Rapier, a river barge captain, to hire her son as a pole boy and waiter. Rapier died ten years later and left money in his will to pay for John's freedom, whereupon the newly freed man took the surname of his deceased benefactor. While John Rapier's choice of last name was probably a heartfelt tribute to his liberator, James's last name attests to the limits of how far Sally would go to humor her white guardians. She readily granted the request that she name her youngest son after the president but also gave him her own last name, probably wishing to give her son a connection with his grandparents, aunts, and uncles, whom she had had to part from when forced to move to Tennessee.[3]

By asserting the independent existence of her family, Sally demonstrated that she had her own resource, an enduring kinship network, a resource that would sustain all three of her sons, each of whom became a barber. The bond among John Rapier, Henry Thomas, and James Thomas withstood a lifetime of separation, an example of how the solidarity among black barbers was rooted in part in fraternal ties. The oldest brother, John, had also been threatened with sale, which prompted his mother to arrange the work on the river barge with Captain Rapier. After receiving his freedom, John settled in Florence, Alabama. The next oldest brother, Henry, at the urging of his concerned mother, fled to the North, settling in Buffalo, New York. The desire of the brothers to remain in touch generated the extensive correspondence that recorded their story. While John had few difficulties keeping in touch with his mother and youngest brother, James, the runaway Henry had to use stealth to communicate with his family, sending letters to John in Alabama, who would pass his brother's news on to their mother. Even these written exchanges involved subterfuge; John prevailed upon sympathetic whites to mail his letters to Henry while on trips to the northern states. The names the oldest two brothers gave their sons also reveal their strong connection, as each named a son after the other. In addition, John called another son James Thomas Rapier.[4]

Sally's grandchildren provided her family's another link. Following the death of his first wife, John found running a barbershop and raising four young boys alone too challenging, so he sent two of his sons to live with his mother and his youngest brother in Nashville, where they could attend a school for free black children. He sent his oldest son, Richard, to live with his brother Henry in Buffalo, where he learned barbering from his uncle.[5] By raising John's sons, his mother and brothers displayed a commitment to maintaining family ties that, in the case of this family, meant giving younger relatives the chance to learn barbering.

Many young black men learned barbering and other trades within a family context. In St. Louis, the Clamorgan brothers founded a barbering dynasty. Louis, Henry, and Cyprian Clamorgan, the free, mixed-race grandsons of Spanish trader Jacques Clamorgan and several of his slave mistresses, had much in common with the Thomas-Rapier family. When the oldest son, Louis, was only ten years old, their unmarried mother Apoline died. Like Sally Thomas, Apoline had a knack for finding white protectors. A white merchant, Charles Collins, not only served as the executor of Apoline's estate, but also raised the three boys, provided for their education, and took Henry into business with him. By 1842, Louis had opened a barbershop. After prospering, he displayed a concern for his brothers reminiscent of the Thomas-Rapier trio. Henry had tried earning a living as a "river man" and had moved his family out west to Milwaukee. River work did not prove satisfactory, and they returned to St. Louis, where Louis opened his house to Henry and his family. Presumably, Louis taught his two brothers the trade, because both began working as barbers. Louis and Henry formed a partnership in 1850, and shortly thereafter they took their youngest brother, Cyprian, into the thriving business. The sudden death of Louis at the young age of thirty-one provided a temporary setback to the brothers' plan to open the most luxurious barbershop and bathhouse in the city, but under Henry's leadership, Clamorgan's became a fixture of downtown St. Louis. In keeping with family tradition, Louis's two surviving sons, Leon and Julius, also became barbers.[6]

A strong-willed mother and family ties also played a role in the start of William Johnson's career as a barber in Natchez, Mississippi. Amy Johnson received her freedom as a gift from her master, William Johnson, in 1814. Six years later, the slave owner petitioned the Mississippi General Assembly to free Amy's son, his namesake. His successful appeal to the legislators was heartfelt, asking permission to do what was "most agreeable to his feelings and consonant with humanity" and continued in a vein that made it clear that the person he sought to emancipate was his own son. Beginning with the 1816 state census, Amy Johnson appears as the head of a free black household. After obtaining a license "to retail in Natchez" in 1819, she operated a small shop or worked as a peddler. Possessing an excellent head for business, she bought and sold a wide variety of items, mostly small, but including slaves. While her son inherited her propensity for earning money, he fortunately did not inherit her stormy disposition. In spite of her diminutive stature (she was five feet tall), Amy had an outsized temper, as evidenced by her habit of "running out in the streets to complete her quarrels." Perhaps her refusal to back down to anyone fueled her son's ambition to enter the front ranks of Natchez society.[7]

William Johnson entered the barbering trade with the help of another family member, his brother-in-law James Miller, a free black man from Philadelphia who ran the most popular barbershop in the city. As evidenced by the willingness of prominent white residents to petition the Mississippi legislature to allow him to remain in the state, Miller had a knack for cultivating white patrons, and he passed that on to his young apprentice along with other barbering skills. Johnson struck out on his own in 1828, moving to nearby Port Gibson and opening a barbershop there. When his brother-in-law decided to relocate to New Orleans two years later, Johnson returned to Natchez to take his place as owner of the city's foremost barbershop. Miller sold Johnson his barbershop for $300, about what the shop cleared in a good month.[8]

Although Johnson's own initiative propelled him to considerable prosperity and renown, his mother and brother-in-law had set him on the path to success, and in turn he displayed a paternal care for his apprentices that reflected his family traditions. Apprentices came to live with Johnson at anywhere from ten to fifteen years of age and worked under him until they were either eighteen or twenty-one. In exchange for their work, Johnson taught them the barber's trade; fed, housed, and sometimes clothed them; and gave them the rudiments of a general education. He also spent an inordinate amount of time riding herd on boisterous teenagers, according to numerous entries in his voluminous diary. On March 21, 1837, Johnson had to placate a white neighbor who had told French Williams, one of the apprentices, that he better not see him around his place again, because "French had been peeping through the fence at One of his Girls on Sunday." William Johnson informed French afterward that he could forget about going to an upcoming party to which he had been invited. On another occasion, Johnson arrived early at his shop and "found that the Boys had Just been smoking some of my Cegars which they Denied. I listened a while and was satisfied that they had stolen them." The transgression earned the boys a few slaps from their master. Johnson had to resort to corporal punishment often, since fights between the boys were his biggest problem. His entry for February 2, 1836, "I had to whip Little Bill & John for fighting in the shop," bore a remarkable similarity to a later entry from the same year, when he wrote, "I had to whip Bill Winston and Bill Nix for fighting in the shop to night when gentlemen was in the Shop." His role as disciplinarian did not prevent him from enjoying his apprentices' company on hunting trips or occasionally indulging them, although the boys sometimes made him regret his generosity. On a busy day in 1835, Johnson had already conducted a brisk business by 11:00, so he took the rest of the day off and told his apprentices that they could keep whatever they earned before closing the barbershop. The surplus funds apparently went to their heads, for two days later he wrote, "William & John & Bill Nix staid out until 1/2 10 O'clock at night. When the[y] came, they knocked so Loud at the Door and made so much noise that I came out with my stick and pounded both of the Williams and J."[9]

Johnson accepted both free African Americans and slaves as apprentices, and unsurprisingly, he took the most interest in the boys who reminded him of himself as a young man. In particular, Bill Winston won his favor. Beginning his apprenticeship at the tender age of twelve (Johnson's diary entry reads, "Little William Winston came to stay with me to Lern the Barbers trade") the boy had much in common with Johnson. Winston had been born a slave, but his master, former lieutenant governor Fountain Winston, freed the boy's mother in his will and included startlingly frank provisions regarding the young slave: "Believing Bill . . . too white to be continued in Slavery," he made provisions for him to be freed after learning a trade. Johnson and Winston shared more than common origins. Unlike his other apprentices, Winston had an innate dignity and trustworthiness that corresponded to Johnson's own ideals. Johnson also admired the young man's toughness. Shortly after he arrived, Winston got into a fight with another apprentice in the back room of the shop. "I Parted them Both and," egging the young man on, "made a greate Deal of fun of Winston. Second fight took place in the Back of the Yard and Bill Winston whipped him fairly and [the other boy] [howled] to have Bill Winston taken off of him." Winston's independent streak could be trying at times, such as when Johnson returned to the shop and "found the Boys in a Contraversy. Tryed to Have an Explanation of the Affair. Winston Continued to talk after being told several times to Hush—Gave Him a slap—He Jump[ed] Out of the front Door and Runs around the Corner and up the Back Alley—I Caught Him opposite to the Bank in the Alley—Slapped Him Like as One would in Such Casses." Yet, when Winston's white guardian came by to discuss the young man's future with Johnson after he had reached eighteen, Johnson readily agreed to employ him as a journeyman barber. In addition, Johnson reported to the guardian that "Winston was a smart boy and that I liked him very much."[10]

This promising young man proved to be Johnson's most apt student. In all likelihood, Winston viewed Johnson as a surrogate father, filling a gap that a twelve-year-old would have felt keenly. The death of his owner more than likely deprived him of his biological father, and his mother Rachel appeared to have difficulty supporting her son. On one occasion, she asked Johnson to send her money for two shirts that she had made her son, "being as I am not able to pay for it myself." Johnson, by contrast, had wealth and connections to the white elite, along with the knowledge of fatherhood that came from having ten children and numerous apprentices. He also enjoyed the company of the bright, upbeat young man, frequently taking Winston along with him for rides in the country, on hunting and fishing expeditions, and to horse races at the track. As the boy became a man, Johnson's admiration for his protégé grew, it seems, for he referred to his former apprentice as "Dr. Winston" in his diary. That Winston had learned Johnson's lessons about dealing with members of the other race was demonstrated when the Mississippi Legislature passed a special law in 1854 allowing William Winston to remain in the state as a free African American. In a decade when leading white Southerners opposed the very idea of manumission, the legislation would have been exceptional but for the precedent established by William Johnson and his mentor James Miller.[11] Miller and Johnson established a tradition of African American barbering in Natchez that they instilled in a younger generation through apprenticeships that combined training with family feeling.

The solidarity and fostering that was developing among black barbers helped apprentices in a climate that saw many abuses. Apprenticeships for black children and youth ostensibly provided support for free children of indigent families and for orphans while ensuring that the young charges learned a useful trade. Over the course of the nineteenth century, however, apprenticeships increasingly became an institution that allowed white masters to coerce labor from free African Americans without preparing them for the future. Many states ceased requiring masters to teach their apprentices to read and write, and courts often ignored this obligation where it did remain in effect. Worst of all, some free black children found themselves assigned by the courts to jobs that involved few skills, such as working as farmhands, so their apprenticeships left them ill-prepared to earn a decent living.[12]

Black apprentice masters appear to have been more conscientious about ensuring that their apprentices received an education and learned valuable trade skills. In part, this solicitude for young charges grew naturally out of blood ties, for masters often accepted relatives as apprentices, such as when John Fernandis of Baltimore took on his nephew as an apprentice barber. Even apprentices without family ties enjoyed connections to skilled blacks from living in tight-knit communities. Since bootblacks and barbers served the same clientele, it was likely that bootblack Isaac Watts knew Baltimore's leading black barber, Thomas Green, before Watt's thirteen-year-old son began an apprenticeship with Green in 1826, pledging that the boy would receive "one years schooling" in addition to learning the tonsorial art.[13]

Barbers and other black tradesmen also had self-interested reasons for taking apprentices, who provided free, albeit semiskilled, labor. Barber John Stanly of New Bern, North Carolina, regularly signed indentures for apprentices in trades other than barbering, such as carpentry, to obtain workers for his numerous properties. Moreover, in 1807, Stanly brought one apprentice back to the court only four months after taking him on, to release him back to the justices, suggesting that the young man had failed to meet Stanly's labor needs. Apprentices also provided a significant portion of William Johnson's workforce in his bathhouse and three barbershops. More than once, Johnson declined to take boys as apprentices even though their parents or white guardians brought them to him, which again suggests that a degree of self-interest informed his thinking.[14] William Johnson, being a good master and a good businessman, combined altruistic and pecuniary motives when dealing with apprentices, and he launched many young barbers on successful careers. The frequency with which black barbershop owners took apprentices and the care they provided for their wards show a commitment among black barbers to fostering their trade and successive generations of African American men.

By maintaining the artisan system, black barbers ensured work and decent prices for all practitioners through a system that took care of them from the moment they entered the trade until their death. They started out as apprentices, then became journeymen entitled to full wages, and finally entered the ranks of master barbers who had their own shops and supported one another through mutual aid societies that, among other assistance, would pay for their funerals. In the nineteenth century, African Americans enjoyed few opportunities to prosper as skilled workers. Since barbers moved among shops as they advanced in their skills, and since barbering could be practiced into old age and barbershop owners remained active practitioners of their trade, all black barbers had a vested interest in maintaining reciprocal obligations that stressed fraternity and fostered harmony in their shops. Even the most prosperous black barbers scraped chins and cut hair every day. Thomas Green, the wealthiest black barber in Baltimore, with a shop valued at over $11,000 and assets exceeding $20,000, worked alongside his employees until he died. Green also followed the venerable tradition of living above his shop and taking apprentices into his home. Bonds of kinship and community also help explain why class distinctions meant little to black barbers. When Cyprian Clamorgan wrote his unique description of the black elite in St. Louis, he counted several journeymen barbers in the ranks of the "colored aristocracy."[15] This inclusiveness sprang from a desire to help relatives, the sons of friends, and promising young African American men.

The black barbers' social network functioned almost like a guild, reserving opportunities for members only. When journeyman barber Walter Thomas moved to Boston in the 1830s, he attended a church service where he had the good fortune to meet one of the city's leading black barbers, Peter Howard, who gave him a job. Black barbershop owners also frequently opened their homes to journeyman and other master barbers. The wealthy barber John J. Smith, for instance, made it easier for journeyman John Robinson to move from Pennsylvania to Boston by allowing him to live with his family. In some cases, a favored young man acquired the experience and contacts necessary to become a barbershop owner himself. Thus, Norton Reynolds worked for Henry Clamorgan, and his connection with Clamorgan helped him to go into business for himself. When Clamorgan died, Reynolds joined forces with the deceased barber's partner and took over the lucrative Clamorgan barbershop and bathhouse. Marrying the daughter of a prosperous black barber offered an even faster way for an ambitious young man to enter the ranks of business owners. After migrating to St. Louis, Robert Wilkinson had toiled with little reward, serving dock workers in his small barbershop. His marriage to a relative of Cyprian Clamorgan secured his admission to black elite society as well as a partnership with his wife's kinsman. After a falling out with Clamorgan, Wilkinson opened another barbershop, which became one of the most popular in the city. The fact that Clamorgan, despite his lingering anger at Wilkinson, made complimentary remarks in print about the way his in-law ran his business illustrates the high value that black barbers placed on solidarity.[16]

Black owners of barbershops sometimes encouraged one of their employees to relocate in order to secure a better position. In his diary, William Johnson recorded several instances when he made his connections available to other barbers. He gave a job to one free black barber who had previously worked for his brother-in-law in New Orleans, while he helped another employee, Bill Nix, become a proprietor when he learned that the barber in a nearby town had died.

Despite Nix's being the most troublesome apprentice Johnson had ever had—he recorded more complaints about Nix in his diary than about any other boy—the barber noted his protégé's departure with the sentiment: "I hope he may do well, I Know he can if He will Only try." An extraordinary arrangement that Johnson had with the other prominent black barber in Natchez testifies to loyalty and cooperation within the barbering brotherhood. They took turns employing a man named Washington Sterns in their barbershops. Although Sterns's high wages attest to his skill as a barber, the two barbershop owners appear to have swapped Sterns between them when one grew tired of his drinking problem. The willingness of master barbers to help apprentices, journeymen, and each other perpetuated the artisan system in their trade and benefited all black barbers.[17]

Maintaining such traditions, however, had little value unless black barbers could attract prosperous white customers. Toward this end, the high level of skill achieved through long, closely supervised apprenticeships proved inestimable. William Johnson demonstrated his concern for skill when he corrected apprentices for lapses in technique. "I had to Beat William," he wrote in 1835, "about being so careless and passionate, whilst shaving." the importance of this emphasis on shaving is understandable, when a gouge from a straight-edged razor could mean serious bloodletting. Accordingly, black barbers strove for a reputation as unparalleled experts at scraping away whiskers. A passage in an antebellum novel about a black-owned barbershop suggests that they achieved their goal. "On taking the chair to be beautified," says a white customer, "the handling was so artistic, so tasteful, so gentlemanly, you wished to be shaved all day; or secretly hoped your hair would grow up as fast as it was cut off!"[18]

Cyprian Clamorgan also stressed the skill of black barbers with the razor in his descriptions of his peers in St. Louis, prefacing his remarks with the assertion that African Americans "certainly make the best barbers in the world. . . . They take white men by the nose [to steady the face] without giving offense, and without causing an effusion of blood." He amplified this testament to black skill in his discussion of fellow barber Byertere Hickman: "He tweaks a man's nose with a dainty finger, as though he regretted being compelled to take hold of the human face by the natural handle, and peels off the beard like a dairy-maid skimming cream." Clamorgan singled out two other barbers for more general praise, giving them the encomium "good workmen." Significantly, his praise for these two colleagues placed equal weight on qualities that had a less obvious connection to skill. Clamorgan complimented Peter Cox for being "very attentive to business," while he lauded Norton Reynolds, Jr., for being "finely formed, and very neat in his dress."[19] Although everyone working in personal service would be well advised to pay attention to the customer and present a good appearance, Clamorgan touched on a key element in the appeal of black barbers to white customers: they played the role of the servant.

Black barbers might have owned their shops, but white customers acted as if they ran them, establishing the tone for the relationship. Reminiscing at the end of his life about "the old time barber shop" of the antebellum period, James Thomas in his autobiography described an environment in which white "gentlemen" insisted on their prerogatives. "The old timer would walk in," Thomas recalled, "take off his coat, hand it to the boy, take off his hat. . . . The boy would brush hat and coat while [the] shave was going on." According to Thomas, gentlemen of the old school would present a "cross and unpleasant appearance" until they had taken the measure of their black barber and decided they liked his demeanor, which they indicated by telling "a little story to the barber or this boy or listen[ing] to his, [the] barber's, yarn with due interest and apparent enjoyment." Rather than passively accepting the service provided by black barbers, "many of the customers were very particular and would lecture the attendant on the slightest occasion. When the customer would come, he would like enough to say, 'Wash your hands.' 'Just washed 'em Judge.' 'Wash 'em again.'" Thomas said that white customers would also inspect the cleanliness of the towels before letting the barber use them and "raised a small row" if the barber's breath smelled of onions or if his hands retained the scent of cheap cigars. Aware of how harsh this treatment sounded, Thomas reassured his readers that the white customers "had no Idea of falling out with the barber. But he was firm in educating the barber to the extent of what a Gentleman was entitled to." Elaborating further, Thomas maintained that "the barber was safe so long as he showed a cheerful willingness to please," or in other words, as long as he acted the part of the deferential servant.[20]

Black barbers accepted their subordinate status because it proved to be an asset. During the 1820s, black-run barbershops emerged as microcosms of the public sphere in the new republic. The enfranchised men of the community, its citizens, gathered for egalitarian camaraderie, and barbershops were one of the favorite gathering places. In James Thomas's Nashville barbershop, for instance, one might encounter businessman E. S. "Squire" Hall, the Reverend William Brownlow, plantation owner William Giles, attorney Francis Fogg, or former governor William Carroll conversing affably with less distinguished white men such as a store clerk or a policeman. Thomas recalled the political topics that animated the conversation and that also underscored the equality of all of the white customers. "Mr. Clay, Mr. Webster, and Mr. Calhoun were much talked of as statesmen. Mr. Tom Corwan of Ohio was not talked of much by the southern people, but Webster and Clay headed the list. . . . Greely of New York was often mentioned but the language in his direction was anything but complimentary."[21] As citizens, all the white men present in the barbershop had the right to participate in these discussions.

The easygoing give-and-take of the barbershop masked inequalities of wealth and status to an extent, but the differences between the men remained apparent in their clothing, their manner of speaking, and their titles. Consequently, the tensions of social hierarchy still reigned in the barbershop, with unspoken resentments and barely concealed snobbery floating in the background. The presence of a black barber diffused this tension, for, whatever the rank of the white customers, they all could feel superior to the staff of the barbershop, and even its owner. Take for example an occasion when Thomas attempted to join a conversation about politics in his own shop. Unfamiliar with the Wilmont Proviso that his customers were discussing, he asked a young lawyer to explain it to him. "The set back I got from him," he remembered, "for asking such a question caused me to be careful as to who I plied questions to with regard to politics. Among other things, he told me I had no right to listen to gentlemen's conversations." The white customer had put Thomas in his place as a black man. Since he was not a citizen, he had no business being concerned with politics. All of the white customers shared an exclusive privilege based on their skin color, a fact reinforced by the presence of an African American. In addition, the privilege of race allowed white men to indulge their baser instincts and take advantage of the opportunity to boss an inferior. An Englishman visiting New York City commented on this phenomenon, observing that white residents preferred hiring black coachmen "because they had no fear that they would assume any thing like equality, because they could order them about in the tone of masters."[22]

In the South, pro-slavery ideology magnified the significance of receiving service from a black barber. Because the institution of slavery freed whites from the necessity of performing menial labor, it preserved their independence. The logic of this argument extended to race relations in general. In 1838, a leading pro-slavery theorist, Robert Barnwell Rhett, declared that "history presents no such combination for republican liberty than that which exists at the South. The African for the laborer—the Anglo-Saxon for the master and ruler." By mitigating class tensions among white southerners, black workers provided the basis for social harmony in a republic. The association of barbering with servitude and of servitude with African Americans made the trade especially repugnant to white southerners who disdained it as "nigger work." According to James Thomas, "a gentleman would not have a white man around him as a waiter or barber. They wanted nothing to do with a white man that could not rise above that." The sight of another white man in personal service apparently revolted them. Thomas's memories of such occurrences involved extreme reactions. "Should a white man attempt to wait on a southern country gentleman in the capacity of a barber, he would go into spasms. If a white man came toward him to shave him, he would jump out of the chair. . . . It was not a white man's place to play the part of a servant."[23] To a certain extent, black barbers played the servant to accommodate white customers, who lined up to enjoy the feeling of superiority.

Humorous anecdotes that white men told of hapless black barbers were among the jokes they made at the expense of the relatively powerless African Americans. In his autobiography, P. T. Barnum relished the memory of hoodwinking a barber during a trip aboard a steamboat. As Barnum recounted it, the barber witnessed the famous showman performing sleight-of-hand tricks and allegedly suspected that Barnum had acquired occult powers through a pact with the Devil. The barber's superstitious beliefs presented an opportunity for ridicule irresistible to Barnum, and he hatched a prank in league with the ship's clerk. He informed the barber, while enjoying a shave, that he had sold his soul, and consequently, "no matter who has money, nor where he keeps it, in his box or till, or anywhere about him, I have only to speak the words, and it comes." Alarmed, the barber transferred his earnings to the ship's safe under the charge of the clerk, who then consulted Barnum and hid the money. Shortly thereafter, intent on testing the showman's nefarious abilities, the barber found Barnum and asked, "Beg pardon, Mr. Barnum, but where is my money? Can you get it?" "I do not want your money," protested Barnum, "It is safe." Triumphantly, the barber replied with a pun, "yes, I know it is safe, Ha! Ha! It is in the iron safe in the clerk's office, safe enough from you!" Barnum assured the barber that his money was no longer in the safe, which prompted the black man to rush to the clerk's office, where he discovered that his funds were indeed gone. When the mystified barber pleaded for the return of his money, Barnum directed him to open a drawer in his cabin, and there lay the sack of coins. Not satisfied with threatening the barber with the loss of his money, Barnum proposed turning him into a cat, which he claimed made the black man flee in terror. The showman only ceased his pranks when the ship's captain expressed concern that the barber might jump overboard. Barnum then explained the trick to his victim, and in his account of how the barber reacted drew heavily on stereotypes: "'By golly!' said the barber, in the exultation characteristic of his race, 'by golly! When I get back to New Orleans, I'll come Barnum over de colored people. Ha! Ha!'"[24]

Although Barnum's tale upheld his own reputation for showmanship, the main thrust of the story concerned how superior intelligence allowed a white man to bamboozle a dim-witted, superstitious black man. Barnum presented the barber as naïve and gullible, failing to suspect that the clerk had hoodwinked him. Moreover, the joke hinged on the barber's falling prey to his own superstition, the antithesis of the hard-nosed rationalism that had become a much-vaunted part of the character of white American men by the antebellum period. Even the way Barnum depicted the barber's response to learning he had been fooled underscored the inequality between the two men. When the barber announced his intention to "come Barnum over the colored people," he implied that every African American could be taken in by the ruse. Barnum's overstatements and clichés suggest that the tale owes more to the conventions of the minstrel stage, on which he once performed, than to the facts of his encounter with a black man working on a steamboat.[25] Barnum cast the barber in the role of the comical fool, of Sambo, in order to amuse and, more importantly, to flatter the egos of his white readers by letting them feel superior.

Certain elements of the tale, however, reveal the audacity and intelligence of the black barber whom Barnum had actually encountered. After securing his money, the barber confronted Barnum and called his bluff, which is hardly in keeping with the role of a deferential subordinate. Moreover, the nimble wordplay of the black barber's challenge to Barnum, recognizing the showman's punning on the meaning of the word safe, displayed his cleverness. And, rather than expressing anger for being made the butt of a joke, the black barber laughed when informed of Barnum's trick. The role that whites prescribed for black barbers left some room for assertiveness but also had its limits. Indirectly, the black barber in the story played another role for whites. His supposedly innate gullibility had tempted Barnum to hatch his prank, which exposed the showman for the confidence man that he was. His skilled execution of the ruse and his glee at having tricked the black barber into believing his outlandish claims let the other passengers on the steamboat know that they should be wary of confidence men.

Nineteenth-century Americans viewed confidence men as a major threat to their society. As deference and hierarchy gave way to the fluid social order of the Jacksonian Age, Americans confronted a dilemma. On the one hand, they strove mightily to take advantage of the opportunities presented by a booming economy to improve their social position and move up in the world. On the other hand, they increasingly lived among strangers in growing cities and on far-flung frontiers, which left them wondering whom they could trust. They would have to trust some of these unfamiliar people, for they needed business associates to prosper and social acquaintances to have status. Yet, they feared being hoodwinked by men who used deceit and guile to win their confidence. Conduct manuals of the time offered a solution to the problem by advocating a scrupulous sincerity that would allow one's character to be transparent. By conducting oneself after the fashion of respectable people, embodying the virtues of industry, piety, and thrift, an individual could establish a good reputation. This advice lessened the contradictions experienced by Americans who celebrated democracy even as they sought class distinctions for themselves. Prosperity and membership in polite society would go to the deserving, while the unworthy would languish in poverty.[26]

In a society that condemned hypocrisy in the strongest terms, the very nature of the barber's trade presented a dilemma. Barbers often helped their customers appear to be someone other than their true selves. By applying hair dyes and arranging wigs, they disguised age. By retailing cosmetics and perfume, they added sparkle to dull countenances and sweetened the malodorous. Were barbers to be trusted? Herman Melville explicitly addressed the tensions between antebellum values and the barbering profession in his novel *The Confidence Man*. When the main character, a mysterious stranger traveling aboard a steamboat, mouthing a philosophy of confidence in others to all who will listen, goes to the ship's barbershop for a shave, he engages the barber in a debate about disguises. The white barber, William Cream, expresses cynicism about human nature, which he justifies by citing his work. "What think you, sir," he asks, "are a thoughtful barber's reflections, when, behind a careful curtain, he shaves the thin, dead stubble off a head, and then dismisses it to the world, radiant in curling auburn?" He answers his own question by contrasting the "shamefaced air behind the curtain, the fearful looking forward to being possibly discovered by a prying acquaintance" with "the cheerful assurance and challenging pride with which the same man steps forth again, a gay deception." Expressing his lack of faith in the public, the barber announces his refusal to extend credit to customers by a plaque above his station reading "No Trust."[27]

Melville presented his fictional barber as a reluctant accomplice in his customers' deceptions. Other contemporary authors and journalists depicted the barber as a morally ambiguous figure, whose congeniality, readers learned, might hide avarice and duplicity. One typical account of a barber, published by *Harper's Magazine*, came prefaced with the editor's observation that in any large city, one could find "your keen barber" with "speculation in his eyes," who plotted to make a "customer" of you in more ways than one. In "Barberised Drama," which followed these remarks, a customer refuses to be cajoled by Oily the barber into buying vegetable extract, a wig, and various brushes, soaps, and scents. The frustrated Oily consoles himself, "That's a rare customer, at any rate." Writers drew, to some extent, on popular wisdom; and in the slang of the period, *barber* meant a thief, who "lathered up" or talked smoothly to his victim before "shaving" or robbing him.[28]

Black barbers were aware of these stereotypes, but also, alert to changes in the ideas of white Americans, observed as new trends in racial thought began to portray African Americans as moral paragons. This new ideology helped white people address the issue of trustworthiness in black servants. To the extent that white men subscribed to the new racial ideology, which historians refer to as "romantic racialism," their suspicion of black barbers changed into affection and sympathy. Proponents of this doctrine extrapolated the well-established dichotomy of white independence and black subservience into a critique of the growing materialism and aggressiveness of white Americans. Influenced by the Romantic movement and by evangelical religion, they reassessed in a favorable light the qualities that whites attributed to African Americans and came up with a new image—forgiving, humble, pious, patient, and selfless. They started from the assumption that nations and races differed fundamentally, each with its own character and destiny. Whereas Anglo-Saxons reputedly possessed a unique gift for promoting democracy and enterprise due to their hard-nosed rationalism, African Americans were thought to be innately religious because of their allegedly emotional, childlike nature. Romantic racialism maintained that black people exerted a positive influence on white people through the example they provided of Christian virtues. Harriet Beecher Stowe penned the best-known literary expression of the doctrine, *Uncle Tom's Cabin,* a novel that contrasted the Christ-like nobility of the slave Uncle Tom with the selfishness and cruelty of the slave owner Simon Legree. The exemplary traits of the romanticized African American included, as one proponent asserted, "a native courtesy, a civility . . . and a capacity for the highest refinement of character." This reassessment transformed what had been a sign of corruption—being of African blood—into evidence of virtue.[29] Consequently, romantic racialism encouraged white men to have confidence in black barbers.

Writing in the same vein as Harriet Beecher Stowe, a white man named Bayard Hall published a novel in 1852 that employed romanticized stereotypes of African Americans to show his readers they could admire a black barber without foregoing their sense of racial superiority. The book, *Frank Freeman's Barber Shop,* focused on the virtues of its protagonist, Frank the Barber. In tones bordering on adulation, Hall described Frank to his readers as a paragon. His commanding appearance and "noble" expression inspired pleasure and confidence in others. Moreover, Frank's intelligence and genteel manners made him "better in all respects than some white men." Nonetheless, Hall qualified his praise by noting attributes that fit with the stereotype of the romantic racialists. Because "Frank was ardent and impulsive" along with having a tendency to be "confiding and unsuspicious," "he could be led into error by those he trusted."[30] Frank, in other words, exhibited childlike qualities that underscored his sincerity, and such qualities of course made white guidance a necessity.

The plot of the novel, which concerns how Frank achieved freedom and business success, combines accurate biographical details about barbers with a far-fetched hope that free African Americans would resolve tensions over slavery between the North and the South by leaving the United States. Like most barbers who began their lives as slaves, Frank won the respect of his owner through his work as a steward and overseer. He also acquired an education and a polished manner through his interaction with the white elite of the South. Traveling North with his owner, Frank seized the opportunity to grasp his freedom. Thereafter, he walked in the footsteps of other black barbers, taking the name Freeman, capitalizing on his knowledge of genteel ways by opening a barbershop, and becoming a leader in the abolitionist movement. Unlike most black barbers, however, Frank embraced the message of the colonizationist movement, that African Americans had no future in the United States, and he emigrated to Liberia, where he became a minister and one of the founding fathers of the independent black republic. The disjuncture between Frank's plausible life history and his implausible support for colonization underscored how even whites knowledgeable about black barbers viewed these men through the twin lenses of stereotype and wishful thinking.

Hall also went to great lengths to assure his readers that commendable African Americans posed no threat to the racial order. While still enslaved, his hero Frank saved the life of his owner and countless other whites by informing on slaves who were plotting a revolt. Frank justified his betrayal of other African Americans by citing the affection he felt for his owner's family. Similarly, after running away from his owner in the North, Frank felt guilty about having forsaken his devoted master and pledged that he would mail remittances with which to buy his freedom. Although in the novel Frank Freeman became an abolitionist, he gave an accomodationist speech at an abolitionist meeting. Not only did Frank refuse to condemn his former owner for holding him in bondage, but he also disavowed bitterness toward whites. "I hate no one," he declared, "but I love my race! I would destroy no one, but I would deliver [my people]!" The author of this fiction sought to present sectional conflict as the result of irresponsible white abolitionists who made slaves long for freedom without providing them with a means to achieve it. He has Frank say, "It is a crime to wake the wrath of my people unless that wrath shall set and establish them free." The responsible black barber, although he demonstrated his manhood by expressing his readiness to die fighting slavery, revealed his peaceable nature when he begged his audience, "Show me . . . the way to free my race without murder and massacre." When, in the end, Frank's white supporters offered to finance his emigration to Liberia, he abandoned his prosperous barbershop without hesitation to help fulfill the destiny of his race.[31] Hall reiterates again and again his message that if African Americans got the respect they deserved, they would gladly accept tutelage from whites and, in the process, validate a kinder, gentler, although still unequal racial order. Although Hall's concerns about sectionalism permeate his novel, *Frank Freeman's Barber Shop* accurately describes the way many whites viewed prominent black barbers, especially Pierre Toussaint, who had become a legend in his own time.

When Toussaint passed away in 1853, after styling the hair of New York City's leading ladies for more than half a century, his obituaries revealed that his white friends and customers had become convinced that he embodied the African American envisioned by romantic racialism. Two of his eulogists specifically referred to fictional characters in describing his praiseworthy qualities. The *New York Post* began its death notice with the heading: "Uncle Tom Not An Apocryphal Character," followed by the suggestion that Toussaint could have served as the model for the protagonist of Harriet Beecher Stowe's novel. The *Home Journal* went even further, proclaiming Toussaint "one whose example is a higher vindication of his race . . . than all the works of fiction that studious invention ever conceived." Showing the influence of contemporary ideas, all of his eulogists praised him for qualities associated with the stereotypes of romantic racialism. One described him as "a man of the warmest and most active benevolence, the gentlest temper, and the most courteous and graceful, yet wholly unassuming manners." Throughout his death notices, the writers also attributed his superior character to his deep religious faith. Toussaint additionally received praise for scrupulously adhering to racial etiquette. According to one eulogist, "no familiarity ever made him forget what was due to his superiors."[32] The portrait that emerged from the obituaries helped explain the success of one of the wealthiest black men in New York City; admirable and pleasant without overstepping his place, Toussaint had cultivated a reputation that abundantly satisfied the expectations of his white customers.

Courting white opinion had had its benefits, for Toussaint had earned an impeccable reputation. One white admirer claimed that Toussaint's respectability made him forget their racial differences. "I never," he wrote, "met with any other of his race who made me forget his color." Explaining the basis of his opinion, the man argued that Toussaint had possessed the qualities of a "perfect gentleman." He had displayed "gentle and courtly" manners, the "most unaffected good humor at all times," and the "most natural and artful conversation." These qualities, significantly, had made it possible for Toussaint to serve without being degraded: he had "the most respectful and polite demeanor without the slightest tincture of servility." One of Toussaint's eulogists repeated this assessment by telling the story of a friend "distinguished for the wit and point of his conversation," who had listened to a lady assert that a well-known Frenchman illustrated her idea of a perfect gentleman. He replied to her, "The most perfect gentleman I have ever known is Pierre Toussaint." Residents of the slave states offered similar praise for the character of black barbers. In St. Louis, Cyprian Clamorgan held up his employee James Thomas as an exemplar due to his refinement. According to his employer, Thomas was "very genteel in his manners," and "his character, moral and intellectual, would do honor to the proudest white man in the land." Clamorgan justified his admiration by referring to a compliment paid to Thomas by a gentleman "occupying the front rank of statesmen in the West." In this distinguished white man's opinion, "all that prevented [Thomas] from being one of the greatest men of the age was his color."[33]

The respectability of black barbers in the eyes of their white customers presented them with a unique opportunity. Their good reputation gave black barbers the credentials to preside over a new type of barbershop. In 1837, George McBride, a black barber in Mobile, Alabama, placed an advertisement in the city directory that publicized the remodeling of his establishment. These improvements placed his shop among the growing number of "first-class" barbershops, where customers enjoyed service in luxurious surroundings. His advertisement also documented that barbershops had become sites for the sale of related items, offering an array of perfume, hair-care products, and cosmetics. Appropriately, McBride located his business in the Alabama Hotel, itself a specimen of a new type of commercial establishments that served as civic centers and showplaces for consumer goods. In an age devoted to commerce, progress entailed a dizzying growth in material goods that Americans could buy, and no one place better symbolized the flowering of a consumer society than the luxury hotel. A marked departure from the inns that preceeded them, hotels installed public parlors that emulated the salons of aristocratic mansions. Despite their grandeur, these new urban

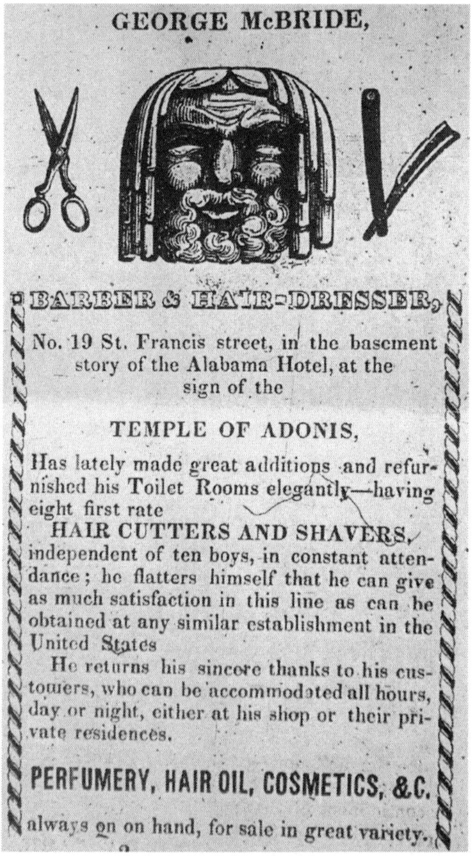

Advertisement for George McBride's first-class barbershop. The reference to Adonis flattered potential customers by implying their familiarity with Greek mythology, an example of the way black barbers validated genteel credentials in their new first-class shops. (From *Fay's Mobile Directory*, 1838; photograph by the author.)

institutions were hailed as "palaces of the people" because they welcomed all (whites) who could afford the bill of fare. Hotels set a trend that other places of business, such as photographer's studios, steamboats, and barbershops followed. As a result, experiencing luxury became part of the service that customers bought. These commercial parlors were the first to feature items that became the hallmarks of Victorian home decor: carpets, window draperies with lace, matched sets of upholstered furniture, "fancy" chairs, a center table, a piano, a decorated mantel, and smaller objects such as framed pictures.[34]

In even greater numbers than they had before, white men flocked to black-owned barbershops. In one novel set in antebellum Philadelphia, published in 1852, the author drew attention to the neat, clean, and comfortable barbershops, stocked with the best newspapers and filled with the best company. Moreover, "when you went in," the writer added, "you felt at once homey and did not want to go out again." The lather mugs that lined the walls of these barbershops contributed to the fraternal atmosphere, for each regular customer would buy his own mug, stamped with his initials in gold letters. Purchasing a shaving mug and keeping it in the barbershop signaled membership in the circle of regular patrons.[35]

Attaining the designation "first class" involved considerable expense and trouble, so black barbers such as McBride often notified the public of their improvements, advertising that they had established a "shaving saloon." A popularization of the term *salon*, referring to the large reception rooms in grand houses, *saloon* in the parlance of the day meant a first-class business. One advertisement for William Roberson's Marble Palace, a "Bathing and Shaving Saloon" in St. Louis, illustrated the lengths to which some black barbers went to ensure that their customers enjoyed the height of fashion. Sitting beneath ceilings with elaborate plaster fretwork, the customers watched the progress of their shave in large, gilt-framed mirrors lit by an enormous chandelier. They might choose to seek additional pampering by walking across the vast brocade carpet in Roberson's capacious shampooing room, where they would find another attendant. Afterward, they had their choice of a sulfur, steam, mercurial, iodine, perfumed, salt, hot, cold, or showered bath. Roberson also discreetly set aside private rooms for removing corns and bunions. Another illustration of a black barbershop revealed similarly genteel accoutrements. Outfitted with heavy Empire-style furnishings, the barbershop also displayed refinement with framed pictures on the wall, elaborate draperies, crown moldings, and a gas chandelier. A new and improved variety of barber's chairs functioned as the centerpieces of the most up-to-date shops. In addition to being upholstered and ornamented, these chairs swiveled and reclined, an innovation quickly copied in railroad parlor cars and in upscale homes.[36]

Black-owned barbershops stimulated desires for a host of products besides reclining chairs, becoming sites of male consumption. Although the items most commonly sold by black barbers—wigs and personal care products—had a connection to the services provided in barbershops, customers might also be tempted to buy fashion accessories such as socks, collars, and suspenders. The size of the orders placed by Jacob White, a leading black barber in Philadelphia, attest to the

Advertisement for William Roberson's first-class barbershop, the Marble Palace Saloon. Note that the proprietor appropriated the title "Professor" for himself, in keeping with the distinguished environment over which he presided. The bottom half of the advertisement features the interior of the "cooling room," the floor plan of the baths, and two illustrations of rooms in the baths. (Rapier Family Papers, series-D cards, box 84-2, file 104; courtesy of Moorland-Spingarn Research Center, Howard University, Washington, D.C.)

Antebellum illustration of black barbers serving white customers in a first-class barbershop. Note the contrast between the realistic depiction of white customers and the caricatured or featureless black barbers and attendant. (Photograph by the author.)

volume of his retail business. In addition to cologne water by the pint and cigars by the thousand, White's ledgers show that he carried a range of personal care products such as hair oil, toothbrushes, and cold cream. Black barbershop owners also played a crucial role in stimulating middle-class Americans to purchase bathtubs and soap. Since washing oneself regularly was uncommon before the 1850s, black barbers had to persuade customers to use their bathhouses by presenting bathing as a genteel entertainment. One black barber informed newspaper readers that he had opened his bathhouse in "an effort to accommodate them with a luxury."[37]

Public parlors like those found in upscale businesses also gave Americans a stage for conducting elaborately scripted performances that demonstrated their respectability. These "genteel performances" not only allowed people to claim an elevated social status but also let them display the sincerity of their character. Sincerity reassured acquaintances that an individual could be trusted, which mattered in an age that expressed concern about imposters who won one's confidence under false pretenses. For antebellum men, inspiring confidence in others had everything to do with manhood, and white men displayed this manhood in public spaces like hotels and barbershops, which were segregated by gender. Middle-class ladies, whose place of display was the domestic parlor, only ventured into certain public parlors, if escorted by men, and avoided others entirely. Hotels maintained ladies' parlors with separate entrances, because the lobbies played host to rowdy men arguing politics and drinking whiskey. As for barbershops, women had no reason to enter, making them ideal settings for white men to define their public identity and masculinity.[38]

White men gathered at first-class barbershops to discuss their lives, and in the process, collectively established standards for manhood and respectability. In William Johnson's barbershop, for example, troubled marriages occupied a prominent role in barbershop gossip. Debates over whether this young man should have eloped or that one should have left his wife provided a forum for clarifying the obligations of husbands and fathers. In many cases, barbershop customers swapped tales that illustrated pitfalls to be avoided, such as bankruptcy or, worst of all, running from a fight. Discussions of politics, while they served the purpose of making all white customers feel equal, also helped define what qualities made a man admirable. Of his customers in the shop he kept in Nashville, James Thomas said that "the old gentlemen who were young men while [Andrew] Jackson was about the town never tired of talking about him." The elders in Thomas's barbershop held up this larger-than-life political figure, whom they admired for his personal magnetism, pluck, and sporting proclivities, as a model for all men to emulate. The presence of a genteel servant dignified these conversations, for a black barber not only kept his customer's chin free of stubble and his hair clipped in the latest fashion but also laughed at his jokes and listened gravely to his philosophical ruminations. Even when a customer failed to act like a gentleman, black barbers tactfully appeared to accept the rightness of what their customers said, along with often boastful claims of accomplishment.[39] Black barbers, through their reputation and their upscale shops, had succeeded in making themselves and their businesses indispensable parts of the forum that white men used to determine status within their community.

The proprietors of first-class barbershops guaranteed their accessibility to affluent white customers by purchasing or leasing buildings in white middle-class neighborhoods. Living on Meeting Street in Charleston amid the city's successful merchants, upwardly mobile tradesmen, and white-collar workers, the free black barber Francis St. Marks stood out not only for his skin color but also for occupying a brick house, in sharp contrast to the wooden houses of his white neighbors. Similarly, the prosperous Thomas Green of Baltimore resided on

Light Street in the merchant district. The proximity to affluent white customers also made Light Street an ideal location for his barbershop. Following a different strategy, several of Green's counterparts acquired a cachet by operating a barbershop somewhere other than from their dwelling. This practice was rare among barbers in general but not among black barbers. Out of almost three hundred barbers of both races listed in the 1860 U.S. Census for Baltimore, only nineteen had an address for a barbershop listed in the city directory in addition to the address for their residence. Black barbers presided over fifteen of these barbershops, which constituted more than three-quarters of all of the barbershops separate from residences within the city.[40]

In 1859, two black barbers had firmly established themselves in genteel, white, precincts of Philadelphia. James Auter's barbershop at 317 Chestnut Street, located a few doors down from the Chestnut Street House Hotel, had a continuous supply of desirable customers close at hand. The upscale character of the surrounding businesses also brought affluent customers his way. On Auter's block alone, retailers sold jewelry, silver, wallpaper, and books. Joshua Eddy, who in time became the wealthiest black barber in America, owned a shop one block farther west on Chestnut, where he too had prestigious neighbors, including a jeweler, a portrait painter, and a French wigmaker. In New York City, one barber even secured a location on Broadway opposite City Hall.[41] That they could occupy these prime locations shows that black barbers had become fixtures on the principal streets of America's cities.

Opening first-class shops allowed black barbers to achieve an unparalleled level of success for nineteenth-century African Americans, but the emotional labor involved in their work exacted a toll on their self-esteem. As James Thomas had confessed, their success, indeed their safety, depended on showing "a cheerful willingness to please" regardless of how their white customers treated them. He discovered how far he would have to go in order to accommodate some customers not long after he opened his own barbershop in Nashville. One day, Colonel A. J. Polk, a relative of the president, made a request of his barber. The colonel explained that he would be traveling to New York City and that he expected Thomas to go along with him as his personal barber. As Thomas recalled, "I told the Colonel that I had just bought a business, and I didn't think I would go," to which the Colonel gruffly replied, "Don't tell me about your business. I'll buy it and shut it up." Thomas had no illusions about who had the upper hand; he abruptly concluded his story of the encounter by saying only, "I got ready," closing his shop and traveling with Polk.[42]

Stung by their customers' willingness to assert their privileges as affluent white men, black barbers felt an understandable resentment toward them. In a letter to

TABLE 1

Businesses on the 300 and 400 Blocks of Chestnut Street, Philadelphia, 1859

One side of Chestnut Street			Other side of Chestnut Street
Louis Belrose, paper hangings	304	303	R. T. Shepard, clothier
J. S. Jardin & Brothers, silver platers	304	311	John Thornley, india rubber goods
Peterson & Brothers, booksellers	306	317	**James M. Auter, black barber**
Goodyear's, india rubber goods	308	321	Eli H. Eldridge, clothier
Bachman & Co., confectioners	310	327	H. A. Dreer, florist
S. Boerum, card and engraving	310	331	Chestnut Street House Hotel
C. Q. Osgood, fancy goods and toys	316	339	Thomas Cousty, tea dealer
		341	Kingsley & Co., express
Adams Express Co.	320	355	William M. Maurice, bookseller
Myron Shew, photographer	322		
Hart & Co., paper hangings	322		
Farr & Thompson, jewelers	324		
A. C. Suplee, card engraving	326		
Thomas C. Garrett, jewelers	326		
Parry & McMillan, booksellers	330		
Wells, Fargo, & Co., express	400	405	J. F. Fouldeaux, hairdresser
Martin Leans, card engraver	402	407	Joseph Huffy, bookseller
E. Borhek, spectacle maker	402	415	**Joshua Eddy, black barber**
Catherine Stringer, dressmaker	430	431	Benjamin Scott, Jr., auctioneer
F. Warburton, hats and caps	432	439	G. G. Evans, bookseller
Lloyd Glover, card engraver	432	441	Frederick Brown, ?
Root, photographer	434		
Wriggins & Warden, jewelers	434		
Charles Cahill, portrait painter	434		

Source: Data from *The Philadelphia Shopping Guide and Housekeeper's Companion* (Philadelphia: S. E. Cohen, 1859).

Pierre Toussaint, an old friend advised him on the issue of conforming to white standards. "You may," he wrote, "indeed change your condition, but you cannot change your complexion." The problem, he continued, sprang from how many white Americans "think that a black skin prevents us from seeing and understanding good from evil," in other words, from being capable of discernment and good judgment. "Courage!" the friend urged Toussaint, "let them think as they please." The correspondent expressed faith in Toussaint's pragmatism, because he knew that the black hairdresser had not deluded himself into believing that "they mistake you for a white man." At rare moments, black barbers expressed feelings of resentment toward their trade. John Rapier, despite being the twelfth wealthiest black man in Alabama after operating a barbershop for thirty years, confided to his son John, Jr., "To tell the truth, I hate the name barber." A compensation for this bitterness was that black barbers could derive satisfaction from understanding white men better than their customers could ever understand black men. The barbers' role-playing attuned them to white feelings of inadequacy and made them aware that they performed an important psychological function for white men.[43]

Another consequence of their relationship to white customers involved the problem of becoming estranged from their own feelings. To avoid internalizing the negative stereotypes they portrayed, black barbers disassociated themselves from their professional demeanor. Resolving this issue, in turn, generated self-doubt regarding their authenticity. Historians of slavery have contended that this "double existence" necessitated irredeemable compromises that scarred the psyche, a view that is borne out to a certain degree by the portrait of alienation found in modern black autobiography and fiction. Yet, as Frederick Douglass observed poignantly in his recollection that slaves told masters what they wanted to hear, "they suppress[ed] the truth rather than take the consequences of telling it, and in so doing prove[d] themselves a part of the human family." Except for the motivation of self-preservation, historians discussing the psychological damage caused by slavery fail to account for the ability of slaves to escape their demeaning role. Black barbers, who enjoyed more freedom, certainly had a variety of other, more fulfilling roles outside their shops, such as father, husband, leader, and mentor, so they had more ways to distance themselves from their job.[44]

The wit of black barbers served an essential function in maintaining their psychological well-being. By injecting a degree of levity into the proceedings of their shops, black barbers could lighten the burden of their role. Some of their humor was dark. When a white friend visiting an ill and bed-ridden Pierre Toussaint asked whether he would like her to draw the curtains so the sun would not shine in his face, his joking reply betrayed self-pity: "Oh no Madame, for then I shall be too black." In other cases, their humor led to a reversal of roles that extracted a symbolic vengeance on whites. Cyprian Clamorgan recalled an occasion when a "pompous little English dancing master" came to town, "hired the Concert Hall and stuck up his name as 'Professor Wells'" across the street from another St. Louis black barber, Gabriel Helms. Clamorgan's colleague put up his own sign, adorned with the title "Professor Helms" in gold letters. As Clamorgan put it, "the joke took." Helms's ridicule of the dancing instructor's pretensions amused his white customers, while the black man undoubtedly relished inflicting on a white man the humiliation that he so often suffered himself. The black barbers may have learned lessons from the trickster tales they had heard as children. In these stories, a small but wily rabbit manipulated larger animals, upending the normal hierarchy, frequently by pretending to be weaker than he actually was.[45]

Herman Melville presented an extreme example of the transgressive disguises black barbers could adopt in his novella, *Benito Cereno*. Told from the perspective of a Massachusetts ship captain named Amasa Delano, the tale satirized the racial stereotypes believed by most Americans. In the tale, Captain Delano came to the aid of a Spanish slave ship that he had found stranded off the coast of Chile. Upon boarding the ship, he was struck by the fact that blacks outnumbered whites "more than could have been expected" before he came upon the Spanish captain, Don Benito Cereno, who was "bearing plain traces of recent sleepless cares and disquietudes." A short black man, named Babo, stood by Don Benito, turning his face up occasionally, "like a shepherd dog's," to glance at the expression of the ship's commander. After hearing Don Benito's woeful tale of a violent gale followed by an outbreak of scurvy, Captain Delano had supplies brought from his own ship and instructed his crew to help dislodge the ship from the reef onto which it had drifted. He had just turned his attention to questioning Don Benito more closely about the many inconsistent details in his story when Babo interrupted to remind his master that he was due for a shave.[46]

As Captain Delano watched Babo loosening Don Benito's cravat and lathering his face, he entered into a reverie on the nature of African Americans. "There is something in the Negro," pondered Captain Delano, "which, in a particular way, fits him for avocations about one's person. Most Negroes are natural valets and hairdressers." He ascribed these gifts to an innate dependency, "that susceptibility of blind attachment sometimes inhering in indisputable inferiors." Describing how black men performed such work, he expressed admiration for their refinement. "There is," he said, "a smooth tact about them in this employment, with a marvelous, noiseless, gliding briskness, not ungraceful in its way, singularly pleasing to behold, and still more so to be the manipulated subject of." In case the reader mistook this compliment as a sign that the captain was qualifying his view of African Americans, Melville added that, "like most men of a good, blithe heart, Captain Delano took to negroes, not philanthropically, but genially, just as other men to Newfoundland dogs."[47]

The American captain did note incongruous elements in the interactions between the devoted slave and contented master. For instance, to keep the lather off of Captain Cereno's clothes, Babo took out the Spanish flag and tucked it under his master's chin before he began stropping the razor. Captain Cereno was "not unaffected by the close sight of the gleaming steel" and shuddered nervously. Lost in his thoughts, Captain Delano, as he gazed upon the two figures, imagined "that in the black he saw a headman, and in the white a man on the block." Yet the shaving began, and the American resumed his questioning of the Spaniard, who involuntarily jerked when asked to explain his predicament, causing Babo's razor to draw blood from his master's throat. Captain Delano noted the terrified look on Captain Cereno's face, but he dismissed it as a sign of the man's cowardice. Only when the American climbed into a boat to return to his ship and Captain Cereno leaped into it from his own ship, followed by Babo with a drawn knife, did Delano realize what had transpired aboard the Spanish vessel. The slaves had taken control of the ship, and the seemingly devoted Babo was their leader.[48] In hinting at what might lurk in the hearts of black servants, Melville returned to one of his favorite themes, mistaken identity. The author presented Babo according to contemporary racial stereotypes that branded African Americans as servile, in order to heighten his reader's surprise upon discovering the true intentions of the seemingly devoted slave. In the process, Melville made it clear that most white Americans had little inkling about the black men and women who catered to their whims. They simply accepted black servants as they presented themselves in interracial situations.

Melville certainly makes it appear that black men had become associated with barbering in the public mind, that white men found the masks worn by black barbers convincing. Yet the duplicity of black barbers should not be mistaken for insincerity. Black barbers embraced the respectability that they forged out of white racial stereotypes to cultivate white guardians and establish first-class barbershops. Rather than being confidence men, black barbers were knights of the razor, complex figures whose bravado and wit dispelled the gloom surrounding them. Their fraternal ties and artisanal traditions made it possible for them to carve out a lucrative niche serving upscale customers. By affirming the racial and class privileges of their white customers, black barbers gained an economic independence that would allow them to withstand growing competition from immigrant barbers. They also established a unique relationship with white men. Cyprian Clamorgan, in his book *The Colored Aristocracy,* pointed out the liberties that black barbers could take with their customers when he called to mind the image of the black man's razor at the white man's throat. Describing the shaving technique of his St. Louis colleague Albert White, he drew attention to the "glittering steel" that White brandished "in *terrorem* over his [customer's] throat."[49] White followed his threatening gesture with conviviality instead of menace, taking advantage of the customer's inability to speak, due to the shaving cream on this mouth, to hold forth on whatever topic caught his interest. He forced a white man to listen to him seriously. Seemingly inconsequential, the act was pregnant with significance in a society that refused to fully recognize the humanity of African Americans. Black barbers would be their own men.

CHAPTER THREE

Caught between Regional Origins and the Barber's Trade

In the summer of 1859, more than a thousand African Americans gathered in Baltimore for a picnic held by the Barbers' Beneficial Association, an example of the close ties between black barbers and their community. The article covering the event in the *Weekly Anglo-African*, a black-owned and -produced newspaper does not give names of who attended, but in all likelihood Jonathan Fernandis, one of city's first-class barbershop owners as well as a founder and lifetime member of the Barbers' Beneficial Association, participated in the outing. Having inherited a prospering shop from his Brazilian-born father, Fernandis was a beneficiary of the cohort of barbers whose skill, persistence, and hard work had allowed them to gain their freedom and establish themselves as leading businessmen in the African American community. Fernandis's young apprentices, Joshua Boone and Samuel Locks, were the next generation to benefit from the tradition and the support of the barbering fraternity. With the heritage of family, trade, and community behind him, Fernandis possessed the resources to protect his business, and his family prospered as barbers at least into the 1950s.[1]

In Maryland, the African American tradition of barbering flourished. The upper South provided more hospitable circumstances to the knights of the razor than any other region in the United States. During the colonial period, regional origins had played a role in the rise of black barbers, who had come from the plantations that had been established between the Chesapeake and the Caribbean. The American Revolution encouraged black barbers to spread throughout the young nation, because the republican stigmatizing of personal service created an economic niche for black men. During the antebellum period, the circumstances of free black people in the North, the upper South, and the lower South diverged enough to make regional origins a major issue in the history of black barbers once again. The demise of slavery in the northern states set them off from their southern counterparts. Within the South, those states bordering the North, along with North Carolina and Tennessee and including Missouri, formed the distinct region of the upper South, where a mixed economy diminished the importance of slavery. The lower South encompassed the rapidly growing states of the Cotton Kingdom. In each region, a distinct free black community developed that shaped barbers' everyday life. Regional differences also influenced whether black barbers viewed their trade positively or negatively. Yet, no matter how different their lives were from one geographical area to another, the fraternal bonds of their barbering tradition and a shared commitment to racial diplomacy united black barbers.

The tension between where they came from and what they did for a living grew over time, forcing black barbers to make compromises as well as principled stands. By the eve of the Civil War, black barbers in each region had charted their own divergent paths. In the North, anti-black feeling, immigrant competition, and a growing inclination among northern free black men to shun personal service worked together to consign the occupational niche of black barbers to a footnote in the region's history. By contrast, white customers in the lower South continued to seek out black barbers until the privations of the Great Depression descended, yet black barbers there enjoyed their success in isolation from the larger black community, limiting their association with African Americans to the tiny elite of mulattos, people of mixed race. Only in the upper South, where circumstances fostered black business ownership and comparatively benign race relations, did black barbers find it possible to reconcile their trade with their commitment to the black community.

The experience of antebellum black barbers mirrored the regional diversity among the lives of free black people. In each of these regions, the nature of emancipation, the character of the economy, and the ratio of blacks to whites played a decisive role in creating the social environment inhabited by free black people. Of these factors, the way that slaves came to be free had the greatest bearing on their prospects for economic success as well as their relationship to white people and to other African Americans. Free black people in each region consequently developed a unique outlook.[2] Although their regional background largely determined the goals black barbers pursued and the values they honored, everywhere their trade made them exceptional. They prospered when other skilled black men could not find work. More importantly, success and the traditions of barbering gave them high self-esteem. This success and self-esteem, along with their ties to the white elite, propelled them into the ranks of black leadership.

In the North, emancipation was complete and therefore indiscriminate, freeing all slaves, whether they were favored house servants, highly trained artisans, or lowly unskilled laborers. Since most of them lacked job skills, they tended to remain in the cities where they had lived as slaves. The egalitarian and evangelical impulses that led every northern state to pass emancipation laws by 1804 sprang more from an abhorrence of the concept of bondage than a concern for African Americans, so the freed people were left to shift for themselves. As one white man remarked about his former slave, "The laws set him free and he left me—now let the laws take care of him." Compounding this bleak employment picture, white artisans, lacking the incentives for employing African Americans that slavery had provided, refused to hire skilled free black workers for anything other than menial jobs.[3]

The restriction of black workers to manual labor and personal service, however, worked to the advantage of black barbers. The persistence of northern black barbers contrasted sharply with the overall decline of skilled black workers in the North. Aware that the large European immigrant population eagerly sought any and all jobs, white Northerners indulged their prejudice against blacks in the workplace. For instance, when a runaway slave from Baltimore, Frederick Douglass, sought to resume his career as a ship caulker in New Bedford, Connecticut, racial discrimination thwarted his efforts. "Such was the strength of prejudice against color, among the white caulkers," he recalled, "that they refused to work with me, and of course I could get no employment." The hostility of white workers in the North led to the exclusion of black men from a range of trades. According to a report by the Pennsylvania Abolition Society in 1856, "less than two-thirds of those [free African Americans in Philadelphia] who have trades follow them." Like Douglass, the author of the report attributed the underemployment of black artisans to "the unrelenting prejudice against their color." Black leaders in Philadelphia also complained that discrimination made placing their sons in apprenticeships difficult, which meant that trade skills in the African American community tended to disappear as skilled black workers grew old and died. To make matters worse, black men found themselves excluded from the manufacturing sector, which absorbed displaced white skilled workers. Less than .5 percent of Philadelphia's black men in 1847, for instance, held manufacturing jobs. Considering the general decline of skilled black workers in the North, the fact that the number of black men in the barbering trade actually increased constitutes a striking departure from the norm. Just 8 percent of Philadelphia's black men worked in skilled jobs in 1850, yet the number of black barbers in the city expanded 111 percent between 1837 and 1850. To cite another example, while only 5 percent of

New York City's black men worked at skilled jobs in 1850—a 24 percent drop from forty years earlier—black barbers outnumbered the combined total of all black butchers, tailors, shoemakers, and carpenters by 1855.[4] Barbering, in short, was one of the few skilled trades open to African Americans in the North.

Although northern black barbers continued to work steadily, they suffered from the deterioration of race relations. A color line developed in social activities that had long been interracial affairs. Churches that had earlier welcomed them as members expelled African Americans or restricted them to segregated seating, while civic parades and festivals became exclusively white events. In response to these challenges, a group of now legendary black leaders, among them Boston's Prince Hall and Philadelphia's Richard Allen, began establishing separate institutions that celebrated black heritage. Black barbers apparently saw no contradiction between operating businesses that excluded African Americans and providing leadership within these exclusively black organizations. In Boston, for example, two leading barbers, James Barbadoes and John Hilton, attended the First African Baptist Church, and Hilton went on to become Grand Master of the Prince Hall Masonic Lodge.[5]

Northern black barbers responded to deteriorating race relations in a variety of ways. Most, like Jacob White, Sr., of Philadelphia, shunned political controversy and continued to serve only whites in their first-class shops, viewing their participation in black organizations as a separate matter entirely. By contrast, barbers such as Pittsburgh's John Vashon formed a substantial minority that vocally supported the antislavery movement and risked alienating their white clientele. A small number resolved the conflict between operating a segregated business and being involved in black activism by reinventing their businesses to serve only African Americans. Because city directories do not record which barbershops served which race, it is difficult to estimate how many black barbers switched to serving African Americans. Only a limited number could have made the change, given the poverty of most black men, who simply lacked the discretionary income to pay someone for shaves and hair cuts. Peter Howard and John Smith of Boston served black men only, and their barbershops became political and social clubs, much like the modern-day black barbershop.

During the 1830s, antiabolitionist violence against the northern African American community struck black-owned businesses, of which the most notable example was barbershops. John Vashon of Pittsburgh had made his barbershop a center for abolitionists, soliciting customers to sign antislavery petitions and carrying abolitionist publications. When an antiabolitionist mob took to the street in the Pennsylvania city, they singled out Vashon's home for a devastating attack. Similarly, in Philadelphia, the barber Frederick Hinton had served on the business committee of Pennsylvania Hall, the headquarters of the state's antislavery society, which a white mob burnt to the ground in 1838. Panicked, the northern African American community, including barbers, considered leaving America for a more hospitable country. Concerned that in emigrating they would be abandoning those in bondage to their fate, leading black abolitionists urged African Americans to stay. One barber, named Lewis Woodson, conveyed how desperate the situation was in his response to these entreaties. "I can do more good," he reasoned, "by living than by dying. . . . Suppose all of the free people of color of the United States were exterminated. What . . . would become of the hope of the slave?" Frederick Hinton disclosed his opinion of the situation by taking a job promoting emigration to Trinidad.[6] Neither Hinton nor Woodson moved, which suggests that they supported emigration out of their commitment to black independence but continued to regard barbering in the United States as their own best vehicle for achieving personal independence.

Northern black barbers turned increasingly to the African American community both for customers and to find outlets for their ambition. As their shops developed into community centers, northern black barbers created the modern-day black barbershop, an institution that would be familiar to African Americans today. Peter Howard's barbershop attracted customers from all segments of Boston's African American community. In addition to getting a shave, black customers could get information about job openings or buy tickets to events such as the African Baptist Church concert featuring Howard as a member of a seven-piece orchestra playing, appropriately enough, the overture to Mozart's *The Marriage of Figaro*. Customers also received a free political education by listening to the shop's heated discussions. Acting on his abolitionist convictions, Howard made his barbershop a station on the Underground Railroad. Another Boston barber committed to abolition, John Smith, turned his shop into a forum for political debates that sometimes included United States Senator Charles Sumner, who occasionally stopped by to learn the concerns of the black community. Hardly unique, Howard and Smith belonged to a cohort of black barbers who played important leadership roles in black churches, fraternal orders, literary and debating societies, colored conventions, moral reform movements such as temperance, and abolition.[7]

Participation in northern black organizations served worthy causes, but it also offered talented men a chance to shine in a society that otherwise deprived them of opportunities for economic and social advancement. Visiting Philadelphia in the 1840s, one black Baltimorean remarked upon "the constant competition among the 'leading men' to take the lead in all matters of concern." The sense that barbering and other service enterprises had a limited potential for improving status often led the children of black barbers into the professions. Even though his father had managed to retain his white customers and operated a lucrative barbershop, Jacob White, Jr., chose not to follow his father's trade but to teach mathematics at Philadelphia's Institute for Colored Youth. He would later become the principal of the Robert Vaux Primary School, which made him the city's most prominent black educator.[8]

In the upper South, two waves of manumissions created distinct free black populations. The first wave, occurring in the two decades after the Revolution, drew inspiration from the same sources as northern emancipation, with the added impetus of the declining profitability of slavery caused by the shift away from the farming of staple crops in the region. Although the movement to end slavery in the Border States was incomplete, it was also indiscriminate, creating a generally dark-skinned, rural, and unskilled free black population that had many ties to the slave community. Just as the larger first wave of manumission receded, a more selective second wave began after 1810 in which a limited number of masters freed slaves out of a personal concern for their welfare. Often the mistresses or children of slave owners, these freed African Americans tended to be light-skinned. Their masters typically ensured that they had a means of supporting themselves, whether by giving them property or by paying for them to learn a trade.

Although immigrants competed with free black workers in port cities in the upper South, their relatively small numbers and the desire of employers to hire the more tractable African Americans allowed free blacks in the upper South to find and keep work more easily than their northern brethren. As in the North, the hostility of white workers worked against the employment of black men, enslaved or free, in skilled trades, although the countervailing interests of slave owners and businessmen slowed the process. Frederick Douglass, who was employed in Baltimore's shipyards as a skilled worker while still a slave, recalled that white shipyard workers began to resist laboring alongside African Americans during the 1830s. Resorting to violence in 1836, white apprentices attacked Douglass and other black workers, hoping to drive them from the work site. He noted that job opportunities for skilled slaves and free black men were intertwined: "had they succeeded in driving the black freemen out of the ship yard, they would have determined also the removal of the black slaves."[9] In addition to engaging in job busting—riots designed to rid workplaces of black workers—white artisans petitioned state legislatures to exclude African Americans from certain trades and pressured employers to discharge black workers.

Their efforts achieved mixed results. To planters in the legislature, proposals limiting the use of black workers threatened the value of their slave property, so they generally opposed such measures. To businessmen who appreciated the relative docility of black workers and their willingness to work for low wages, switching to white workers made little sense. The tug-of-war over skilled black workers created occupational segregation, with black men dominating certain trades and being excluded from others. For example, one-third of Richmond's free African Americans worked at skilled jobs in 1860, but they were confined to just six trades—barbering, plastering, carpentry, blacksmithing, shoemaking, and bricklaying. More than half of those skilled black workers were barbers. Similarly, approximately 18 percent of free African Americans in Baltimore found employment at skilled jobs in 1860, congregated in less than a dozen trades. Employment trends in Baltimore, as recorded in city directories of 1850 and 1860, did not bode well for skilled black workers, whose numbers declined overall. Only bricklayers and barbers increased their numbers during the 1850s. In fact, the city's black barbers flourished, their numbers increasing by 75 percent between 1827 and 1860.[10]

Black barbers held their ground in Baltimore's job market, but in the meantime, white Southerners were lashing out against free African Americans, which caused black barbers in both the lower and upper South to wonder if it was wise to stay in the United States. Following the gruesome murders of fifty-seven white men, women, and children in 1831 by Nat Turner and his band of rebellious slaves in Southampton County, Virginia, legislators in Maryland and Virginia faced a deafening cry for the removal of free African Americans. Maryland legislators broke new ground in 1831 when they appropriated $200,000 to promote an African colony where free African Americans might settle, a move duplicated by Virginia lawmakers the following year. Baltimore's free African Americans had earlier protested against colonization, yet by 1839, troubled by the lingering effects of the 1837 depression and a race riot, they considered obliging state lawmakers, at a public meeting on the subject of emigration. In spite of his wealth and his successful business, the city's leading barber, Thomas Green, chaired the meeting, which appointed two men to travel to Trindad and size up the island's prospects for black immigrants. They reported back favorably, and a group of 256 free African Americans from Baltimore emigrated to Trinidad in 1840. Green remained in Baltimore. Perhaps hearing that everyone who had gone to Trinidad was satisfied except for a small number of barbers dissuaded him from packing his bags.[11]

The overwhelming majority of black barbers in the upper South decided against emigration, which reflected the strength of community ties and the unique opportunities for black barbers in the region. Along the Mason-Dixon Line, the large free black population maintained its ties to the slave community, creating a strong feeling of racial solidarity that did not exist in other parts of the nation. The relative poverty of the free black community in the upper South partially explains this lack of separation. In Baltimore, low wages and the fact that many of the jobs available to black people were seasonal prevented the social stratification among free black people found in other cities, such as Philadelphia, Charleston, and New Orleans. A comparison of property ownership by blacks reveals the difference between Baltimore and these other cities. In 1837, 282 black residents of Philadelphia owned property worth at least $1,000, while more than a decade later, in 1850, Baltimore's tax records show just 101 free African Americans owning any property at all. Among fourteen antebellum cities in the North and throughout the South, Baltimore ranked next to last in percentage of free African Americans who owned property. In the absence of a wealthy free black elite, occupation became the chief marker for status among free black people in antebellum Baltimore.[12]

Craftsmen in particular enjoyed elevated status, regardless of the size or financial success of their business, as is shown by their prominence in black organizations, especially churches. Out of the nineteen black ministers listed in Baltimore's city directory between 1816 and 1850, fifteen worked in a trade. Black barbers fit into this pattern of church leadership. In addition to contributing one-quarter of the money used to purchase land for a new church for his congregation, Thomas Green opened his commodious home on Light Street to fellow church members for prayer meetings on Thursday evenings. Skilled black workers emulated their white counterparts, who set themselves apart from other members of the working classes by following a creed predicated on self-discipline, sobriety, and thrift.[13] Since craftsmen tended to demonstrate these virtues in their workplace, the trades acquired an association with respectability and thus class status.

Free blacks in the upper South suffered fewer restrictions in the marketplace than in other areas of their lives. Although a white majority in Maryland prevented free blacks there from appearing too threatening, the slave state had a restrictive code of laws for free black people. White legislators were particularly suspicious of any large gathering of African Americans, so they limited freedom of association, inhibiting the growth of black organizations. Yet, the importance of free black labor to the state's economy gave black barbers, bricklayers, caulkers, coachmen, porters, and mechanics the leverage to operate benevolent associations that helped members and their families when they were ill, unemployed, or deceased. As the 1859 Barbers' Beneficial Association picnic demonstrates, however, trade organizations did more than pass the hat to pay for a member's burial. These trade groups held picnics, cakewalks, fancy balls, and other social events that drew the black community together. At the same time, such affairs underscored the higher status of the hosts; and the organizations placed restrictions on who could join their ranks, starting with free status as a condition for membership. Black community leaders typically belonged to several organizations, establishing a web of relationships that formed the leadership structure of the African American community.[14] The circumstance of living as free African Americans in a region where African Americans were still kept as slaves made occupation central to black identity.

Since the economic arena offered free black men in the upper South the greatest scope for activity, most focused on achieving business success. Again, barbering offered exceptional opportunity for profits. On the eve of the Civil War, one out of eight African Americans in the upper South worth at least $2,000, the standard for affluence at that time, owned a barbershop. Cyprian Clamorgan emphasized wealth in his profile of the black elite in St. Louis, starting each biographical sketch with an estimate of the individual's net worth. He also quoted a motto of one of his subjects approvingly: "Wealth makes the man, the want of it the fellow." Describing the city's prosperous African Americans as a "colored aristocracy," he expressed pride that the majority of members of this group belonged to the "tonsorial profession." His sketches of individual barbers traced their careers, and those who ventured into other livelihoods, such as the two St. Louis barbers who moved to California during the Gold Rush, almost invariably returned to barbering, since the trade offered free black men a way to prosper without inspiring white animosity. In fact, white men in the upper South found much to admire in the financial success of their black barbers, and this admiration provided another incentive to enter the trade. James Thomas, in Nashville, declared that once free black men had accumulated enough wealth, they were eligible to be "spoken of in the highest terms, of being honest, upright, truthful, and gentlemanly in manner."[15]

The fraternal ties among black barbers also made the trade attractive. Clamorgan underscored the link between occupation and identity by referring to his colleagues with the name that was gaining usage among them, "knights of the razor." Despite a regard for wealth, black barbers in the upper South counted every member of the trade as an equal, helping to erase distinctions between journeymen and shop owners. St. Louis barbers welcomed promising younger colleagues into black society regardless of their wealth or skin color. Although

Clamorgan described Richard Merrin as dark enough to resemble "a Moor," he said that the young man was a "universal favorite." "Dick," he continued, "must have a hand in every pleasure party and picnic."[16] For all of the emphasis placed on skin color by free blacks, black barbers appeared to ignore it.

The egalitarianism among black barbers in the upper South contrasted sharply with their counterparts in the lower South. Masters in the lower South, amassing great wealth from cotton, rice, and sugar plantations, found little reason to contemplate freeing their slaves. Indeed, they viewed discussion of emancipation as tantamount to promoting servile insurrection, reflecting the fears occasioned by living in the midst of a black majority. Following the pattern of freeing only a few slaves for personal reasons (often blood relation), they created a light-skinned free black population that had considerable resources for providing for themselves. The plantation's dominance of the economy, which gave white immigrants few incentives to settle in the region, provided ample opportunities for free African Americans to work in almost every level of the skilled trades.[17]

Measured against their counterparts farther north, skilled black workers in the lower South thrived. Charleston was their apex in the region. Somewhere between two-thirds and three-quarters of Charleston's free black men in 1860 worked at skilled jobs, and they dominated a few trades outright. Despite making up only 15 percent of the free male workforce in the city, free black men comprised 75 percent of the millwrights and 80 percent of the barbers. The unique position of mulattos in the region accounted, to a great extent, for the success that free black men in skilled trades enjoyed. Whether they were the colored heirs of French and Spanish colonists or favored slaves whose masters provided for their future after emancipation by securing an apprenticeship for them, free mulatto tradesmen in the lower South generally had close ties to white patrons who sent them customers and sheltered them from discrimination. The racial composition of Charleston's free black barbers attests to the value of these contacts: three out of four had mixed racial origins. Likewise, both of Mobile's free black barbers in 1860 were mulattos, although they occupied a less dominant position than Charleston's free black barbers due to the competition presented by fourteen slave barbers.[18]

Relatively low barriers to black employment in the trades meant that skilled free African Americans often faced competition from slaves. In Charleston and Mobile, skilled slave workers outnumbered their free counterparts. The trend extended to barbering, in which slave barbers eventually displaced free black barbers in both cities. Between 1839 and 1860, the number of free black barbers in Mobile declined from five to two.[19] Slave barbers in Mobile appear to have operated their own businesses, and their presence sheds light on the substantial proportion of black barbers in the lower South who were enslaved. Municipal ordinances such as one enacted in Savannah required slave owners to purchase badges for slaves hired out as barbers, which suggests that a considerable number of slave barbers worked in the city. In Mobile, an estimated 1,000 of the city's 6,900 slaves lived apart from their masters by 1855. The following year, city leaders deemed it necessary to pass an ordinance requiring slave owners to register their slave barbers with the city clerk. The ordinance also prescribed twenty lashes for any slave who opened a barbershop without the consent or knowledge of his owner. Unlike Charleston, where most prosperous black barbers owned slaves of their own who worked in their shops, only one Mobile barber, a white man, owned any slaves in 1860. It is unlikely that his slaves, a twenty-two-year-old woman and three boys under fourteen, worked as barbers.[20] In all likelihood, slave barbers in Mobile hired their own time, bringing a set amount of money to their owners on a regular basis, which underscored the opportunities available even for enslaved black artisans to practice their trade in the lower South.

Free black barbers played for higher stakes in the lower South when race relations deteriorated in the 1830s and 1840s, as can be seen in free barber William Johnson's experience in Natchez. Living on a sparsely settled, lawless frontier that still contained roving gangs of thieves, white Mississippians understandably experienced anxieties about maintaining control as they expanded their slaveholdings to the point that the state had a black majority. In 1835 an insurrectionary panic was sparked in Madison County when a plantation mistress overheard one of her slaves say that "she was tired of waiting on white folks and wanted to be her own mistress the balance of her days." The panic engulfed the whole state after wide circulation of a pamphlet claiming that the notorious outlaw John Murrell planned to begin a slave revolt as a cover for his gang to loot and pillage. In Natchez and Vicksburg, the fear inspired assaults on professional gamblers and itinerant medicine men, whose status as outsiders made them suspect.[21] William Johnson discovered even a few years later that the remnants of that frenzy of alarmed slave owners negated his patient efforts to win a higher status. As a free black man, he remained an outsider in the lower South.

After news that several African Americans in St. Louis had murdered a white family reached Natchez in 1841, a white vigilance committee formed to drive free African Americans from the city. Meanwhile, the Board of Police met to consider revoking licenses that entitled free African Americans to reside in the county. Johnson recorded in his diary: "all sorts of trials going on . . . the offices have been full all day and they continue to arrest people." On the next day, he vividly expressed his feelings about the proceedings: "The horrors of the Inquisition are still going on in this city." White authorities eventually summoned free African Americans of substance, people like Johnson, to appear before them. A month into the judicial proceedings, Johnson noted that two of his friends, emancipated by their white father and endowed with property, had been ordered to leave town. "They are," he wrote in a tone of disbelief, "as far as I know innocent and harmless people." An investigation into the status of a free black child revealed that Charles Lynch, a former governor, had accepted money from the boy's mother for his purchase but had provided her with an ambiguous contract that failed to grant the child his freedom. For Johnson, who had placed much faith in the honor of the planter elite, the affair proved disheartening. He saw that the white man had cynically ensured that he could "do as he pleases in the affair," and concluded, "Oh what a Country we Live in." Then, just when Johnson feared that he would be expelled from Natchez, the white persecution ceased as quickly as it had begun. He had survived the purge of free blacks, but he had lost the illusion that he was anything more than a marginal figure in Natchez society. Just five days later, Johnson recorded news about race riots in Cincinnati in a lengthy diary entry, noting that the white mob had employed two cannons in their assault on a black church. He offered no comment on this troubling event, and he remained in Mississippi.[22]

Perhaps Johnson stayed put because he aspired to recognition as a member of a distinct social group. In 1840, Johnson and other free African Americans in Mississippi comprised less than 1 percent of the population. Elsewhere in the lower South they formed no more than roughly 3 percent of the population, except in Louisiana. Consequently, they found security in numbers, clustering together in towns and cities, away from the countryside where most African Americans labored as slaves. They deliberately placed some distance between themselves and slaves because they sought recognition from whites as a separate caste based on their loyalty to the planters' regime.[23]

Ties to influential white men and women offered protection for free black barbers in the lower South and often proved lucrative as well. William Johnson cultivated beneficial relationships with white patrons. In addition to the wide circle of white acquaintances whom he knew from his shop—and who, in some cases, borrowed money at interest from Johnson—he counted Dr. Luke Blackburn, who later became governor of Kentucky, as a patron; the two even exchanged small gifts. He also formed a longstanding friendship with Colonel Adam Bingaman, a Harvard graduate, wealthy planter, leading Whig politician, and nationally known horseman. A shared passion for racehorses and hunting bound the two men. After

Johnson's death, Bingaman helped administer Johnson's estate and ensured that his black friend's eldest son, who had been committed to a mental asylum, received proper care.[24]

Just as black barbers in the lower South took shelter from prejudice in their relationships with individual whites, they also warded off suspicions about their allegiances by identifying with the slave-owning class. By emulating planters, free African Americans demonstrated that they posed no threat to the social order, which in turn shielded them from white oppression. Black barbers in the lower South displayed a zeal for purchasing agricultural land that exceeded reasonable expectations of the profits they would reap, suggesting that they had nonpecuniary motives. In the case of John Stanly, he had only begun to acquire urban real estate when he began his drive to transform himself into a planter. He followed up his purchase of 196 acres in 1805 with 130 more acres later the same year. In 1811, Stanly bought 450 more acres, and seven years later added another 602 acres to his holdings. All together Stanly acquired 2,600 acres on which his slaves raised cotton and manufactured turpentine. Even after the value of real estate began to drop precipitously as part of a gradual economic decline in eastern North Carolina, Stanly continued to buy farmland. William Johnson also yearned to be known as a planter. Uncharacteristic of black barbers, Johnson displayed a penchant for speculation in his earlier years. He bought 162 acres of farmland in 1835 only to sell it at a profit six weeks later. In 1845, sobered by the loss of his investment when the Mississippi Railroad went bankrupt, Johnson turned his attention to becoming a planter, buying a 120-acre tract along the Mississippi River. He bought rural land in an area that he called "the Swamp," a partially wooded area southwest of Natchez pocked with many shallow lakes, which created the dampness for which the land was known. Johnson named his latest purchase, tongue-in-check, Hard Scrabble. Thirteen months later, he bought another 242 acres that adjoined his land and shortly thereafter, obtained a 99-year lease on 403 more acres.

Johnson employed an overseer and the occasional white laborer along with his slaves to work his land, revealing the degree to which a free black barber could act the part of the planter. In his contracts with white men, the outlines of profitable activity at Hard Scrabble emerge distinctly. One agreement that Johnson made with W. H. Stump in 1847 gave the overseer a third of "what is made on the ground" and a third of the profit from lumber operations. After entering this agreement, the relationship between the two men steadily declined. Stump may have resented taking orders from a black man, or he may have been lazy; either way he did little for his employer. In January of 1849, Johnson rode out to Hard

Scrabble and stirred people to work, which led him to observe that "there is Scarcly anything down there done when I am not there, I found Mr. Stump and Little Winn going down the Road when I came down this morning." Twelve days later, he rode out to the country in the evening to ask Stump whether he would stay another year, and the overseer declined "under the Circumstances." Increasingly consumed by a desire to reap profits from the countryside, Johnson died while arguing with his neighbor over the boundary of his land. His neighbor shot him dead.[25] The murder underscores the risks free African Americans in the lower South took when they sought to appropriate the title "planter."

Owning slaves was the surest way of proving fidelity to the slave-owner class, and of augmenting one's wealth. John Stanly displayed unquestioning loyalty to the slave owners' regime by owning as many as 163 slaves in 1830, twice as many slaves as the second largest black slave owner in the South. While most of his bondsmen labored in the fields, Stanly trained two, Brister and Boston, in the tonsorial arts and eventually let them manage his shop, which freed him from working as a barber on a regular basis. William Johnson also purchased slaves, thirty-one over the course of his lifetime; when he died in 1851 he owned fifteen bondsmen. While most of Johnson's slaves toiled in his fields at Hard Scrabble or in his house on State Street, he let slave barbers run one of his shops.[26]

In Charleston, the majority of prosperous free black barbers owned slaves. These slaves worked as barbers, but they also represented an investment vehicle, because free barbers bought and sold them for a profit, just like white slave owners. Moreover, when a slave learned the tonsorial arts, he increased in value. Slave barbers also generated income when they were hired out. For example, William Johnson paid $150 a year for the services of a slave barber named Charles, the average wage that he paid to free men working in his shop. Johnson employed Charles to run his one-man, Natchez-under-the-Hill shop during most of the 1840s, and their business arrangements suggested the degree of trust between the two men. Charles turned in the proceeds of the shop every two weeks, and Johnson often let him keep 10 to 20 percent of the money.[27]

Because Johnson had a variety of relationships with slaves, his diary provides a unique insight on the experience of being a free African American who owned slaves in the heart of the Cotton Kingdom. Having been born a slave, Johnson knew vividly what it meant to go without freedom, and he often expressed sympathy for individual slaves when they encountered hardship, yet he never let anyone forget that he was a free man known to the most prominent men in Natchez. He socialized only with a small circle of free African Americans and white tradesmen. Out of this group, his only true equal was Robert McCary, a free, light-skinned barber had served his apprenticeship alongside Johnson in the barbershop of Johnson's brother-in-law, James Miller. Johnson and McCary shared the distinction of being the town's leading black barbers. The bonds of a shared youth and the barbering trade made them fast friends.[28]

Perhaps Johnson's insistence on his rights in the hierarchical society of Natchez explains his contempt for the disreputable carousing among other African Americans, free and slaves. On more than one occasion Johnson scribbled in his diary a comment about free black barbers who worked for him attending what he called "darky parties." In one such entry, Johnson listed who had attended "a Darky Ball," before concluding with "Oh what a Set." Several comments in that vein hint at Johnson's own views about race. When his free black apprentice Bill Nix got in trouble for the umpteenth time, Johnson wrote, "Bill Nix is up to this day a pure, pure Negro at heart and in action." Yet Johnson had warm relationships with slaves who adhered to his idea of respectability. Before he made the slave barber Charles the operator of his Under-the-Hill shop, Johnson had raised him in his house and as an apprentice barber. When Charles's owner, Major Young, told Johnson that he wanted to free Charles and set him up in his own business, the master barber approved.[29] Johnson had an even closer relationship with his slave apprentice Bill Winston, although he viewed Winston as a free person because his late master's will directed that the boy be freed upon reaching manhood.

Only one slave, a man named Steven, made Johnson lose his composure as a slave owner. On January 3, 1836, Johnson brought Steven to his shop in order to teach him barbering. Before the week ended, Steven revealed that he was not a docile slave, when the slave patrol caught him out at night, which was forbidden, and whipped him. Johnson concluded his account of the incident with evidence of his determination to master Steven: "I whipped him myself in the morning afterward." Steven's independence showed itself again in September, when Johnson complained that it had been "precisely three weeks since I received any wages from Steven." After being whipped "prety severely" by Johnson, Steven confessed that he had received his wages and kept them for himself. The next month, a neighbor of Johnson's found Steven returning from a camp meeting and gave him "a genteel whipping for me." Deprived of the profits of his labors and cursed with a predilection for alcohol, Steven took to drinking unabated. Johnson discovered his slave lying unconscious in a wagon and sent for Dr. Hogg to tend to him. According to Johnson, "the Dr pronounced him Drunk at first site."

Steven remained uncontrollable over the years. In 1841, another master had hired him from Johnson to haul wood out of a swamp, but Steven left the job site and came to town for a visit. Johnson's account of corralling the wandering slave demonstrates his public conduct when disciplining a slave and the ties that existed between slave owners regardless of their race. After learning that Steven was in Natchez, Johnson rode around town on his horse until he found the slave and "Gave him a tap or two with my wriding whip." He brought the wayward slave back to his barbershop, where a white neighbor, Mr. Vernon, came in and told Johnson that Steven had stolen a watch from one of his men. Johnson searched Steven's pockets immediately, retrieving the watch from his coat pocket. Giving the watch to Mr. Vernon, Johnson said that he was "Glad that he Came So Soon for it." On one level, Johnson's comment probably represents an attempt to make clear that he was not, like Fagin in *Oliver Twist*, teaching his apprentices to "shave," or steal from, the inhabitants of Natchez. On another level, Johnson also needed to express his solidarity as a slave owner, which he did more emphatically by sending Steven to Mr. Vernon's place for a "good Flogging with [a] Big whip."

The relationship between Johnson and Steven finally ended on the last day of 1843. Although Johnson appears at the start of his diary entry to be minimizing the significance of what he was about to record, opening the entry with "Nothing new," on that day he had arranged for Steven's sale, and he grew emotional as he wrote. Asking, "And what is the Cause of my parting with him," he furnished the answer "nothing but Liquor, Liquor." Waxing philosophical, Johnson wrote, "There are many worse fellows than poor Steven is, God Bless Him." Johnson, appearing to feel pangs of guilt, added, "Tis his Own fault." In the morning, as Johnson took his slave to the ferry landing, he confessed that "many tears was in my Eyes to day On acct. of Selling poor Steven." They missed the boat, and Steven got drunk while they waited. Realizing that he would have to come back the next day, Johnson helped Steven walk home and "made him Sleep in the garret and Kept him safe." Johnson surely meant to prevent the slave from running away again, but the tone of the entry also suggests a desire to protect Steven from his own weaknesses.[30] By recording his ambivalence about selling Steven, Johnson's account adds nuance to generalizations about black slave ownership and the social exclusiveness of free African Americans in the lower South.

Johnson's diary furnishes a portrait of a man torn between the aspirations nurtured by his regional background and his identity as a barber. Johnson exhibited a paternal concern for the slaves who worked in his barbershop and showed solidarity with other slave owners, but his best friends were Robert McCary and his much-admired brother-in-law, who were barbers. Moreover, it was Johnson's success as a barber that made it possible for him to seek recognition as a gentleman, the ideal of his region. He failed to achieve status as a planter, though, because his non-barbering enterprises were truck farms and a lumber operation rather than a cotton plantation. Slavery's strength in the lower South restricted black opportunity, and Johnson's life was no exception to that rule. Johnson's diary offers perhaps the most striking illustration of a black barber's inner turmoil. In his effort to gain recognition from whites by distinguishing himself from the mass of African Americans, he cut himself off from the black community, with the exception of other elite free blacks, ending in a social limbo. Isolation might well explain Johnson's devotion to recording his life in more than two thousand pages. Unable to confide in others, he expressed himself, sometimes cryptically, in writing. Johnson, along with black barbers in the North as well as others in the lower South, was caught between his regional origin and his trade.

One could reasonably ask whether the preceding survey overstates the significance of regional identity for black barbers. For example, William Johnson may have simply been offering pragmatic concessions to the social order in which he found himself rather than embracing its values as his own. If he had left the lower South, perhaps his ideas would have changed. Black barbers from the upper South did move outside their native region, but they tended to maintain their regional outlook and values. The affluence of black barbers from the upper South who migrated to other regions suggests that they shared a focus on business. Migrating from Virginia to Boston, Massachusetts, John J. Smith acquired a sizeable $3,000 worth of real estate. Barbers often relocated more than once to find their fortunes. Born a slave in Virginia, Lewis Woodson moved to Ohio after gaining his freedom and moved again to Pittsburgh in 1830, where he and his sons operated several barbershops in prestigious hotels. The presence of other migrants from Virginia, such as his good friend and fellow barber John Vashon (who owned $4,000 worth of real estate in 1850) must have made Woodson feel at home in a new city.[31]

Because they had a worldview that equated prosperity with success, black barbers from the upper South could flourish outside their region. Their success came in part from the network they formed in the northern black communities to which they moved. Although black barbers had homes in most of Philadelphia's wards in 1860, fifteen of them who came from Maryland and Virginia lived in the same ward, many on the same block. This small group of men also apparently shared a spirit of enterprise, because they thrived in the City of Brotherly Love. Out of the sixteen black barbers in the city who owned real estate, seven came from the upper South. Joshua Eddy illustrates the heights to which free blacks who migrated from the upper South could climb in the North. Born a slave in Virginia in 1798, he moved to Philadelphia in the 1820s, established his own barbershop, and married the daughter of the most prominent black leader in the city, Richard Allen. He died in 1882, leaving an estate worth $100,000.[32]

The story of John Rapier, Sr., demonstrates the tenacity of regional identity, because he retained his upper South values of artisanal customs, mutuality, and identification with slaves, even though he found himself at the epicenter of lower South cotton production and planter hegemony. Originally from Nashville, Rapier gained his freedom in Florence, Alabama, where he ran a barbershop and became the twelfth wealthiest black person in the state. Although his stature as a barber equaled that of William Johnson, Rapier made decisions that revealed values sharply at odds with those of his counterpart in Natchez. He maintained personal, lifelong relationships with slaves. As a youth, he had learned his trade from a slave barber named Frank Parrish, and Rapier kept up the connection with Parrish, eventually apprenticing his own son James to his old master. Johnson, by contrast, refused to socialize with slaves unless they were his apprentices. Rapier, following the death of his free black wife, married his slave housekeeper. Although he was unable to secure legal freedom for his new wife or their children, he remained faithful to her for the rest of his life. Moreover, Rapier expressed the values of black barbers from the upper South, trying to inculcate the spirit of enterprise in his sons. In a letter to his son, John Junior, Rapier wrote, "I hope you will . . . try and get a better [life] than your father has." When his son proposed going into business with his uncle, he expressed hope that it would be "a paying business for I long to see some of my boys making money."[33] His desire to see John Junior become financially independent, although a commonplace sentiment among fathers of young men, also reflected the values of Rapier's youth in Virginia and Tennessee. John Junior eventually followed the barbering trade, whereas Johnson's sons shared their father's interest in farming. Juxtaposing Rapier and William Johnson provides a study in contrasts that underscores the significance of regional identities.

Although regional differences influenced the lives of black barbers, as a group they shared distinctive characteristics. Most black barbers, regardless of where they were geographically, came from the small group of slaves freed selectively with the help of their master. These men were most likely to be light-skinned. In turn, skin color may have helped bridge the social divide with white customers and convince them to feel comfortable entering their barbershops in the first place. Whatever the causes for their success, black barbers certainly found many more opportunities to work than did other free black men, even other skilled workers. Prospering businesses also gave black barbers an uncommonly high self-esteem, and their occupational identity united them.

Nevertheless, black barbers lived in very different societies depending upon their region, which gave them different outlooks. Northern black barbers displayed their regional background by focusing on their activities in the African American community, helping to create separate black institutions and supporting moral reform, even though some reformers criticized the accommodation of white people that was part of their trade. In the upper South, black barbers participated in institution building only when they could do so legally, not as reformers, and occupation played a much larger role in the selection of black community leaders than it did farther north. The collection of trade associations in Baltimore attests to the greater economic opportunities of the region, which helps explain why occupation formed such an important part of free black identity. Although free blacks in the upper South worshiped with slaves, they kept them out of their fraternal orders, revealing the fault lines in a mixed, slave and free, society. Black barbers in the lower South enjoyed fraternal ties among themselves but remained aloof from most of the African American community, preferring instead to cultivate relationships with members of the white elite. In part, they may have been attempting to distinguish themselves from the many slave barbers operating barbershops. Their aspirations to become planters and their slave ownership set them apart from black barbers in other parts of the country.

CHAPTER FOUR

Self-Improvement and Self-Loathing before the War

John Rapier, Sr., had everything that a free black man could reasonably hope for in Alabama in 1857. Not only had he managed to operate his barbershop in Florence for more than thirty years, but he had also prospered, becoming the twelfth wealthiest African American in the state. His quiet dignity and good judgment had won him the respect of the white planters who sat in his barber chair. He had sons attending college. He had traveled throughout the United States and had even visited Canada. Yet, in 1857, he wrote to his son John, Jr., that he had had enough of barbering. "To tell the truth," he declared, "I hate the name barber. A farmer I look on as a superior occupation to a barber." He informed his son, "the time has come for me to act."[1]

Rapier's sentiments about occupations reveal a powerful current in African American thought. In the minds of many black leaders, including Frederick Douglass and Martin Delany, "menial" labor degraded African Americans by reinforcing the conviction among white people that "colored men are only fit for such employments."[2] Many black leaders expressed particularly harsh views about black barbers. Since most black barbers, deferring to the prejudices of their white customers, barred African Americans from their shops, they were, in the opinion of the delegates to the 1852 Ohio Colored Convention, "much worse than a white man who refuses to eat, drink, ride, walk, or be educated with a colored man," because they themselves were African Americans.[3] Farming, on the other hand, symbolized independence. For example, the delegates to the 1843 National Convention of Colored Citizens asserted that a farmer is "upon the same level as his neighbors," who "see him now, not as in other situations [he might] have done as a servant, but as an independent man." The delegates also identified what they valued most about farming as an occupation: "the business of farming . . . is the shortest, surest road to respectability."[4]

Black leaders looked to class status and its essential nineteenth-century value, respectability, for their deliverance from second-class citizenship. Pursuing respectability duplicated trends among the middling sort of white Americans, who embraced parlors and parlor etiquette during the middle decades of the century. At the same time, the strategy addressed the circumstances faced by free African Americans. Overcoming racism, at that time, required responding to assumptions and allegations about the character of black people. Although a few pseudoscientists advanced biological theories of racial inferiority, white opinion generally cited the debased condition of impoverished free African Americans to justify discrimination. Black leaders thought that moral and social reform would disprove such claims, thereby knocking down the barriers to equality. If such efforts enhanced the social status of the black elite, all the better; they felt entitled to claim respectability, as members of an emerging black middle class.[5] Beyond this general consensus, black leaders disagreed on much else, including the definition of respectability.

Black barbers angrily rejected charges that their work degraded the race; nevertheless, they still found value in pursuing social distinction on white terms. A good reputation allowed them to win the confidence of white customers and gave them the credentials to preside over commercial parlors in first-class barbershops. In turn, the income from their thriving businesses allowed them to meet nineteenth-century standards of manhood by keeping their wives at home and their children in school. They also possessed the leisure time to serve as leaders in community organizations. Despite the occasional embarrassment or humiliation that came with serving white men, they expressed pride in their accomplishments as barbers, men, and leaders. Even John Rapier, despite his misgivings, remained in barbering. Observing the rules of etiquette and acquiring the material basis for middle-class status, at least as members of the petite bourgeoisie, had the virtue of giving otherwise marginal men a definite, if modest, social standing. Black barbers pragmatically developed their own conception of respectability based on what they had accomplished through their trade.

Later in the antebellum period, several developments threatened to undermine the distinct status of black barbers. White Americans, in the North as well as in the South, repeatedly made free African Americans the scapegoat for their frustrations and guilt about the contentious issue of slavery. Despite their ties to the white elite, black barbers were not immune from the white backlash, and the nature of their work intensified their experience of deteriorating race relations.

Many of them seriously considered abandoning the trade. To make matters worse, they faced unprecedented competition from white barbers, even in the lower South. Barbering changed dramatically as a result; black men went from being the majority of barbers as late as 1850 to becoming the minority by 1860. Even as the knights of the razor parried the attack from white competitors, they engaged in the most heated antebellum debate over barbering to occur within the African American community. The significance of this debate became clear during the Civil War and Reconstruction, when black barbers emerged as more influential leaders and made their conception of respectability and race relations integral to their leadership.

Regional differences shaped how the black elite pursued respectability. In the North, African Americans enjoyed the right of association and had built an impressive array of institutions that facilitated reform. They also found white allies in the abolitionist movement, which led the northern black elite to view achieving black respectability as just one facet of a campaign to reform American society. Swept up by the fervor of white abolitionists and the optimism generated by their own comparative respectability, many black leaders expressed unwavering faith in the promise of elevating their race.[6] Although black barbers helped lead reform organizations in the North, they dismissed the goal of a colorblind society as unattainable and therefore rejected the call for black men to quit menial jobs.

The Cincinnati race riot of 1829 symbolized the beginning of the erosion in northern race relations that inspired pessimism in black barbers. On July 1 of that year, Cincinnati officials announced that they would begin enforcing a set of dormant "black laws" passed twenty years earlier. All black residents of Cincinnati had thirty days to register with the county clerk, furnish proof of their freedom, and secure $500 bonds from two bondsmen who would guarantee their good behavior and ability to support themselves. While black notables petitioned the state legislature for the repeal of "those obnoxious laws," two black residents journeyed to Canada in search of a refuge for their beleaguered community. City officials extended the deadline for meeting their ultimatum to the beginning of September, but white workingmen punctuated this period of reprieve by repeatedly attacking the main black neighborhood, commonly known as Little Africa. At the climax of the raids, during the weekend of August 22, two hundred to three hundred white men invaded the district. Having given up on receiving protection from city officials, the African American residents had armed themselves. On Saturday, the fighting between blacks and whites broke out around midnight and continued throughout Sunday. Only one of the five daily newspapers in Cincinnati bothered to report the clash. By winter, after the passions of the white mobs had cooled, at least 1,100 African Americans had fled the city, where they had made up ten percent of the population, and resettled in Wilberforce, Canada.[7] The eviction of half of the black population of Cincinnati through legal repression and mob violence attests to the degree to which many northern whites thought that African Americans had no place in American society.

The marginalization of African Americans during the 1820s and 1830s, which labeled black people as degraded, jeopardized the profitable relationship that black barbers enjoyed with their white customers. In Cincinnati, as in the rest of the North, the American Colonization Society led the way in turning white public opinion against black people. The small but influential membership of the Cincinnati Colonization Society used newspaper editorials and church pulpits to offer a rationale for seeing African Americans as "a serious evil among us" to promote their exile to Africa. The issue was the failure of northern blacks to rise above poverty and crime after slavery ended. Consequently, they were seen by national leaders of the Colonization Society such as Henry Clay as "the most corrupt, depraved, and abandoned element in the population." Clay and other colonizationists denied being racists, maintaining instead that the degradation of African Americans was "not so much their fault as a consequence of their anomalous condition" as ex-slaves surrounded by hostility and discrimination. The social conservatism of colonizationists, whose background often included Calvinism and the Federalist Party, made white prejudice seem to them unalterable, so in their view, sending African Americans back to their native land was a humanitarian undertaking. As northern state legislators restricted African Americans' voting rights, legal standing, and freedom of migration during the 1820s and 1830s, the colonizationists' pessimism about ever diminishing white prejudice was understandable. The supposedly humanitarian position ignored the fact that arguments in favor of African American removal implicitly claimed the United States as a white man's country.[8]

The Cincinnati riot only hinted at the destruction that white mobs would inflict on the African American community there during the 1830s. Nevertheless, the prosperous town offered economic opportunity, and the black portion of the city's population grew from 2 percent back to 10 percent over the decade. With that growth, white anxiety mounted. A writer for a local newspaper expressed one fear: that "we shall be overwhelmed."[9] In addition to concern over job competition from African Americans, whites in Cincinnati may have resented the progress the African American community had made toward equality, receiving public funds to educate their children and establishing two churches of their own.

White mobs in other cities habitually targeted African American institutions and the property of well-to-do black residents. In at least two instances, in New York City and in Pittsburgh, rioters attacked black-owned barbershops. The abolition movement also incited white animosity, which explains why John Vashon, a black barber and mob victim, was targeted.[10]

Although black barbers stood to lose much from physical and financial injury at the hands of a mob, they expressed more concern about the impact that public disorder had on their credibility as leaders. Prominent black leaders realized that the increasingly troubled race relations of the late 1820s and 1830s challenged their legitimacy by denying their claims to respectability. For example, less than a month after the Cincinnati Race Riot, one of the city's newspaper editors noted a lessening "of the moral restraint which the presence of respectable persons of their own color imposed" on the African American community. The editor's association of morality with respectability captured how black leaders had defined the term since the 1790s. Defined by cultivation rather than by economic class, respectability was the sum of attributes such as temperance, observing the Sabbath, a reputation for integrity, and particularly education. Black leaders invoked their respectability to claim equality from whites; furthermore, as the editor observed, respectability formed the basis for the authority of black leaders within their own community. So when white mobs destroyed the property that entitled members of the black elite to vote, when white editors characterized the entire black population as degraded, and when white minstrels ridiculed the genteel aspirations of respectable blacks, they obliterated the distinctions that had set certain members of the black community apart as leaders.[11] The peaceable efforts of a few distinguished African American leaders, like the petition against black registration in Cincinnati, proved insufficient to deal with the collective threat.

The exodus of African Americans from Cincinnati included black leaders, and this flight alarmed their peers around the country, so they met in Philadelphia for the first in a series of national conventions that stretched into the postbellum era. The Reverend Richard Allen, one of the founders of the African Methodist Episcopal (A.M.E.) Church, called the 1830 convention to order at his church and presented the agenda for the meeting. Although the initial reason for the gathering was to debate whether to support emigration to Canada like that which had occurred in the aftermath of the Cincinnati race riots, the distinguished black minister used the opportunity to call for moral reform. Black barbers supported Allen's vision of uplifting their community, and they figured prominently in the leadership of the convention movement as well as the American Moral Reform Society, an organization created in 1835 as an outgrowth of the national conventions. Shocked by the events in Cincinnati, these leaders, come from throughout the North, sought a new strategy for the African American community. Black barbers, including Frederick Hinton, John Bowers, and Joseph Cassey of Philadelphia and Alfred Niger of Newport, Rhode Island, played important roles at the convention. Although most of the deliberations concerned how to aid those African Americans who had fled Cincinnati, the delegates also spoke of the need for concerted national action. They stated their goal "of more effectively strengthening the general union among Free People of Color."[12] For the rest of the antebellum period, unity and collective action served as the rallying cry for northern black leaders.

Black barbers played important roles in the National Negro Convention, as the gatherings became known. After the first convention, Richard Allen personally recruited Cassey and two other leading Philadelphia barbers, John P. Burr and Thomas Butler, to the permanent organization that carried on the work of the convention. Black delegates representing churches and other black organizations gathered again the following year and elected some of their number to carry on their work after they disbanded. Black barbers elected were Joseph Cassey, and two barbers from New England. In the American Moral Reform Society, three Philadelphia barbers—Joseph Cassey, Frederick Hinton, and Jacob White—served as officers while Alfred Niger, who went on to lead a victorious black suffrage movement in Rhode Island, helped compose a memorandum that expressed the goals of the organization.[13]

The resolutions passed at the 1831 national meeting succinctly expressed the concerns that animated the convention movement. Genuinely worried about the future of African Americans, the convention members bemoaned "the present ignorant and degraded condition of many of our brethren in these United States." Accordingly, they devoted most of the convention to making plans to improve the situation of free blacks in the North. They also made it clear that they blamed white Americans for the plight of people of color in the United States. The problems of their communities could "excite no astonishment," given the discrimination and prejudice that free African Americans confronted. Nevertheless, they objected to "our enemies" using the example of destitute African Americans as an indication of black peoples' "inferiority in the scale of human beings." The members of the convention's Committee of Inquiry elaborated on this sentiment, referring to those who "improperly class[ed] the virtuous of our colour with the abandoned."[14] To concede that African Americans had a long way to go as a people before achieving respectability, they argued, should not diminish accomplishments that had been achieved.

Black leaders participating in the movement had legitimate reasons for objecting to their association, in the minds of white people, with "the abandoned," because they came from the upper echelons of the African American community. According to one study of black delegates to state and national black conventions, 51 percent owned property, while only 22 percent of the general free black population in five leading northern cities owned property. Moreover, the average value of property owned by those delegates, $1,446, was nearly six times greater than the average value of property held by free African Americans in those cities. Most significantly, 79 percent of the delegates earned a living in skilled or professional occupations as compared to only 29 percent of the general black population in those cities. This elite group set about promoting "intelligence, industry, economy, and moral worth"; in other words, they sought to make their people respectable.[15] By adopting this mission, black leaders implied that they already possessed the virtues that they pledged to instill in the broader African American community, underscoring their own higher status.

The link between class formation and moral reform exposed a penchant for self-aggrandizement at the expense of non-elite African Americans. On occasion, the attendees at the 1831 convention used language that revealed a condescending, elitist attitude toward the less fortunate; one report cited the "dissolute, intemperate, and ignorant condition of a large portion" of free African Americans. Black barbers, whose affluence and status as businessmen made them part of the elite, voiced similar attitudes. For example, Lewis Woodson, who served as the secretary of the Pittsburgh chapter of the American Moral Reform Society in addition to barbering and ministering to an A.M.E. congregation, claimed that "want of attention to cleanliness and neatness of dress" among black people caused white prejudice against them. His remarks about proper attire revealed a class bias when he added that a shabby appearance would "entirely exclude us from the society of all persons of taste and refinement." Woodson's comments displayed a resolve to establish class distinctions within black society, but his innumerable labors on behalf of the African American community in Pittsburgh suggest that he had other motives for participating in reform efforts as well. One explanation for why black barbers participated in the moral reform movement is that they agreed with its philosophy of self-help.[16]

The activism of Lewis Woodson and his fellow knight of the razor John Vashon illustrates why many African Americans thought self-help worked. Both natives of Virginia, they arrived in Pittsburgh by circuitous paths. Woodson, as a young boy, had moved with his free black family to Chillicothe, Ohio, where he lived for almost twenty years before relocating to the future home of steel manufacturing in 1830 or 1831. He brought with him a commitment to activism, having helped organize the African Educational and Benevolent Society before he left Ohio. According to one source, Woodson came to Pittsburgh so he could teach in the school sponsored by the city's African Educational Society. Although he taught children during the day and adults at night, few students could afford to pay tuition. Woodson had recently married, so, after only a few months of teaching, he turned to barbering to earn a living.

Vashon, who had helped found the Pittsburgh school, quickly became one of Woodson's closest friends. The son of a free black woman and a white man, Vashon had grown up in Virginia and fought in the War of 1812. After the war, new restrictions on free African Americans convinced him to move north, first to Carlisle, Pennsylvania, and then to Pittsburgh in 1829. He supported William Lloyd Garrison's efforts to establish the antislavery newspaper *The Liberator,* which he sold at his barbershop along with another newspaper, the *Rights of All,* and David Walker's notorious *Appeal to the Colored Citizens of the World,* which called for slaves to revolt. As previously noted, an antiabolitionist mob attacked his home, an action that had a symbolic value for two reasons. The ownership of a home was the outward sign of the respectability to which Vashon aspired, so his house made a better target for a racist mob than his business. It also happened to be where the young Martin Delany, a fiery black nationalist, first lived when he moved to Pittsburgh.

Although Delany went on to become a physician, the first black major in the Union army, and a political leader during Reconstruction, he did share a common background with his barber mentors, Vashon and Woodson. Like them, Delany began his life in Virginia, the child of a free black woman and an enslaved man in Charlestown, Virginia. He lived in Charlestown until he was eleven, when his mother fled to Chambersburg, Pennsylvania, to avoid being punished for violating a law against educating black children. At age nineteen, Delany left his family to continue his education in Pittsburgh, becoming one of Woodson's first students. Delany quickly emerged as Woodson's partner in activism. Teacher and student threw themselves into supporting moral reform, attending the organizational meeting of the Pittsburgh chapter of the American Moral Reform Society, where they were elected officers. A year later, both men participated in a series of meetings that urged black leaders statewide to gather for a convention to protest the disfranchisement of black voters. Woodson and Delany also worked together on the agenda for an 1841 state black convention held in Pittsburgh. Woodson, as an ordained minister and the only one of the three activists then writing articles for black newspapers, spoke for them all. The extent to which

Woodson spoke for Delany can be seen in how many of his ideas recurred in Delany's speeches and writings in the 1850s.[17]

Perhaps this meeting of minds attested to the influence of regional values, for the three men evinced a belief in self-help that echoed the priorities and strategies of free African Americans in the upper South. Woodson expressed great pride in what the black residents of Pittsburgh had accomplished for themselves. Unlike political activism such as participation in the abolition movement, nonpolitical black improvement could be accomplished entirely through black agency. Woodson underscored this point by celebrating the growing number of black community organizations successfully pursuing moral reform. In an article that he wrote for the *Liberator* in 1833, he dwelled on how far the African American community had come since the demise of slavery, which had taken three decades after passage of the 1780 gradual emancipation law. "Our forefathers were brought up in abject bondage," he reminded readers, "and [they] were deprived of every means of moral improvement. In this condition, they were liberated." Now, he continued, African Americans in Pittsburgh had established a regular school and a Sunday school for their children. Four years later, he and his friend John Vashon authored a report with the same theme, extolling the respectability of black Pittsburgh. They wrote about the temperance society, the black school with its university-educated teacher, and the A.M.E. Church. When discussing their house of worship, they emphasized its refinement, noting that it occupied a "substantial brick building" and had been outfitted with "comfortable pews, carpets, Venetian window blinds, and opaque lamps." The two barbers discussed these hallmarks of Victorian respectability to make it clear that self-improvement extended to social mobility as well as to moral uplift. By showing that African Americans observed a "manner of living" like the white residents of the city, they claimed to have erased the degraded legacy of slavery. Black Pittsburgh, they contended, honored family ties, worshiped God, obeyed the laws, and felt "a warm interest in the peace, safety, honor and prosperity of the Commonwealth."[18] Their respectable behavior, in other words, made them good citizens who deserved equal rights.

Frederick Hinton, echoed the arguments of his Pittsburgh counterparts in an 1838 petition that he took the lead role in drafting. Fearful that the state constitutional convention would disfranchise black property owners, Hinton and other black leaders stated their case for black suffrage. The petition invoked Pennsylvania's tradition of safeguarding individual liberties, then challenged the white delegates' assumptions about race. African Americans, Hinton asserted, had "been much misrepresented" by white leaders, who had attacked their moral character to justify excluding them from citizenship. He countered these slanders by declaring that African Americans were, in his words, "a rapidly rising people, in morals, in intelligence . . . and in the comforts and refinements of life." That is to say, they were becoming respectable, which Hinton contended gave them a right to a higher social status.[19] Black leaders recognized that white legislators could not be persuaded to extend suffrage to all black men, so they employed a more conservative strategy that advocated keeping property qualifications for voting. At least, they reasoned, the black elite would be able to participate in civic life and, they hoped, pave the way for greater racial equality in the future.

Yet, even as northern black barbers endorsed the strategy of racial uplift, they did not seek assimilation. Lewis Woodson, for example, responded to black leaders who contended that maintaining a separate identity hampered the cause of African American uplift by arguing that the greater danger lay in forgetting the realities of prejudice: "The condition in which we have for generations been living in this land constitutes us as a distinct class. We have been held as slaves, while those around us have been free. They have been our holders, and we the held. Every power and privilege has been invested with them, while we have been divested of every right."[20]

Woodson also believed that African Americans contributed to their own misfortune: "CONDITION and not color is the chief cause of prejudice under which we suffer." He thought that if young black men would assume the responsibility for changing their condition, they would appreciate the value of being respectable. Returning once again to the issue of dress, Woodson established a distinction between the outward trappings of clothing and appearance and the inner character reflected in behavior and thought. He said that young black men "would find that elegant language and polished manners would give them greater currency in society than a smooth beaver or a golden headed rattan and that a cultivated mind is of higher consideration than dollars and cents." Woodson blamed black poverty and ignorance on white racism even as he told African Americans that their failure to improve themselves fostered prejudice. In view of his livelihood, he was merely acknowledging contradictions with which he struggled daily. Black barbers led a double life. In their first-class barbershops, they conformed to the stereotyped roles dictated by their white customers, even as in their communities, they led and inspired others.[21] For barbers like Woodson, therefore, prejudice was offensive, but it was also unavoidable.

The tolerance of black barbers for living with double consciousness, that awareness of the difference between how they appeared to white people and their actual identity, also placed them in conflict with their more idealistic brethren.

Even before the convention movement began, some influential black leaders had demanded that African Americans refuse to be exploited by white Americans, regardless of the price. David Walker, in his 1829 *Appeal*, derided free African Americans who served whites in a menial capacity. To make his point, Walker recounted a conversation with a bootblack to whom he had complained that "we are so subjected under the whites, that we cannot obtain the comforts of life, but by cleaning their boots and shoes, waiting on them, shaving them, etc." When the bootblack replied that he only wanted enough business to live well, Walker was appalled. He said the bootblack exemplified a debilitating problem within the northern free black community: "our glorying and being happy in such low employments." In contending that the man who had no higher aspirations than "wielding the razor and cleaning boots and shoes" was "ignorant and wretched," Walker invoked common stereotypes about those who worked in service jobs. He specifically objected to the dependence inherent in such work. In his mind, the deference of barbers and bootblacks to their white customers differed little from the submissiveness of slaves to their masters. He only respected African Americans who insisted on full equality with white people. Walker revealed why the issue of jobs touched a raw nerve when he asked, "Are we Men? How we could be so submissive . . . I never could conceive."[22]

Walker's statement reflected the tendency of Victorian Americans to conflate citizenship with manhood. Since nineteenth-century America recognized only independent men as citizens, the dependence of most free black workers on white employers made them appear to have fallen short of the ideal of manhood. Richard Allen articulated these ideas in a speech at the first national convention in 1830. Drawing a connection between "our deplorable situation" and the need to "pursue all legal means for the speedy elevation of ourselves and brethren to the scale and standing of men," Allen implied that the status quo left black men symbolically castrated. The distinguished minister agreed with David Walker that working in menial occupations posed the greatest obstacle to demonstrating black manhood, and he proposed, "we cannot devise any plan more likely to accomplish this end" than seeking to work in agriculture and the mechanical trades, which would raise the "moral and political standing" of the African American community.[23] That a conservative clergyman and a militant abolitionist both linked black manhood to abandoning most of the occupational niches available to free black men is a reflection of an emerging consensus among black leaders, one that saw black barbers as less than men and as impediments to black progress.

In adopting this critique of what they saw as menial labor, black leaders were responding to currents running through the industrializing northern economy.

A new dichotomy assigned status in society based on whether an individual worked with his hands or his head. By lifting clerks, salesmen, and shopkeepers above the disdain of the elite, this distinction between manual and nonmanual work played an instrumental role in creating the American middle class. A physical division between the two groups of workers developed in which ornamental storefronts, elaborate furnishings, and the respectable attire of clerks set them off from manual workers, who increasingly labored behind the scenes. Although the separation between manual and nonmanual workers owed much to the unintentional effect of increasing specialization, Americans who worked in the public spaces where business was conducted quickly laid a claim to higher status. The resulting class distinctions extended the disrespect white workers had earlier shown for personal service to all manual labor. In the labor newspapers of the Jacksonian Era, workers frequently bemoaned the humiliation they suffered because they worked with their hands.[24] This enhanced stratification magnified the plight of African Americans because the overwhelming majority of them worked as casual laborers and domestics. Since many black leaders had achieved the distinction of wearing a white collar, they eagerly sought to remove the stigma gained through their association with the black masses and urged their brethren to find more respectable jobs.

Even though the criticisms of Walker and Allen stung, northern black barbers waited twenty years before rising to public defense of their trade, because they moved in the same social circles as their critics. For example, prominent black barber and moral reform leader James Barbadoes of Boston was a neighbor of David Walker, and William Henry, apparently a hairdresser, lived in Walker's home. Similarly, Richard Allen's daughter married Joshua Eddy, a prominent black barber in Philadelphia. Black barbers ultimately retained their allegiance to the rest of the black elite through a shared commitment to respectability. By the 1830s, a handful of black ministers, small business owners, and teachers in virtually every city in the North and South had accumulated enough leisure and property to seek respect from white society on the basis of their refinement. They purchased homes, educated their children, and supported morally laudable black organizations.[25] While these accomplishments had practical value, they were pursued also with an eye toward reducing white prejudice toward themselves by distinguishing these ambitious free African Americans from the uncouth. The northern black elite clung to the accepted standard of respectability as if it were a life preserver that would keep them from drowning in a sea of racism.

In the South, "black codes" generally prohibited the formation of black organizations, and even where they did exist, self-preservation dictated that black leaders deemphasize any involvement with them, focusing instead on maintaining good relations with the white community. Black leaders in the Border States participated in northern-organized reform activities, but they remained mute during jobs debates. It would appear that, like black barbers, they had developed circumspection. In the lower South, the generally mulatto free black elite pursued respectability in exclusive organizations that largely served the function of distinguishing members from the general black population. Sporadic panics over alleged slave insurrections resulted in crackdowns that included enforcement of laws that were otherwise seldom observed. As leading free African Americans were forced to leave the lower South or chose to emigrate, the African American community in that region lost key members who had worked to organize collective efforts. Shaky ties within the black community and the general absence of black-controlled institutions prompted southern black leaders to guide the community through informal networks of family and neighborhood.

In the 1830s, the situation of free black people in the upper South was bleak. Even as advocates of colonization lobbied for African Americans to leave the United States, white mobs lashed out at them, especially in Baltimore. It was in 1831 that the Maryland legislature appropriated $200,000 to send emancipated slaves and free African Americans to Africa, as did Virginia in 1832. Free African Americans in Tennessee and North Carolina lost the right to vote in 1835, as suffrage was expanded to all white males. That same year, a North Carolina legislator, a proponent of disfranchisement of blacks, made clear the sentiment that free African Americans had no place in American society: "This is a nation of white people," he declared, "its offices, honors, dignities, and privileges are alone open to, and to be enjoyed by, white people." To deal with this climate and legal restraints, free African Americans turned to white patrons for protection.[26] This reliance on individual white men constrained free African Americans when they spoke publicly, none more so than barbers, whose businesses operated under the aegis of white patrons.

In both the South and the North, black barbers served as a bridge, as mediators, between the white and black communities, helping to settle disputes between individuals of different races. Since such disagreements often involved sensitive issues better left out of public view, the barbers seldom recorded the details of the disputes. They did leave tantalizing glimpses into the day-to-day negotiation of race relations during this period, and out of this fragmentary documentation emerges a portrait of shrewd black men testing their wits in dealings with powerful antagonists. Occasionally, their delicate position made them grow despondent and contemplate greener pastures elsewhere. Several left accounts of travels across the nation and abroad in search of a better life, but the trips inevitably ended up with the men working as barbers. Practical men by nature, they accepted that the state of affairs was less than ideal and decided to make the best of it.

To preserve their status, free blacks in the lower South drew closer to white allies and shunned slaves. Ironically, the abolitionist movement to an extent strengthened the ties between free African Americans and white patrons. For the first time, southern proslavery spokesmen began in the 1830s to defend slavery as an institution that protected an inferior race. The belief in African American inferiority made free blacks seem less threatening and fostered compassion for a group living with a natural disability. This stimulus to paternalistic feelings reinforced the relationships between black barbers and their white patrons. Free blacks in the lower South sought out the company of whites. Mulattos aimed to form a distinct class through exclusive organizations such as the Creole Fire Company of Mobile. Creole firemen went so far as to consider motions for expelling or fining members who associated with slaves.[27]

Over the course of the 1830s, a sectional divide had opened among free African Americans, and the subgroups adopted contrasting strategies and goals. A privileged group of mulattos in the lower South carried on as they had since their emancipation, carving out a middle ground for themselves between slaves and whites by cultivating white allies and their own respectability. Farther north, white mobs and elected officials undermined this traditional strategy with violence and repressive legislation, while colonizationists denied that free African Americans even had a place in American society. Free blacks in the North and upper South responded to these threats by endorsing the need for communitywide protest and action, but those in the upper South states faced two unique constraints. The threat of enslavement—laws were proposed to enslave free blacks—and consequent need for white patrons inhibited the push toward collective effort while the close ties between free African Americans and slaves ruled out the exclusionary tactics pursued by free blacks in the lower South. Whether they lived north or south of the Mason-Dixon Line, free African Americans in the North and upper South experienced a white backlash against their claims to respectability, a stinging rebuke that engaged both regional groups in a thoroughgoing reassessment of how to elevate their race.

The last decade before the Civil War transformed barbering in the United States, as the number of white men in the trade surpassed the number of black men. The drastic change struck Frederick Douglass, who remarked, "A few years ago, . . . a white barber would have been a curiosity—now their poles stand on every street." In Boston, New York, Philadelphia, Baltimore, Richmond, and Mo-

TABLE 2
Number of Barbers by Race, 1850 and 1860

City	1850	1860
Philadelphia		
White	36 (21%)	358 (53%)
Black	137 (79%)	315 (47%)
Baltimore		
White	40 (19%)	150 (51%)
Black	170 (81%)	142 (49%)
Mobile		
White	9	21 (57%)
Black	n.a.[a]	16 (43%)

Source: Seventh and Eighth Censuses of the United States, 1850, 1860. Population, Slave, Manufacturing Schedules, Records of the Bureau of the Census, Record Group 29, National Archives, Washington, D.C.

[a]Not calculable because number of slave barbers is unknown.

bile, white men displaced some black men in the trade, but northern black barbers fared the worst. Between 1850 and 1855, the number of black barbers in New York City declined by more than a third. By 1855, more than nine out of ten barbers there were white. Black Bostonians held just one-third of all the barbering jobs in 1860; the proportion of foreign-born white barbers alone grew from one-fifth to one-third during the 1850s. In Philadelphia, black men went from being the majority of barbers to being the minority between 1850 and 1860, but unlike their counterparts in other northern cities, their ranks continued to grow.[28]

Black barbers throughout the South hung onto their jobs better overall than did those in the North, but they experienced a decline also. In Baltimore, white men achieved a razor-thin majority within the trade at the end of the 1850s, and the number of black barbers shrank. Black barbers in Richmond fared a little better in 1860, making up just slightly more than half of all tonsorial artists in the city. In Mobile, white barbers had taken the lead by 1860, although the presence of slave barbers attested to the different circumstances in the lower South. Just one out of eight black barbers enjoyed freedom, reflecting the city's heavy reliance on slave labor. In fact, out of all the cities in the South, Mobile alone had a growing slave population when the war began. Free black barbers in Charleston stood out for their strong position, comprising 80 percent of the city's barbers in 1860. With the exception of free black millwrights, who represented a full 75 percent of the men in their trade, no other group of free skilled

African Americans in Charleston comprised more than 41 percent of their trade.[29]

Charlestonians had employed free and enslaved black artisans since the eighteenth century, giving black barbers a remarkably strong position at the beginning of the 1850s; however, Charleston's free black barbers might also have used slave ownership to reinforce the association of their trade with African Americans. Although the number of black barbers owning slaves declined over the decade, in 1860 some black barbers continued to own slaves. Barbers Peter Brown, John Francis, and Francis St. Mark owned eleven slaves among them on the eve of the Civil War. As late as 1864, only one had divested himself of his slaves. Given the tradition of black barbers' employing slaves in their shops, many if not most of these bondsmen probably worked as barbers, which potentially expanded the number of black barbers in Charleston by a third.[30] Whatever the reason for the continuing predominance of black barbers in Charleston, they had become anachronisms, because the half-century-old American tradition of associating barbering with African Americans ended during the 1850s.

According to trends in Philadelphia, Baltimore, and Mobile, the prospects of black barbers seemed likely to grow worse. While young white men were entering the trade in droves, the average black man in the trade in the 1850s was middle aged. The men who represented the future of barbering were disproportionately white. Black men who entered the trade, moreover, rarely stood behind a barber's chair for an entire decade. In Baltimore, less than one in ten worked as a barber for the entire decade of the 1850s, while a little more than one in twenty remained barbers in Philadelphia during the same period.[31] With a smaller, aging group of black men moving into barbering, and then in many cases out again, it appeared that white barbers would eventually claim the trade.

TABLE 3
Percentage of Barbers under the Age of 25, 1860

City	White	Black
Philadelphia	44	37
Baltimore	45	33
Mobile[a]	33	0

Source: Eighth Census of the United States, 1860. Population, Slave, and Manufacturing Schedules, Records of the Bureau of the Census, Record Group 29, National Archives, Washington, D.C.

[a]Free barbers only.

The upswing in the number of white barbers resulted from European immigration. In the North, the upper South, and the lower South, more than two-thirds of the white barbers in 1860 were foreign-born. Germans predominated in Philadelphia, Baltimore, and Mobile, providing a counterpoint to the Irish, who were the chief rivals of black men in other occupations. Out of the hundreds of white men in Philadelphia earning a livelihood as barbers in 1860, for example, only eight came from Ireland. German barbers, in spite of their growing numbers, appear to have had trouble breaking into the higher end of barbering, and enjoyed only modest prosperity in the 1850s. For example, one Mississippi barber reported that a newly arrived German competitor advertised his willingness to shave customers for a fraction of the going rate. One black barber, when referring to the German-owned barbershops in St. Louis, spoke derisively of "little shops."[32]

When James Thomas experimented with hiring German barbers, the barriers the immigrants faced became apparent to him. He observed that his German employees had to learn "the American way of serving their patrons," yet even after they completed their lessons, they still had a hard time winning over white

TABLE 4
Birthplace of White Barbers, 1860

Place of Birth	Philadelphia (%)	Baltimore (%)	Mobile (%)
United States	26.5	12	23.8
Austria	0.6	0.7	0
Belgium	0.3	0	0
Canada	0.3	0	0
Denmark	0	0.7	0
England	2	0.7	4.8
France	1.7	0.7	14.3
Germany	64	80	28.6
Holland	0.3	0	0
Ireland	2.2	0.7	4.8
Italy	0.3	2	0
Scotland	0	0	9.5
Spain	0.3	0	9.5
Sweden	0	0	4.8
Switzerland	0.6	0	0
West Indies	0	0.7	0
Uncertain	1.1	2	0

Source: Eighth Census of the United States, 1860. Population, Slave, and Manufacturing Schedules, Records of the Bureau of the Census, Record Group 29, National Archives, Washington, D.C.

customers. Customers used to ask him, "What are you doing with that [German] here?" He told the customers of his need for employees and, in a conciliatory tone, assured them, "He seems to be a clever boy, and I thought I would try him." Even with these reassuring comments from the black barber, many customers said, "I don't want him to touch me." The prejudice of his customers grew so burdensome that the German barbers resorted to making plaintive appeals. As customers waited for an open chair, one German pleaded with them: "I can wait on you as well as that other fellow. Why not take my chair all of the time? I'm poor and want to work."[33] The reason German barbers had to beg for work was that black barbers had become entrenched in their first-class barbershops, dominating the upscale segment of the market.

The affluence of the select number of black barbers who owned property reveals that they bested their white competitors. In Philadelphia and Baltimore, the value of the business and residential real estate that black barbers owned equaled or surpassed the value of white barbers' real estate. Moreover, Baltimore's black tonsorial artists outstripped their white counterparts in the total value of their personal property—everything not counted as real estate. Black barbers held the upper hand because they were more likely to own a freestanding barbershop. Of 292 barbers listed in the 1860 Baltimore census, only nineteen had an address for their barbershop listed in the city directory along with an address for a residence. Black barbers presided over fifteen of these freestanding barbershops, which constituted about four-fifths of all of the barbershops not attached to residences within the city.[34] To operate a first-class shop required more than just the front room of a row house outfitted with a barber's chair; it required the space and trappings

TABLE 5
Wealth of Barbers, 1860

City	Race	Median Value of Real Estate	Total Value of Real Estate	Median Value of Personal Property	Total Value of Personal Property
Philadelphia	White	$1,800	$42,850	$300	$71,305
	Black	$1,800	$61,400	$200	$33,455
Baltimore	White	$1,000	$23,375	$225	$35,980
	Black	$3,600	$20,200	$100	$44,275

Source: Eighth Census of the United States, 1860. Population, Slave, and Manufacturing Schedules, Records of the Bureau of the Census, Record Group 29, National Archives, Washington, D.C.

befitting the designation "first-class." Where black barbers had cornered the upscale market, they continued to do well.

Black barbers in the upper South were the most affluent group of free African Americans in the region after those who owned farms. By 1850, one out of every eight free black property owners in the upper South who had accumulated at least $2,000 was a barber. Barbers crossed this threshold of prosperity in almost every one of the region's cities. Examples were Thomas Green in Baltimore, Washington Spalding in Louisville, Joseph Causton in Memphis, John Thomas and James Thomas in Nashville, and Reuben West in Richmond. In St. Louis, where Henry Clamorgan, Barriter Hickman, William Johnson, and Albert White each accumulated at least $2,000 in wealth, barbers formed the majority of prosperous free African Americans in the city. Virginia's barbers surpassed this achievement by becoming the wealthiest group of free black people in the entire state.[35]

In comparison with the lower South, where less than a dozen black barbers in the whole region had accumulated $2,000 by 1850, black barbers from the upper South appeared to be phenomenally successful. More of them owned property than did black barbers in the lower South, and the value of their property was higher. During the 1850s, the disparity between these two regions in black barbers worth at least $2,000 grew even more pronounced. The average value of the real estate owned by the most prosperous black barbers in the upper South was worth two-and-a-half times that of their counterparts in the lower South. In Mobile, the modest circumstances of black barbers—not one of them owned any real estate—underscored this trend. Yet the almost total lack of property ownership in Mobile among barbers of either race in 1860 shows that the city provided fewer opportunities for barbers to accumulate wealth. Out of the thirty-six men working in the trade, only two barbers, both white men, owned real estate, so black barbers in

TABLE 6
Southern Black Barbers Owning Real Estate, 1850 and 1860

Year	Region	Number Owning Real Estate	Median Value of Real Estate
1850	Upper South	91	$1,538
	Lower South	14	$1,293
1860	Upper South	114	$2,866
	Lower South	18	$1,750

Source: Adapted from Loren Schweninger, *Black Property Owners in the South, 1790–1915* (Urbana: University of Illinois Press, 1990), 82.

Mobile fared no worse than white barbers. The disparity in prosperity of black barbers in the two parts of the South fit into a larger pattern. While free African Americans made notable gains in wealth during the 1850s in the upper South, the fortunes of even black property owners in the lower South declined. The growing prosperity of free African Americans in the upper South was an expression of a regional identity that oriented talented black men toward the marketplace and material gains,[36] and it helped the region's black barbers dominate the first-class sector of their trade.

During the 1850s, the sophistication of the barbershop in which a man worked made a significant difference. The fortunes of those who owned or worked in first-class barbershops waxed, and the condition of black barbers who did not waned. Most black barbers did not work in first-class barbershops, so they bore the full brunt of white competition. In sharp contrast to the affluent proprietors of first-rate barbershops, the majority of black barbers possessed little, if any, wealth. Less than one out of twenty black barbers in Baltimore held title to any real estate, while less than one out of a hundred owned real estate in Philadelphia. Economic hardship also seems to have prevented most black barbers from establishing their own households. Although more than half of the black barbers in the two cities were over twenty-four years old, just a slim majority in Baltimore headed their own household and even fewer did in Philadelphia. They consequently had a difficult time starting their own families. While barely more than half of Baltimore's black barbers had a wife, most in Philadelphia did not.[37]

As the records of the Philadelphia Almshouse and County Prison attest, some black barbers faced graver problems than establishing themselves as the head of their own household. The almshouse provided care for individuals with nowhere else to turn, and the barbers who took shelter there suffered from a variety of afflictions, including mental illness and untreated wounds and disease, not just

TABLE 7

Percentage of Black Barbers Who Were Husbands or Heads of Households, 1860

City	Household Head (%)	Married (%)
Philadelphia	45	40
Baltimore	54	52

Source: Eighth Census of the United States, 1860. Population, Slave, and Manufacturing Schedules, Records of the Bureau of the Census, Record Group 29, National Archives, Washington, D.C.

poverty. Charles Penn died in the almshouse at thirty-three, leaving a child whose mother had already died. John Peter had lived to see his eightieth year only to die of frostbite in the almshouse, bearing witness to the kinds of privation that awaited many black barbers in their old age. The descriptions of black barbers who were incarcerated in the Philadelphia County Prison also reveal hard lives. Even the presumably jaded prison clerk found the scar behind Barney Russell's left ear "remarkable." In prison for the second time, Russell had been convicted of larceny.[38] Almost all of the incarcerated black barbers in Philadelphia served time for crimes against property, which implied their poverty. Those black barbers unable to secure positions in first-class shops eked out livings on the margin, while those fortunate enough to work in first-class shops prospered.

Poor black barbers appear to have viewed barbering as part of a repertoire of jobs they could use to survive. The Convict Description Dockets of the Philadelphia County Prison contain hints about what kinds of work these men took up. At a time when "tattoos were virtually never seen save on the weather-beaten skin of a seafaring man," prison clerks noted that several black barbers in the prison had extensive tattoos. One of these men even bore a crude design that resembled a ship. Black men formed a substantial portion of Philadelphia's seamen, and black sailors may have worked as black barbers and vice versa. Perhaps barbering was a way station for black men who had recently migrated to the city. Nineteen-year-old black barber David Brown must have only recently moved from Lancaster, Pennsylvania, when he checked into the Philadelphia Almshouse, since his home county assumed responsibility for the cost of his medical treatment.[39] These examples of down-and-out black barbers in Philadelphia are extreme cases of hardship in the region of the nation where immigrant barbers had made their greatest inroads on the trade. Nevertheless, they illustrate the very different prospects of ordinary black barbers and those working in first-class barbershops.

Up until the 1850s, black barbers had led a charmed existence when compared to other free skilled black men. They had plenty of white customers, even in the North, long after other black tradesmen despaired of finding work. Their fellowship as knights of the razor encompassed black barbers across the nation, lessening the isolation of prominent free black men in the lower South such as William Johnson. Although black barbers in each region faced growing white hostility in the 1830s and 1840s, they weighed their options and then plainly decided that this trade remained their best bet. However, the growing sectionalism of the 1850s and increasing tendency for whites to lash out at free African Americans, combined with the first serious competition from immigrants, made it impossible for barbers to continue being exceptional among black workers and artisans.

The passage of the Fugitive Slave Act in 1850 caused some African Americans in the North to again consider leaving the United States, a sign that they were losing faith that they would win acceptance and prosperity in this country. There were black barbers among the emigrants, and several actually led a group of several hundred who fled to Canada. The Fugitive Slave Law obligated local law enforcement officials to help capture runaway slaves. After prospering in Buffalo, operating the barbershop in the elegant Niagara Hotel, Henry Thomas began to worry that his status as a fugitive slave from Tennessee might catch up with him. When a Tennessee slave owner visited his shop and remembered him from Nashville, Thomas realized that his origins were known, so he could be recaptured. Thomas helped organize a meeting in Buffalo of free African Americans to denounce the new law. He gave the first speech and helped draft resolutions that declared the law unconstitutional and asserted that it placed every African American in the North in danger of being enslaved. One year later, alarmed by a highly publicized case of a fugitive slave who was arrested, Thomas and other black leaders organized another meeting, this one in Toronto, that encouraged African Americans to emigrate to Canada. One of the most outspoken advocates of emigration, Mary Shadd Cary, received support for her leadership from her husband, a black barber. In the fall of 1851, Henry Thomas closed his barbershop and moved with his family to Canada, where they took up farming. Thomas's focus on community activism—he also participated in a convention that demanded the vote for African Americans—showed that he had taken up the assertive independence of the northern black community, which helps explain why he walked away from his business as well as his country.[40]

Henry Thomas's half-brother, John Rapier, despite living in Alabama, displayed his upper South, Nashville, origins when he too considered emigration as race relations deteriorated. He had many good reasons to leave. Although Rapier owned his second wife and children, restrictions on manumissions in Alabama prevented him from securing freedom for his family. He feared that, if he died, they would remain enslaved and perhaps become the property of a white man. Rapier also dreamed of reuniting the dispersed free members of his family in a free country. He hoped that he, his son, and his half-brother James Thomas could join Henry and find a place where they could all settle and become neighbors. Writing to his son, he said, "I am in hopes that your uncle [Henry] will settle down, and when he does that, I shall be his neighbor." Rapier had considered emigration before. Earlier in the 1850s, he had subscribed to the journal of the American Colonization Society, which tried to convince free African Americans to move to Africa. He seriously considered going to Africa but concluded that the motives of the society were suspect. Writing to the president of the society, he declared his belief that the members would not care "if all of the free negroes in the United States were at the bottom of the sea so long as they were out of the United States." Rapier bought land in Buxton, Canada, where Henry and his family had joined a community of African American émigrés. Yet, as Rapier, sick of barbering, prepared for his life as a farmer, he encountered many obstacles. Henry failed to clear John's land as promised. Rapier's son John Junior failed to pay the sum due for his share of the family land. Rapier finally gave up on becoming a farmer when he learned that the Canadian government had not given the settlers already living in the émigré colony titles for their land, and he ultimately abandoned the idea of emigration, mistrustful of the white men who offered to help him relocate and discouraged by his prospects elsewhere. In the South, Rapier had an occupational niche; but more importantly, he occupied a social niche where he could raise his family with a minimum of white interference. He stayed in Alabama and worked in his barbershop until his death in 1869.[41]

In John Rapier, Sr.'s family, dissatisfaction with both the South and barbering proved contagious. His other half-brother, James Thomas, also a barber, and his son John Junior shared aspirations quite unlike his own; they longed for adventure. In 1855, General William Walker, a Nashville native, illegally seized control of Nicaragua with a private army, and the Nashville paper featured advertisements that promised free passage to Nicaragua, 250 acres of land, and $30 a month for each American immigrant who remained in the country for one year. Carrying a letter for the general from his father, presumably a customer of his barbershop, James Thomas departed for Nicaragua along with his nephew John Junior. Three days out of port, they encountered an unpleasant reminder of their second-class status when the ship's officers and a large crowd of passengers demanded that the two men prove they were free. They apparently managed to do so, and they quickly regained their composure and idyllic dreams of living in a tropical paradise where "the people do nothing but lay in hammocks all the day, eat delicious fruits, sing songs, and dedicate poetry to the moon by night." The campaign in Nicaragua proved disastrous, however, and left Thomas asking himself, "What did I come here for?"[42]

Thomas, never one to discourage easily, returned to the United States and set out for the Midwest to make his fortune as a land speculator. He sold all of his property in Nashville and traveled through Wisconsin and Iowa before arriving in Kansas just after the bloody 1855 fighting over whether the state would be free or have slavery. When Thomas inquired about preempting 160 acres, he discovered that the law allocating land to settlers excluded African Americans. He did obtain twenty-seven lots in Topeka as payment for a loan he had made, but it took three years before he could get his property recorded. At Lecompton, the proslavery stronghold in Kansas, a narrow escape from kidnappers turned his disgust with racism into fear. He was standing on the platform of a train station when a man came up to him and told Thomas in hushed tones that he had a group of slaves he was taking across the border to sell in Missouri. As soon as he could, Thomas left the man's company and went to sleep in the station. The sound of a dozen men approaching awakened Thomas shortly thereafter, and the man he had spoken to earlier pointed out Thomas, saying, "there is the one who wants to be taken away." Thomas reported that he had not made any such request and denied that he was from Missouri as the man claimed. At that moment, a young colonel, the leader of the group, spoke on behalf of Thomas. "He is not from Missouri," he said, "I know everyone in Missouri." The colonel's prestige induced the group to release Thomas, who later contemplated how badly the situation might have turned out had the white man not intervened on his behalf. Perhaps his near enslavement caused him to miss the secure position he had enjoyed as a barber, or perhaps it made him reflect on how far he had drifted from the regional values that had informed his youth. Whatever the case, Thomas left Kansas and took up residence in St. Louis, where he toiled once more as a barber, this time on a luxury steamboat.[43]

John Junior remained adventurous longer than his uncle, but he eventually returned to the barbering fold as well. He had secured a job as the personal secretary of Colonel Parker French, the ambassador to the United States from Walker's Nicaragua, and, the two men began traveling across America. However, just a few months later, the ambassador and his secretary parted following an acrimonious dispute. French refused to pay John his wages and then denounced him publicly, in the newspaper, as a thief. With little money and even less faith in swashbuckling adventurers, the young Rapier found himself unemployed in Minnesota during the winter. He tried unsuccessfully to earn a living as a gambler but ended up working as a barber, like his father and uncles. In his diary, the young man also began to sound like his father, because he embraced the values that his father had striven to impress on him. Disgusted with "crawling in the dust before wealth" in order to make money for someone else, he saved his wages and opened his own barbershop, pursuing the goal of economic independence. His diary also reveals that his ambitions had changed. Whereas he had earlier sought adventure and famous associates, he now sought money. He declared that, with money in your pocket, "the most reserved and select parlors are thrown open to you. Your faults are never seen through your gold, your virtues are enhanced a hundred times by its omnipotence." Having failed to overcome the constraints on free black life, the young man came to see the wisdom in confining his ambitions to the marketplace, where he was allowed to compete.[44] John also emphasized wealth and business ownership, because these two qualities undergirded the respectability of black barbers.

The differences between barbers and other respectable African Americans came to a head when the controversy over menial labor renewed itself with new furor during the 1850s. The barbers had to swim against the current to gain a hearing for their views in black leadership circles. They specifically had to contend with prevailing conceptions of respectability. Although black barbers had forged a common cause with leaders such as Frederick Douglass through a shared commitment to make the African American community more respectable, they disagreed over how to achieve that goal. The barbers ultimately dissented from the orthodoxy of racial uplift, advocating separatism and self-help instead. Drawing on their identity as knights of the razor, black barbers argued for a conception of respectability that focused on obtaining the means for achieving a middle-class lifestyle and on celebrating how they embodied the virtues of small businessmen.

During the 1840s, another generation of black leaders had emerged in the North that brought a more pragmatic agenda to the fight for black equality. The split within the abolitionist movement over the issues of moral perfectionism and women's rights had the effect of making African Americans feel freer to criticize the shortcomings of the moral reform movement. Having emerged from working-class backgrounds, leaders such as Frederick Douglass saw skilled manual labor as a path to greater equality. Douglass, when writing of his life as a slave, stressed the dignity conferred by working as a ship caulker. His subsequent rise to international celebrity as an abolitionist lecturer and newspaper editor, moreover, suggested that skilled labor could also furnish a vehicle for acquiring middle-class respectability. At national conventions and in newspaper articles, Douglass led a chorus of black leaders demanding that African Americans enter the professions and skilled trades. His tactics failed to endear him to black barbers. Although Douglass offered a conciliatory response to a sweeping condemnation of African Americans who worked as servants, made at the 1848 national black convention, his editorials on the subject pulled few punches in painting the dangers of personal service jobs.[45]

In 1853, Douglass penned his most stinging attack on personal service when he urged parents to keep their sons from becoming waiters, porters, and barbers. Douglas contended that such occupations sapped men of their energies and enfeebled their intellect. Forever waiting to serve whatever pale face beckoned, he contended, young men became accustomed to passing their day in idleness. Douglass went on to express concern about the effect of working in such trades. "To shave a half dozen faces in the morning and sleep or play the guitar in the afternoon—all this may be easy," Douglas acknowledged, "but is it noble, is it manly, and does it improve and elevate us?"[46]

Douglass repeatedly urged African Americans to demonstrate their worth by achieving success in the new market economy. Given that he depended on support from white middle-class abolitionists whose opposition to slavery was inextricably connected to the creation of an industrial society, his allegiance to bourgeois views was understandable, and it formed the basis for his criticisms of black barbers. He focused on what he saw as flaws in the barbers' work ethic and argued that they failed to reflect credit on their community. In an attempt to be sympathetic, Douglass diverted his scorn from the men he criticized to the circumstances of their employment. They spent innumerable hours every day waiting for their next customer, which he asserted left them "peculiarly exposed and liable to be led into temptation, for idleness is the parent of vice." Infected by ennui, they found diversion in admiring the lifestyle of their well-heeled customers. Douglass speculated on the impact of such tastes: "We spend our all in trying to emulate the customs and follow the fashions of the rich with whom our vocations bring us in contact." Douglass spurned extravagance and fashion, believing them to be a poor substitute for the cultivation of inner character. By putting on airs, he reasoned, African Americans invited whites to condemn them for attempting to rise above their station, and he went on to imply that such displays had goaded whites to hatch colonization schemes and pass laws barring African Americans from settling in midwestern states. Douglass concluded his editorial by reminding parents what was at stake: either their sons learned some "useful and honorable calling" in the skilled crafts, or they would forfeit "their manhood and respectability."[47]

As Douglass's harsh words in the 1850s showed, black leaders remained concerned about the association of black men with servility, but issues of masculinity had loomed even larger before then. Martin Delany played a major role in gendering the debate. Speaking words that electrified the atmosphere at the 1848 national black convention, Delany claimed that "he would rather receive a telegraphic dispatch that his wife and two children had fallen victims to a loathsome disease, than to hear that they had become the servants of any man." The issue of black women working as domestics was complicated. Due to the impoverishment of black men, most northern black women had to work as domestics, which limited their ability to fulfill the nineteenth-century woman's role as caretaker of the household. Black women, moreover, always risked sexual assault when they worked for a white family. Hence, Delany further gored the wounded pride of black men when he reminded them that they failed their women as protectors and providers. He argued that reversing this situation would be the litmus test for black progress. In his 1852 book on the condition of African Americans, he wrote, "Until colored men attain a position above permitting their mothers, sisters, wives, and daughters to do the drudgery and menial offices of other men's wives and daughters, it is useless, it is nonsense, it is pitiable mockery, to talk about equality and elevation." Black barbers working in first-class shops, however, were able to keep the women in their family from working as domestics. As Leslie Harris has noted in her discussion of the antebellum jobs debate among African Americans, black barbers "potentially exemplified an alternative model of independent manhood" because they owned their own shops and tools. They drew down lightning from black critics, she argued, due to their policy of segregation.[48]

Since northern black barbers occupied such a prominent role as leaders, they undoubtedly experienced inner conflict over their refusal to serve African Americans in their shops. The implacable opposition of white customers to sharing their barber with African Americans made the issue moot, as one English traveler's account of a visit to a New York City barbershop demonstrated. Shortly after the Englishman, Henry Fearon, took his seat in the barber's chair, a black man, "very respectably dressed," entered the shop. The barber inquired whether the man wanted to see the proprietor, and he replied that he wanted a haircut. According to Fearon, "my man turned upon his heel, and with the greatest contempt, muttered in a tone of importance, 'We do not cut coloured men here, Sir.'" The Englishman grew self-conscious and asked if the man had been denied service because of his presence, hoping that the black man could be called back to the shop. After ascertaining that Fearon was not an American, the barber explained, "My boss would not have a single ugly or clever gentleman come to his store if he cut coloured men." That evening at dinner, Fearon related the incident to three Americans whom he regarded as "men of education and of liberal opinion." They exclaimed, "Ay right, perfectly right, I would never go to a barbers' where a coloured man was cut!" With the overwhelming majority of northern black men living in poverty, they hardly offered an alternative customer base for black barbers. Nevertheless, black leaders deeply resented being excluded from a black-owned business. The delegates at an 1852 black convention in Ohio passed a resolution condemning any "colored man who refuses to shave a colored man because he is colored" as "much worse than a white man who refuses to eat, drink, ride, walk, or be educated with a colored man . . . for the former is a party *de facto* to riveting chains around his own neck and the necks of his much injured race." Yet, the same convention urged African Americans to rival white men as business owners.[49]

Black barbers were caught in a dilemma not of their own making, and they eventually dropped the restraint they had so long maintained toward their critics. Black barbers did not let Frederick Douglass's comments go unanswered, although some offered up no more than expressions of wounded pride. One barber wrote to Douglass, "We know our position and feel it." Uriah Boston, on the other hand, dashed off a rebuttal to the black editor in which he barely contained his outrage. As the owner of a barbershop in Poughkeepsie, New York, as well as being the most prominent black leader in his black community, Boston felt entitled to have his opinion published in Douglass's newspaper, a conviction that the editor only came to share after publicly ridiculing the grammatical errors in the barber's first letter. Boston denounced the famous leader's articles as an attack in "blazing capitals" on barbers for being a "servile class" in a business "derogatory to the interests of the race," which he emphatically denied. "On the contrary," he continued, "they are, in every way, as intelligent and respectable as any other class of businessmen and much more so than some others."[50] The barber's claim to the title of businessman was very significant, for the prevailing racial ideology defined the characteristics needed to succeed in business, such as ambition and competitiveness, as inherently white.

In Boston's opinion, Douglass obscured the real issues when he attempted to distinguish between worthy and unworthy occupations for African Americans since owning a business required intelligence and made one respectable. He shared a belief with Douglass that white prejudice stemmed from the demoralized, impoverished condition of African Americans, but their agreement ended at that point. In his own article, Douglass admitted that whites refused to train black workers in the skilled trades that he admired, weakly contending that "if most men will not teach our sable children trades in this country, some men will; and of the aid of the latter we should quickly avail ourselves." His dubious proposal suggested that he was more concerned with moving up an occupational scale that whites considered respectable than with finding work for his people. By contrast, Boston appealed to pragmatism, noting in his letter to Douglass that barbers made up "a very large class of businessmen among our people." Black businessmen, even if whites failed to take them seriously, could derive satisfaction from achieving economic independence and serving as capable breadwinners to their families. In other words, they could appropriate white standards for success and achieve them in a different, black, context.[51]

Boston was not alone when he expressed impatience with the concerns of some leaders about respectability and cultural attainments. According to Lewis Woodson, business should be the chief concern of African Americans because it provided "an easy, practical, and certain means" of bettering the condition of the race. He noted tartly, "Our efforts to obtain wealth have not been equal to our efforts to obtain knowledge," a jab at underemployed leaders with some formal education who criticized barbers. Woodson probably drew additional satisfaction from the fact that he wrote these words in an article for Frederick Douglass's newspaper. After a national antislavery meeting, the representatives decided to establish the American League of Colored Laborers, which would lend money to black men so they could go into business. Woodson and Douglass were the vice-presidents of the new organization, and Douglass's support fit his rhetoric, because the organization also sought to promote the education of young black men in agriculture and the mechanical arts. Woodson, however, appeared to view the league as a new departure, one that fit his philosophy of self-help. He concluded his outline of the organization's purposes by observing, "This, I believe, was the first time that the necessity of possessing wealth, as a means of our elevation, was, as a distinct proposition, presented to the consideration of such a meeting."[52] Finally, black leaders appeared open to the point of view of black barbers.

Notwithstanding the cooperation of Douglass and Woodson, they remained divided, because the jobs debate was only part of a larger argument over who would define black America. For their part, middle-class black professionals such as Douglass sought to demonstrate that African Americans were qualified for inclusion in mainstream society. They defiantly proclaimed from the podium and the pulpit that American ideals were not for whites only. While contesting ideologies of citizenship and race to claim equality, they placed their stamp upon the nation's moral heritage by extending the principles of Christianity and the Declaration of Independence to their logical conclusion. Black barbers, in sharp contrast, formed an enduring part of a black lower middle class of artisans and shopkeepers who had their own ethos, life style, and worldview. As members of a social group keenly aware of how they were distinct from other African Americans, black barbers sought independence on their own terms. Like other black middle-class artisans and professionals, they reinterpreted ideology to change their status, yet they focused on different strains of antebellum ideology. Rather than invoking republicanism or the emerging free labor ideology as Douglass and his counterparts did, black barbers such as Uriah Boston laid a claim to the independence and virtue associated with successful small businessmen in American society. Black barbers sought to define themselves as enterprising, self-made men. Out of this decision flowed different tactics. Instead of attempting to persuade white Americans to grant them more rights, black barbers ingratiated themselves with affluent white men in order to obtain the financial and social capital necessary for upward mobility, even if this meant adopting the politics of subterfuge and accommodating white racial stereotypes. They regretted the need to wear masks to earn a living and worked to create a society that would judge them according to the standards of class instead of race. In the meantime, they remained faithful to their conception of respectability.

CHAPTER FIVE

Defining the Meaning of Freedom

Few men heard the drumbeat for war more incessantly than black barbers in the tumultuous years before Confederate guns opened fire on Fort Sumter. In his St. Louis barbershop, James Thomas heard the mayor debate whether the Yankees would fight if war broke out and asked customers visiting from up north questions about their politics. The snippets of conversation that he recorded in his autobiography capture the passions of the day like a fly preserved in amber. Customers proclaimed their sentiments freely. "If that kind [Yankees] went to heaven," announced one bellicose Southerner, "[I wouldn't] want to go there." Northern customers held up their end, one declaring, "New York men said they wouldn't need help to thrash them Fire Eaters." Thomas also recorded his anger over proposals to expel free African Americans from Missouri. In the way he chose to express his sentiments, Thomas captured black barbers' divided loyalties during the Civil War and Reconstruction: "I like the southern people individually, but collectively and politically, Dam 'em."[1]

Black barbers, like African Americans throughout the nation, struggled to define the meaning of freedom as the Civil War destroyed slavery. They sought nothing less than complete equality, and several barbers played leading roles in the quest for suffrage. Yet they labored under the burden imposed on them by their occupation and, more generally, by their conservative approach to race relations. They had to balance their proud identity as black men and businessmen against their determination to maintain their status as respectable people, which hinged on the income they derived from segregated barbershops. Again, regional differences shaped their experiences. Northern black barbers, having long played a role in the abolitionist movement, embraced the Republican Party and prayed for Union victory. For them, obtaining the right to vote was the culmination of a long effort to be deemed worthy of citizenship, that symbol of nineteenth-century American manhood. Southern black barbers, notwithstanding their close ties to prominent whites who served the Confederacy, shared the African American community's excitement about the Emancipation Proclamation, black troops, and advancing Union forces.

The experience of black barbers during Reconstruction and the Gilded Age also fit into larger patterns shaping the African American community. Because the free black elite decided to form common cause with the new freedmen, the organizing principle of the community changed. Whereas during the antebellum period color and freedom had defined black status, during Reconstruction the African American community was increasingly stratified by class. The free-born artisans, ministers, and teachers that composed the leadership of this new community formed a nascent black middle class. While these men had made great strides on behalf of their people, their leadership reflected their class interests and prior experiences, representing postbellum variations of antebellum themes. Disagreements about how to define respectability continued as well, with the barbers' point of view gaining a wider following after it became clear that the promise of Reconstruction would remain unfulfilled. Regardless of how black leaders understood racial uplift, their emphasis on social distinctions proved as divisive as before.[2]

The owners of first-class barbershops, in particular, found themselves in a quandary. At last they possessed full legal rights, so they could pursue their careers as businessmen without restriction, or more accurately, without infringement of their legal ability to make contracts and settle business disputes in court. They capitalized on their new rights by elevating the first-class barbershop to its highest form, and the investments they made in ever more luxurious shops made these establishments the pinnacle of black business achievement in the late nineteenth century. They also played important roles in the Republican Party. What Reconstruction granted in the political realm, however, it withheld in the social realm. No constitutional amendment or law could force white customers to purchase the services of a black barber in an integrated shop, and freedmen generally lacked the disposable income to keep black barbers in business. First-class barbershops consequently remained unreconstructed, serving affluent white customers exclusively, a symbol of continuity in a time of changing race relations. For the black barbers who owned these shops, their livelihood and the class status that it secured ultimately took precedence over their commitment to black equality, although, as before the war, they strove valiantly to reconcile the conflict between these two goals.

Black barbers first experienced these tensions during the months immediately preceding the Civil War. The comments of James Thomas of St. Louis illustrate the barbers' predicament. Across the river from the free state of Illinois and in a state bordering Kansas, where there was bloody guerilla warfare over whether to be a free or a slave state, St. Louis was a microcosm of the forces tearing the Union apart. Thomas himself noted that the "social, financial, and political fabric" of his hometown had undergone great strain, and "the time had come when everybody was expected to show his hand." St. Louis residents generally expressed their loyalties quite volubly. The large German immigrant population demonstrated their support for free-soil politics and abolition by marching in the home guard every Sunday. On two or three occasions, Thomas wrote, southern sympathizers opened fire on the parading Germans, who shot back, wounding innocent bystanders.[3]

Thomas's description of the Germans and other immigrants in St. Louis betrays a mixture of contempt and jealousy. While noting that the Germans could speak only a pidgin English, such as saying that they were waiting for a chance to kill the "Seush" (secessionists), he pointed out that they had the right to defend "my country's flag" but that he did not. His animosity extended to the Irish also. Of them he wrote that "they were 'dimocrats'" who blindly supported "Dooglass" because his wife was Catholic. It must have vexed the black barber that greenhorns could participate in politics when he could not. While immigrants, in his view, mouthed whatever slogan their leaders gave them and had a poor understanding of the issues, Thomas possessed a detailed knowledge of both the secession crisis and politics in general. He chafed at the restraints placed on African Americans.[4]

At one point, however, it appeared that the sectional controversy would give him an opportunity to become a participant in the momentous events swirling around him. When secessionists invited Thomas to visit their armed camp outside St. Louis for brandy and cigars, the black barber faced a dilemma. These representatives of the white elite, men that Thomas called "Aristocrats," had asked him, in effect, to support their cause publicly, implicitly granting him recognition as someone entitled to a voice in politics. At the same time, these men also represented the slaveholders' regime. Thomas pondered the offer long and hard, writing a letter to John Rapier, Jr., seeking his advice. Rapier's response was unequivocal: "Do no such thing, for can you not see that the Hand of Him who ruleth the world is directing this war, to His own good purposes." In addition, Rapier contended that if slave owners won the war, they would expel free blacks from the South. Thomas ultimately declined joining the southern party even though it undoubtedly included many of his customers. Perhaps his skepticism toward white men ran too deep, a view that his comments on St. Louis abolitionists suggest. Thomas recalled that the true abolitionists, those opposed to slavery on moral grounds, "were few in number." There was, however, "another stripe of Abolitionist . . . [who] would like to see the Negro get away just to laugh at the discomfiture of his owner." These men, in his opinion, cared little for the plight of African Americans, supporting abolition to strike a blow against the wealthy or to create more opportunities for white people.[5] Thanks to his intimate knowledge of white prejudice from the barbershop, when it came to transforming race relations, Thomas did not experience divided loyalties in the Civil War; he doubted the sincerity of both sides.

Cyprian Clamorgan, Thomas's boss and the owner of one of the most successful barbershops in St. Louis, may have influenced his employee's views. In 1858, Clamorgan published a denunciation of racial hypocrisy in the introduction to his short book *The Colored Aristocracy of St. Louis*. His opening lines invoked abolitionist emblems such as *Uncle Tom's Cabin* and the autobiography of Solomon Northrup to make the case "that the colored race are not without their friends and admirers," before ending sarcastically—"even in this land of liberty." Although many free African Americans were "separated from the white race by a line of division so faint that it can be traced only by the keen eye of prejudice," they possessed no rights that white men were bound to respect. Clamorgan drove this point home in his discussion of the Dred Scott decision of the United States Supreme Court, which had ruled that African Americans "had no political rights under the Constitution." With masterful indirectness, he expressed respect for the court, saying that he did not intend to "call into question the judgment of the learned Chief Justice," but then noted that Justice Taney had "kindred of a darker hue than himself."[6] Clamorgan implied that white supremacy was based on a lie because it required men such as Taney to deny the existence of their own black brothers and sisters.

For the rest of his book, Clamorgan presented the argument that people should be judged by their degree of respectability instead of by their race. Clamorgan intended his sketches of individual members of the colored aristocracy to win over readers to his point of view. For example, he drew attention to genteel qualities such as Samuel Mordecai's impeccable manners and "aristocratic" feelings. Clamorgan also noted that Mordecai was "one of the most energetic business men to be met with anywhere," linking business success to respectability. In his descriptions of black barbers, who, he observed, formed the majority of the colored aristocracy, Clamorgan emphasized their virtues as small businessmen. He remarked that his fellow barber Elenius Henley was "a pattern of a business man." Along with wealth, enterprise apparently formed a prerequisite for membership in the black elite of St. Louis, revealing notions of respectability in line with those of other black barbers. This worldview, based on the material accomplishments of artisans and shopkeepers, provided an objective basis for granting status. Unsurprisingly, Clamorgan wrote that colored aristocrats supported free labor ideology because they knew it "would remove a stigma from their race, and elevate them in the scale of society."[7]

James Thomas ultimately embraced Clamorgan's faith in the Union cause, showing how momentous events shook even jaded black barbers to the core. Even before the war began, secessionists had alienated Thomas from their cause. The proposed expulsion of free African Americans, intended to remove people of dubious loyalty to the South, spurred county courts to begin rounding up those who might be affected by the law. Observing that many "Indians, Spaniards, [and] French, whose chocolate mothers had lived under the three flags," were exempted from proving their status as free people, Thomas expressed disgust at such capricious definitions of race. The same white men who volunteered to help the courts appointed themselves the duty of monitoring the free black population. According to Thomas, they made their views quite clear, never tiring of saying, "You fellows must remember this is a white man's country yet." Then everything changed. "The [Emancipation] proclamation came and black troops followed," Thomas remembered forty years later with a tone of amazement; a black man could be the "protector" of his government. The implications stunned him: "The black man purchased two years previous at a good price [was] now hunting his former owners with a deadly weapon." He remembered African Americans singing, "It must be now that the Kingdom's coming, the year of Jubilee." As Thomas looked back in his autobiography, his words make it clear that he had chosen sides. Many, he said, blamed the African American for causing the war, but "if that is so, he was the cause of this becoming a better country."[8]

The Civil War experience of James Thomas gave him a political education in the issues that would dominate Reconstruction. Age probably discouraged Thomas and Clamorgan from enlisting in the Union army. Both left St. Louis during the war to earn high wages as barbers aboard commercial steamboats. The war came to Thomas directly while he served on the maiden voyage of the passenger steamer *Ruth*. After Union General Clinton Fisk commandeered the boat as his flagship, he directed his flotilla of sixty transports on an expedition up the White River that culminated in the Battle of Arkansas Post on January 10–11, 1863. The Union forces encountered little opposition. What struck Thomas the most was that the Confederate prisoners needed someone to read the newspaper to them, because they were illiterate. While this incident made Thomas realize that Confederate military forces did not live up to their vaunted reputation, not long afterward he also grew disheartened with his liberators in the Union army. Runaway slaves began trickling into the army camp seeking an audience with the "Gineral." After they had been thoroughly questioned by the ladies of the Sanitary Commission, the general would come out offering his hand to his "colored brother." Following the warm handshake and unexpected greeting, General Fisk would inquire whether the slave knew the location of any hidden cotton bales.[9] The northern friends of the slaves appeared more interested in confiscating southern wealth than in liberating African Americans.

His war experience also introduced Thomas to the freedmen's struggle to grasp the meaning of free labor. With labor in short supply, able-bodied young freedmen sought work aboard steamboats, although Thomas contended that it was events that had forced them to look for new employment: "Those blacks would have remained on the plantations and worked, but the planters were out of business for the time being." Thomas considered the freedmen "an awkward set at times" because they were unfamiliar with the ways free laborers worked. At first, they attempted to labor in fits and starts, as they had during slavery, before they learned the routine of paid labor. He took his fellow black shipmates' quickly acquired taste for finer things as evidence of advancement.[10]

When he visited St. Louis during breaks from serving on steamboats, Thomas found the city full of freedmen eager to find jobs or serve as substitutes for white men in the army. These "new made citizens" won his sympathy, for they "had just left the corn and cotton plantations and little knew about what they had to encounter." They had arrived in a city unprepared to house them, and Thomas felt special compassion for older freed people, who "found [freedom] awkward." For younger skilled freedmen such as carpenters, emancipation meant unemployment, since bosses refused to hire them. Thomas remembered that when a black man received a job that a white man was willing to do, "somebody would say, 'You have given a nigger work when white men are starving.'" The situation foreshadowed heightened discrimination after the war. He concluded his account of the Civil War with complaints that also anticipated disappointments to come: "There are many things the Negro could do, but it would not be given to him. That would be too good for a Negro. In many cases where he has accumulated something, [white people] will use some means to reach it and destroy it. Sometimes the Negro is destroyed with it."[11] His pessimism about white people outweighed his optimism about the abilities of freed people.

In the early years of the Civil War, plying his trade on the Mississippi River and in St. Louis, James Thomas could examine the merits of both sides in the conflict. Black barbers living north of the Border States tended to see only the dominant viewpoint within their region and, as a result, had different perspectives on the war's meaning. In Boston, black barbers had switched to serving black customers and formed strong ties to the abolitionist movement, so they saw the Civil War with a moral clarity that was impossible for people like Thomas who lived in a slave state. John Smith's regular customers, having made their barbershop a hub of antislavery activities, decided as a group to enlist in a Massachusetts regiment. Their solidarity became clear when, after signing up, they naturally drifted back to the barbershop for a celebration. "Some got a trim," one participant recalled, "but most got drunk." At the opposite extreme, in the lower South black barbers had divided loyalties due to their close ties to white planters, as the career of South Carolinian Robert DeLarge illustrates. DeLarge earned a substantial sum of money for serving the Confederate Navy as a barber during the war, and after the fighting he displayed sympathy for white southerners. In a resolution that he coauthored at a convention of black leaders, DeLarge expressed "our sorrow" that freedom for African Americans also meant "the ruin of thousands of those for whom, notwithstanding the bitterness of the past, and of the present, we cherish feelings of respect and affection." Moreover, as a delegate to the state's constitutional convention, DeLarge argued in favor of debt relief for white planters. He balanced his support for South Carolina's antebellum rulers with an unequivocal commitment to the defense of black rights. During his short career in Congress, he promoted the use of federal authority to suppress the Ku Klux Klan and other terrorist groups. He was not inconsistent when adopting these positions. Rather, he was a conservative politician who envisioned a racially integrated middle class restoring the state's plantation economy. White planters, DeLarge argued, had to be brought back within the fold, which he thought could be done by readmitting ex-Confederates to political life, so they would have a vested interest in the Reconstruction governments and, more importantly, a reconstructed southern society.[12]

Even among black barbers in the lower South, such an unambiguous relationship with white southerners was unusual. For Joseph Hayne Rainey, a prosperous black barber from a slaveholding family in Charleston, the sectional controversy and subsequent military conflict brought the full realization that white southerners defined him by his race when it seemed expedient. On the eve of the war, he ran afoul of the South Carolina law prohibiting free African Americans from traveling to a free state without prior authorization. Although friends solved this particular legal problem, his troubles had just begun. Rainey had barely resumed working with his father at the family barbershop when he was conscripted as a steward on a Confederate blockade runner. He served this duty and returned to Charleston only to be drafted again to work on harbor defenses. Although nominally a free man, Rainey plotted his escape from the reach of the Confederate government. He eventually slipped away with his wife to Bermuda, where the islanders held him in such high regard that they renamed the street where his shop was located "Barber's Alley." The Civil War having underscored the deficiencies of his second-class citizenship, Rainey sought to improve his prospects in the new southern society that was emerging after the war. After hearing encouraging reports from South Carolina that African Americans were moving into public life, Joseph Rainey left Bermuda for home in 1866 and entered politics. The next year he served on the central committee of the newly formed state Republican Party, and the following year he won election as a delegate to the state constitutional convention, where his distinguished service helped him run successfully for the state senate. In 1870, Republican Party leaders nominated him to fill a vacancy in the U.S. House of Representatives, and he handily won the off-year election, becoming the first African American to serve in the chamber.[13]

Rainey's commitment to the Republican Party may well have been a product of his mistreatment during the war, but he shared the conservative views of his white Republican colleagues as befit his class status; moreover, he encountered hostility among the freedmen when a political opponent questioned his loyalty to his race. When Joseph Rainey stood for Congress in South Carolina, he discovered that his light skin could be a liability. At a public meeting in 1870, a dark-skinned state legislator accused Rainey of caring nothing about poor African Americans, driving home his point by alleging that the candidate had tried to pass as white at the National Negro Laborers Convention. When Rainey attempted to defend himself, the mostly dark-skinned audience booed him off the podium. Divisions based on skin color also emerged at the state's 1865 colored convention, where the light-skinned black barbers John Chesnut and Robert DeLarge argued successfully for the deletion of a reference to color prejudices among the African Americans. Since both men belonged to Charleston's Brown Fellowship Society, which excluded those with darker skin, the charge of racial bias struck home.[14] The conversion of black barbers from the lower South to membership in a unified African American community was halting and incomplete.

Given the ties that black barbers in the upper South had enjoyed with the less fortunate members of their community, it was unsurprising that other blacks chose them as political representatives during Reconstruction. In the lower South, because freeborn barbers constituted such a small fraction of the black population, the achievements of South Carolinians like DeLarge in Reconstruction politics were atypical. In Louisiana, but nowhere else in the lower South, a few freeborn barbers achieved similar political success. In general, black barbers who entered politics held lower public offices. The four barbers who served on Richmond's city council provide a typical example.[15]

In all regions of the nation, black barbers pragmatically sought to maintain and strengthen their position by working for evolutionary instead of revolutionary change within the American social order. As a result, they stayed on the path they had followed in the antebellum period, cooperating with whites rather than submitting to them. They sought incremental changes in race relations and focused primarily on securing the influential white allies and financial resources that would make black self-help possible. Nowhere was this better demonstrated than in their involvement with the Republican Party. Having long served as hosts in the premier forums of political debate, their first-class shops, black barbers were ideally situated to enter politics themselves. They not only knew the important local politicians but also had spent many years analyzing platforms and criticizing strategies. Most importantly, they had developed relationship skills that enabled them to pursue their interests so tactfully that whites found their ambitions unobjectionable.

This behavioral quality facilitated the political debut of southern black barbers. In the immediate aftermath of the war, the political awakening of the African American community infused a variety of gatherings with a quasi-political character, and hence raised concerns among southern whites. One white editor in Alabama expressed relief when he learned that the head of a benevolent aid association recently established by freedmen was someone he knew and trusted, "John Tyre, our barber." At an 1867 meeting of freedmen in Alabama, the nominating committee selected the black barber John Rapier, Sr., for the office of voter registrar, an appointment that those at the gathering supported enthusiastically. Rapier became the first black public official in the history of the state. In addition to having the backing of the African American community, Rapier received the endorsement of conservative white southerners. The editor of the *Florence Journal* praised the appointment of "Uncle John," the name by which his white customers addressed him, because all classes of people respected him. Similarly, after Sampson Keeble became the first African American member of the state legislature in Tennessee, the editor of the *Nashville Union and American-Conservative* praised the black barber for respecting white sensibilities. "He is by no means," declared the editor, "a 'bigoted nigger' as might reasonably be expected, but upon the contrary, while he knows the laws of the country guarantee him equal political rights with other members [of the legislature], he is fully conversant of the fact that there is a social difference between them as great as the difference between night and day."[16] Because of their skillful handling of white men and their good reputation in the community, black barbers were naturally drawn and well suited to politics.

Being local leaders, when southern black barbers attained positions of political power, they focused on their communities' immediate well-being; and drawing on lessons of their own careers, they advocated self-help. In Charles Chesnutt's short story "The March of Progress," a barber named Frank Gillespie chairs a committee overseeing the black school of a little southern town, and his character accurately portrays the inclination of barbers from the upper South to advocate self-help. Gillespie, as the story opens, calls to order a public meeting held to employ a teacher for the upcoming school year. The residents have a choice between Henrietta Noble, the elderly white northern spinster who came south with the Freedmen's Bureau and opened a local school for black children, and Andrew Williams, a young, well-dressed black man who studied under Miss Noble before leaving home to obtain his college degree. After reading the applications of both candidates aloud to the gathering, Gillespie offers his own recommendation for hiring Williams. "The time has come in the history of our people," he says, "when we should stand together." Continuing his remarks, Gillespie declares, "The march of progress requires that we help ourselves or be forever left behind."[17]

In the story, Gillespie argues that self-preservation dictates hiring the black candidate, and he explains his reasoning with a frank discussion of racial inequality. In order for black people to improve their condition, he maintains, they must educate their young men and women. Yet, because of discrimination, black college graduates could only find jobs as ministers and teachers in black institutions, for which he is glad, because otherwise "they would have to go on forever waiting on white folks like their forefathers." By penning these lines for Gillespie, Chesnutt tacitly acknowledged that black barbers still felt the onus of earning a living by bowing and scraping to white men and sought more dignified occupations for the next generation whenever possible. The barber noted that the community had an opportunity to find employment for one of its own, whose eloquent letter of application, Gillespie adds, "ought to make us feel proud of him and of our race." By contrast, the other candidate, although she had done much good for the community, was "white and has got her own people to look after her; they got all the money and all the offices and all the everything."[18] Gillespie's analysis of the options available to young black men revealed the author's understanding of the outlook of black barbers. Skeptical about the possibility of improving race relations, Chesnutt thought the African American community needed to provide for itself, a belief that black barbers in the South expressed with greater and greater conviction.

Northern black barbers had more choices than their southern counterparts in the long run, but they also began the postwar era with grave disabilities. Until the enactment of the Fifteenth Amendment in 1870, African Americans lacked the franchise in most northern states, and afterward occasionally found it dangerous to exercise the right. As the 1870 election approached, General E. M. Gregory, U.S. Marshal for the Eastern District of Pennsylvania, invoked the Force Act, which Congress had passed to suppress Klan activities in the South, sending marines into Philadelphia to protect black voters. On their first trip to the polls, the city's African Americans voted without incident; however, the influence of their ballots angered Irish residents, who correctly attributed Republican victories to black voters. Democratic politicians in Philadelphia further inflamed Celtic voters, telling them in one instance that Republicans looked "upon a working white man as no better than a Negro." The stage had been set for confrontation. Even in a city known for mob violence, Election Day 1871 stood out as one of the bloodiest days in Philadelphia history. In the fourth and fifth wards, whites assaulted blacks attempting to vote, and the largely Irish police force sided with the rioters. The mayor refused to call out the state militia. In the ensuing gunfire, Octavius Catto, the most dynamic black leader in Philadelphia, was mortally wounded. The black barber and civil rights activist Isaiah Wears stepped into the leadership vacuum created by Catto's death and became the most visible black Republican leader in the city.[19]

Isaiah Wears's leadership illustrates the connection between elite black antebellum organizations and the mass black political movements of the postbellum era. As a young man, Wears had attracted notice in Philadelphia's black literary societies for his skill in debates. These organizations acquainted him with the cream of black society, including such leading black barbers as Joseph Cassey and Jacob White, Sr. Between 1845 and 1861, Wears led the debates at the Philadelphia Library Company, where his forceful attacks on colonization and the critics of William Lloyd Garrison swept aside the opposition. While helping to organize the General Vigilance Committee, he struck up a friendship with the prominent black abolitionist Robert Purvis, who helped Wears get elected to the 1846 Pennsylvania State Negro

Suffrage Convention. Wears received praise in *Frederick Douglass' Paper* eight years later for his participation in the National Negro Suffrage Convention. According to the newspaper's correspondent, Wears was "not only an elegant and vigorous speaker but [also] one of the best debaters in the house."[20]

The advent of the Civil War shifted the focus of Wears's activism toward issues affecting the black masses. As president of the newly formed Social, Civil, and Statistical Association, he continued to agitate for black suffrage and in 1867 lobbied successfully for the enactment of a state law desegregating street cars. The defeat of the Confederacy and Republican victories at the polls convinced Wears that African Americans could form a mass political movement, so he redoubled his push for enfranchisement. In an 1869 letter to a state senator, Wears made such a compelling argument for granting African Americans the vote that the elected official had it read into the proceedings of the Pennsylvania Senate. Wears also had the honor of addressing the Judiciary Committee of the United States Senate as the representative from the 1869 National Convention of Colored Men. Presenting a detailed constitutional analysis to the committee members, Wears ended his remarks on a positive note. Those who opposed black suffrage, he argued, would fall before the inevitable "march of progress." From modest beginnings, he noted, the antislavery cause had grown, through the unity generated by the war, into "one grand knighthood for the rights of men." Political equality, Wears concluded, was the future of America.[21]

The success that northern black barbers enjoyed as politicians vindicated Wears's optimism about the future. Like their southern counterparts, northern knights of the razor displayed an aptitude for winning votes and shaping public opinion, tasks made easier by the more enlightened racial climate in the North following the Civil War. Ohio's leading black barber, George Myers, explained the influence of his peers succinctly: "We come into contact with perhaps more people than any other class of [black tradesmen]. Our influence has always been exerted in behalf of the Republican Party." Barbershops in Philadelphia acquired a reputation as centers for political debate, and the ratification of the Fifteenth Amendment cleared the way for black barbers to become candidates. Detroit provides a case study of black barbers in postbellum politics. In the first election with black candidates, Thomas Owens ran for office, and in 1870, George Baptiste became the first African American to attend the Republican Party state convention in Michigan. In the years that followed, black barbers continued to distinguish themselves in politics, as when Henry Eubanks became the only African American from Cleveland elected to the Ohio Legislature in 1904, a feat that he repeated in 1908.[22]

Serving as an elected official granted northern black barbers a measure of prestige and influence that lingered beyond their generally short tenures in office, but patronage offered them an alternative career. Well-connected black barbers who rendered valuable services to the Republican Party expected to be rewarded, and in an age that regarded government jobs as so many plums to be divided among loyal party operatives, many expected that their reward would come from the public payroll. For example, in March of 1869, even before African Americans received the vote in Michigan, a black barber in Detroit named W. G. Winn got appointed as a clerk in the Freedmen's Bureau in March of 1869, and four months later his employer, John Richards, became a customs inspector. Another Detroit barber, George Barrier, parlayed a fortuitous marriage to the daughter of a local politician and service on the Third Ward Republican Committee into a lifetime of pubic employment in the city's sidewalk department, rising from inspector to clerk to department head. In Philadelphia, rumor had it that Isaiah Wears lived off a stipend from the Republican Party and the proceeds from his appointment as a notary public.[23]

Men like Wears entered politics for reasons besides pecuniary gain, however. More loyal to his party than it was to him, Wears evinced a determination to make the Republican Party his outpost in Philadelphia's civic life. Money, regardless of whispers about a Republican subsidy, probably did not influence Wears, who owned a prospering barbershop and later received the bulk of his uncle's estate, purportedly worth $100,000. When the Republican hierarchy turned a deaf ear to calls in the black press that Wears be nominated as a candidate, he must have recognized that elected office would remain beyond his grasp. He explained his devotion to the G.O.P. in pragmatic terms: "For myself, I only use it as a tool. It is a knife [that] has the sharpest edge and does my cutting. I use it as I do the church to which I belong, as a means to attain something higher." In other words, he classified the party along with the black church as an institution that could lend stability to the African American community but was a means rather than an end. He also agreed by and large with Republican policies. Whenever critics denounced Republican shortcomings, Wears drew on his pragmatic viewpoint as a black barber and replied that no decent alternative existed. He never tired of reminding black audiences that a Republican president had emancipated the slaves and a Republican Congress had passed the constitutional amendments that gave African Americans equality before the law. In Philadelphia, Republican mayors, he argued, offered the best guarantee against the mob violence that had taken the life of his friend Octavius Catto during the 1871 election. He also supported Republican measures to promote temperance by restricting the sale of alcohol, a move in keeping with the tenets of African Methodist Episcopal practice and his commitment to middle-class respectability. At critical moments, Wears kept black voters from leaving the Republican fold by expressing his convictions about the party at public forums, which made him a prominent leader in the city. His care in preserving keepsakes from his long political career—invitations to the governor's inauguration, a request from the *Philadelphia Sentinel* that he serve as a special editor, his appointment to the Citizens' Advisory Committee to the Mayor—suggests that he relished the limelight. Furthermore, his association with leading Philadelphians, such as John Wanamaker, burnished his stature within the African American community.[24] Wears's faith in the party of Lincoln, an amalgam of deeply held convictions and a thirst for recognition, remained unshakable throughout his life, which set him apart from many of his peers.

Unlike Wears, Ohio barber George Myers looked to the Republican Party for access to the social elite and ultimately assimilation into white society. His involvement in politics stemmed from personal relationships with white customers and the influence that he derived from them. Myers might have charted a quite different course in politics had he not felt the need to get out from under the shadow of his father, Isaac Myers. The Myerses lived in Baltimore, where Isaac, working with some of the leading black businessmen of the city, organized a plan to open a black-owned shipyard and persuaded members of the African American community to contribute $10,000 toward the venture. In 1866, the Chesapeake Marine Railway and Dry Dock Company opened. This cooperative business, drawing on the resources of the African American community to provide employment for black men as well as profits, anticipated the black-owned banks and insurance companies that would be founded a generation later. Not long afterward, Myers also proved instrumental in the foundation of the short-lived but precedent-setting Colored National Labor Union, and he played an active role in Republican politics. The fortunes of the collective shipyard enterprise ran aground in 1879, when several investors filed a suit against the officers of the company. The shareholders alleged that the officers had "grossly mismanaged" the company, "wastefully squandered its money," and misled investors into believing that the company owned rather than leased its property on the waterfront. The confusion stemmed from the challenges the organizers of the company had faced. Since no white property owners would sell land to African Americans, the organizers had to negotiate through a white intermediary. It is unclear whether this individual duped them or if they took a lease hoping that a concrete demonstration of black industry would change the hearts of white landowners; either way, racial discrimination had prevented them from obtaining all the resources they needed for an industrial enterprise. Although the lawsuit was dismissed, it had succeeded in undermining public confidence in the firm, which closed when its lease ran out in 1884.[25]

The suit may also have undermined George Myers's faith in his father and in independent black initiatives. During the same year that the Chesapeake shareholders began the court battle that led to the dissolution of the largest black-owned industrial venture of the day, George Myers made a fateful decision of his own, abandoning the city of his birth and moving to Cleveland at the age of twenty, just as Cleveland resident John D. Rockefeller consolidated his monopoly in oil refineries. George's move constituted a youthful rebellion against his father. Although he had finished high school, George was barred from entering college in Baltimore because of his race, and instead of pursuing a degree in medicine at Cornell as his father urged, George learned the barber's trade. After moving to Cleveland, he worked for nine years at the Wendell House barbershop, where influential white patrons took an interest in the his future, eventually lending him $2,000 to purchase the barbershop in the newly opened Hollenden Hotel. Unlike his father, who demanded that whites recognize his equality, George Myers built his career by recruiting influential white men as his patrons, starting with Mark Hanna, the architect of Republican dominance in the early twentieth century. Myers affectionately referred to his idol as "Uncle Mark" and, by his own description, became an "apt pupil" of the conservative, pro-business politician, adopting his opposition to unions and support for high tariffs. In 1896 at a Republican state convention, Myers cast the decisive vote that allowed Hanna to take control of the Republican Party in Ohio. Myers placed his mentor further in his debt two years later by securing the votes of black delegates to nominate Hanna's protégé, William McKinley, for the presidency and to give Hanna a seat in the United States Senate. Although Hanna and McKinley repeatedly offered to reward Myers, he declined their offers, "being in a business that was far more remunerative than any position that either would have given me." Instead he secured government appointments for his friends. While Hanna and McKinley remained in office, Myers exercised so much influence that his critics labeled his political network "Little Black Tammany."[26]

The contrast between the younger and elder Myerses illustrates how black barbers adopted more pragmatic, albeit more cynical, tactics than more populist black leaders. Whereas Isaac spent his life trying to open trade unions to African Americans and urged those who had been discriminated against to start cooperative ventures like the Baltimore shipyard, George counted among his customers Rutherford B. Hayes, the American president who had dispatched troops to Baltimore during the great strike of 1877, and kept a non-union shop. Father and son shared a devotion to the Republican Party, but George embraced the party's conservative turn in the late nineteenth century. Judging from his actions and opinions, George had concluded that his father's convictions were impractical, naïve, and out of touch with changes in American society. Myers thought his acquaintances in the white elite of Cleveland and the fruits of his own hard work provided the most certain means for achieving equality. As he wrote to a white friend, historian James Ford Rhodes, a "wide and beneficial acquaintance" had sheltered him from much of the discrimination that African Americans generally faced. He earned over $3,000 a year, lived in a fashionable white neighborhood, and belonged to the exclusive City Club, a popular spot for white businessmen and politicians. Because he had, in his own mind, transcended race, he had little patience with African Americans who complained about racism. He urged working-class blacks, in an article entitled "Our Lack of Initiative," to "cease crying about discrimination and confounding it with a lack of initiative." Instead, he argued that the secret to success lay in "concentration, courtesy, and efficiency," which was the "trinity that will break down every barrier of race prejudice in the industrial world." The theme underlying Myers's commentary was that African Americans needed to shoulder the burden of integrating themselves into the white majority. Despite his embrace of bourgeois values, Myers also retained the family ethos of black barbers, mentoring young protégés and postponing his retirement to ensure that his staff of thirty would have employment.[27]

James Ford Rhodes moved away from Cleveland in 1910, but the historian and his old barber kept up a wide-ranging correspondence for the next thirteen years; the letters attest to the indignities that Myers suffered in order to secure his privileged status. The letters include gossip about mutual acquaintances, but also more serious debates over Rhodes's interpretation of Reconstruction. While Myers clearly drew satisfaction from these intellectual exchanges and the respect that a leading historian accorded him by discussing his research, he must have winced when, twice annually, Rhodes would include some of his old ties along with his letter to Myers. Such gifts were a practice common between gentlemen and their favored servants, and they reminded the black barber of his subordinate status. Myers did not need hand-me-down clothing, yet he graciously accepted Rhodes's old ties in order to maintain his relationship with an important white patron. On one occasion he dutifully wrote Rhodes, "I beg to assure you that I appreciate the ties, and shall clean them up with a little elbow grease and gasoline."[28] Myers never dwelled on such rituals or the fact that he was the junior partner in his friendships with prominent whites, apparently viewing them as minor inconveniences that he endured to achieve his ends. Following the advice that he gave others, he stressed personal initiative and refused to complain about discrimination.

Isaiah Wears agreed with George Myers about the need to stop emphasizing distinctions of color, warning black audiences that politics based on race would be their undoing. "Descending to the low and marshy grounds of mere race advocacy," he maintained, "would justify the enemy in acting on the same lines for his own deportment toward us." When "race shriekers" complained about the so-called Negro problem, they revealed that they had been, according to Wears, duped by southern white supremacists. "The idea of a 'Negro problem,'" Wears argued, was nothing more than a "fig leaf" covering up the "disloyal and . . . cowardly efforts [of white southerners] to make the Negro pay the penalty [for] aiding the National government in crushing the life out of the Southern Confederacy." Since the Declaration of Independence and the United States Constitution made no reference to skin color, he contended, to embrace an African identity "qualified" a black person's American citizenship. Wears particularly disliked the vogue at the time for using the prefix "Afro-," predicting that "the colored man and woman of the next generation will be addressed as 'Afros' for short, which will be as respectful in sound as 'Sambo.'" Privately, he wondered why black people in America would want to identify with Africa. What had the continent or the inhabitants of Africa done, he wrote in his notebook, when measured by the "standards . . . of the nineteenth century," that "demands, justifies, or even invites the adoption" of the label "Afro-Americans"?[29] To Wears, black people were Americans and assimilating the norms of white middle-class society was the only sure way to win complete acceptance for African Americans as equals.

Wears might be accused of confusing the perspective of his comfortable middle-class existence with the situation that the majority of African Americans faced in the North, but if so, the accusation could be levied against many other northern black barbers. Perhaps success in politics had inspired in them dreams of a color-blind society; whatever the cause may have been, northern black barbers assimilated white middle-class standards eagerly, in large part by seeking more respectable occupations for themselves and their children. Wears himself had by 1874 become a real estate dealer and speculated in land at Cape May, New Jersey. Coming to Denver in 1860, Barney Ford worked as a successful barber, restaurant owner, and boardinghouse operator before opening, in 1874, the Inter-Ocean Hotel, which acquired a reputation as the "aristocratic hostelry" of the city. The two men's career changes mirrored the black elite's general inclination to invest in real estate. Although entrepreneurs could acquire status within the

African American community, entering the professions seemed to present a better way to gain social acceptance. Cleveland barber Thomas Fleming displayed the scope of his ambitions by joining the legal profession and becoming active in politics. After earning a law degree and founding the influential Attucks Republican Club, in 1909 he became the first African American member of the Cleveland City Council, a post he held until 1929. Jeremiah Sanderson, to cite another example, abandoned barbering in favor of teaching school not long after settling in San Francisco. Like many of his peers throughout the country, he also worked part-time as a minister. The sons and daughters of northern black barbers were more likely than their fathers to be upwardly mobile, aspiring to become educators, physicians, and attorneys. In his book of advice for young black people, *Don't Tell White Folks; or Light Out of Darkness*, the black Boston doctor James Still helped explain why the children of barbers were reluctant to follow in their father's footsteps. "How," he asked, "is the Negro family to rise to manhood and manliness through the barber's 'profession,' . . . any more than the white man has?"[30] Even as prosperous black barbers and their children climbed to the top of the black social structure, the arrival of growing numbers of impoverished black migrants dramatically altered circumstances in the North, exposing as an illusion the conviction that race would cease to define their lives.

Black barbers would not have been torn between their class interests and their racial identity if the Civil War had severed their relationship with white customers. In fact, some white men did break with tradition by shunning black barbers after the war. "Formerly, we had only colored barbers," observed the editor of the *Petersburg (Virginia) Daily Index* in 1865, "now, the native whites seek generally barbers of their own color." Although white immigrant barbers had made inroads on the trade during the 1850s, black barbers held on to their economic niche by serving white customers tenaciously, and they regained some of the ground they had lost to immigrant white barbers. The strength of black barbers in Richmond, where the number of their barbershops doubled following the Civil War, suggests that the Petersburg editor had overstated the gains made by Virginia's white barbers. Farther south, black barbers remained competitive in the trade, and in some places, they enjoyed a resurgence. In New Orleans, despite its teeming immigrant population, a third of its barbers were black. In Mobile, black barbers regained lost ground and displaced their white competitors. They went from being the minority in 1860 to majority status in 1870, when two out of three barbers were African American. In Savannah, black barbers also gained the upper hand, albeit more gradually; although black men made up less than half of the city's barbers in 1870, eight out of ten barbers in 1880 were black. Even the ranks of Charleston's long-predominant black barbers swelled. Between 1860 and 1880, the proportion of African Americans employed as barbers rose from a healthy 80 percent to an overwhelming 96 percent of the whole. Outside the South, the prospects for black barbers improved as they moved westward. While black men in 1870 held only one-sixth of Boston's barbering jobs and one-third of Philadelphia's, roughly half of the barbers in Detroit and Cleveland were black as were two-thirds of all of the barbers in the state of Colorado. The West Coast provided an even more hospitable climate for black barbers. For example, the first black resident of Seattle was also the city's first barber, and by 1870 nearly half of the city's small black population worked as barbers, attesting to the strongly competitive position of black men in the trade outside the northeastern states.[31]

During the Gilded Age, growing affluence and the rise of mass consumption transformed the marketplace in which black barbers operated, raising the bar for attracting prosperous white customers.[32] Those who wished to remain competitive had to keep pace with the growing American appetite for luxury. The most prosperous black barbers rose to the challenge, making the first-class barbershop of the late nineteenth century into a palatial establishment befitting the robber barons and political bosses who mingled there. At any given time in Alonzo Herndon's Atlanta barbershop on Peachtree Street, reputed to be the finest in the South, one might encounter state supreme court judges, influential lawyers, planters, ministers, and politicians from every Georgia community. Customers entered through two sixteen-foot tall mahogany doors with beveled glass that Herndon had had made by special commission to resemble a pair that he had admired while visiting Paris. Once inside, they walked across a vast expanse of white marble to reach one of the twenty-three barber chairs. Electric chandeliers illuminated their passage. After their shave, they could visit the bathhouse downstairs. In Cleveland, George Myers surpassed even this level of luxury according to the author Elbert Hubbard, who proclaimed Myers's establishment at the Hollenden Hotel "the best barbershop in America." Myers outfitted each chair with a marble wash basin and a telephone. In addition to using the latest in sterilizing equipment, Myers claimed to have given the Koken Barber Supply Company the inspiration for the modern barber chair and to have been the first barber to provide the services of manicurists. He even employed a stenographer to take dictation from busy customers.[33]

The number and diverse roles of Myers's staff probably impressed customers as much as the surroundings. A foreman greeted most customers, directing them to the chair of a waiting barber, but Myers provided personal service to noteworthy customers, who each kept monogrammed shaving mugs in a rack by Myers's chair. In all, Myers shaved eight presidents (Hayes, Harrison, Cleveland, McKinley, Theodore Roosevelt, Taft, Wilson, and Harding), dozens of congressmen, and other notables, such as Mark Twain and Lloyd George. The size of his staff, which included as many as thirty barbers at a time, formed the upper end of the spectrum; other first-class barbershops in Cleveland employed between twelve and twenty men. Elsewhere, large staffs were commonplace. For example, Moses Bentley, one of Alonzo Herndon's competitors in Atlanta, kept eighteen barbers working in his shop, while James Cragwell, the leading barber of Seattle, employed twenty men at two shops located in downtown hotels. Information about the number of black barbers and black-owned shops in Louisville reveals an average of six men per establishment.[34] By expanding their capital investment and introducing a division of labor, first-class barbershops emulated on a small scale the trend toward bigness in late-nineteenth-century business.

These firms were the cutting edge of black businesses in the country at the time. Whereas most black businessmen failed to expand their customer base beyond the African American community, black barbers attracted more white customers than did black men in any other line of business. At a time when most black businessmen lacked capital, first-class barbershop owners committed substantial investments to outfitting their stylish establishments. Dunn and Barlow, a nineteenth-century credit-rating agency, declined assigning credit ratings in 1889 to almost three out of four black-owned businesses operating in North Carolina because the firms lacked sufficient funds to be deemed credit worthy. By contrast, an 1899 study found that more barbers had at least $500 invested in their business than black men in any other line of business except for grocers and general store owners, and barbers nearly tied for second place. Furthermore, there were roughly twice as many barbers in this investment category than members of the next three businesses in the ranking: publishers, undertakers, and saloon keepers. More than half of the barbers included in the study also had $1,000 or more invested in their shops. In some cities, barbers towered over their fellow black businessmen in terms of capital. Three Cleveland barbers individually had more capital invested than any other black-owned business in the city. Collectively, the $21,000 capitalization of their barbershops surpassed the combined investment that black businessmen had made in all other types of establishments in the Ohio city.[35] The investments that barbers made in their shops assumed greater significance when compared to other black businessmen, such as grocers, whose capital was tied up in stock obtained on credit from wholesalers. By contrast, barbers kept little inventory and spent lavishly on creating shops that in luxury were on a par with department stores.

The transformation of boss barbers into businessmen, while necessary to maintain a competitive edge, had the negative side effect of eroding the black

TABLE 8
Black-Owned First-Class Barbershops by Capital Invested, 1899, Nationwide

Amount of Capital Invested	Number
$500–$1,000	60
$1,000–$2,500	63
$2,500–$5,000	12
$5,000–$10,000	3
Undisclosed amount over $500	24

Source: W. E. B. DuBois, *The Negro in Business* (Atlanta: Atlanta University Press, 1899), 9, 16.

barbers' fraternity by replacing cooperation between journeymen and employers with conflict. By the late nineteenth century, first-class barbershop proprietors operated on an entirely different scale than did their humbler peers. W. E. B. DuBois noted this distinction in his study of black businesses. Although the 1890 census reported that 17,480 black men across the United States worked as barbers, DuBois pointed out that the vast majority were tradesmen rather than businessmen. They either worked for wages or ran small shops working alone or with one helper who came in on Saturday night. These men worked in barbershops that cost approximately $20 to equip and typically occupied a ten-foot by twelve-foot space. By contrast, he estimated, three hundred or so barbers had at least $500 invested in large, ornate shops, employed three to eight journeymen, and attracted well-heeled customers. Only these barbers, in his opinion, were "really businessmen."[36] As distinctions arose between entrepreneurs, petty shopkeepers, and employees, the common bonds that had held black barbers together for half a century dissolved.

Class differences lay at the heart of the conflicts among black master barbers and journeymen. For most journeymen, life was a dull grind of long hours and short pay. An 1886 survey found that Detroit journeymen barbers worked an average of thirteen hours a day in a work week that included Saturday evenings and Sundays. For their efforts, most barbers earned meager rewards. Only three out of the forty-seven barbers questioned in the Detroit survey owned their own homes, and only one had a bank account. In Philadelphia's first-class barbershops, the best journeymen could earn $8 to $10 a week, although a few made up to $15, equivalent to the wages of the city's black teamsters and janitors.[37] The men handing out the pay packets, on the other hand, appeared flush with cash.

Sometimes, the wealth of black barbershop owners even attracted comment in white newspapers. A Nashville reporter observed Sampson Keeble sporting a $100 gold watch, and the *Atlanta Constitution* noted in 1877 that "there are colored barbers . . . who wear diamonds that weigh two ounces." When Joshua Eddy died in 1882, the *Philadelphia Evening Bulletin* devoted almost two full columns to his obituary topped by the headline, "Money His God," along with an estimate that the black barber left an estate worth $100,000. The U.S. Census substantiated these anecdotal stories about the wealth of black barbershop owners. In the South, where most of the country's black population lived in the decade after the war, black barbers made up a substantial percentage of black property owners: 290 southern black barbers owned an average of more than $2,000 worth of real estate in 1870. Their wealth rose over time as well. Whereas James Thomas had begun accumulating his $100,000 fortune in St. Louis during the antebellum period, Alfred Billingslea started his Birmingham barbershop after the Civil War and had equaled Thomas's wealth by the 1880s. Such affluence funded a manner of living beyond the dreams of most journeymen. Thomas resided in a large suburban house furnished with lace curtains, imported Persian carpets, mahogany furniture, and a rosewood piano, the whole cared for by a full-time gardner and a Prussian-born servant. Thomas also traveled extensively, visiting London, Paris, Rome, Florence, Naples, Vienna, and Berlin on one European tour.[38]

The growing chasm between journeymen and employers nurtured mutual resentment, especially over working conditions. In response, journeymen barbers used time-honored traditions of workplace resistance. Moving between employers and even cities furnished one means of maintaining independence. In a conversation with a white customer, one black barbershop owner described these itinerant barbers, who knew how to shave and cut hair "first rate," but of whom he disapproved otherwise. Arriving broke, they would "maybe work steady for two weeks. By that time he's got a collar that scrapes all the hair of his black jaw without a razor and shoes so pointy that he must pare his black feet to get into them. He's a great man then. Wants days off and evenings out until you can't rest and cuts it mighty fine with the women." According to the proprietor, such men invariably left town: "I've about made my mind [that] they are mostly tramps." Wendel Dabney, a black chronicler of African American life in Cincinnati also commented on arrogant, lazy journeymen barbers. "On Mondays, many barbers failed to show up for work, and if they had enough cash on hand, they did not even show up on Tuesday." In the barbershop, if the journeyman "got into a little poker game . . . , the customer simply had to wait if he wanted his services." To barbershop owners preoccupied with competition, fixed overhead costs, and the bottom line, it seemed like "half the time the barbers are loafing." George Myers dealt with high-handed barbers in Cleveland by recruiting employees from the South and keeping a strictly non-union shop.[39] With fewer employers controlling larger barbershops that required greater amounts of capital investment, proprietors held the upper hand in workplace disputes, a coercive authority that further dissipated mutuality among black barbers.

Journeymen barbers turned to the collective strength of their own unions to gain more leverage over employers, discontinuing a tradition of cooperation with shop owners in trade associations. For example, class tensions roiled the Tennessee Barbers' Association at the close of Reconstruction. The journeymen were on strike, seeking not only higher pay but to alter the balance of power between themselves and their employers. On July 31, 1877, the striking barbers declared that they would accept nothing less than 65 percent of barbershop revenues. They did consent to meet with a wealthy barbershop owner, Sampson Keeble, whose role as the first African American elected to the Tennessee State Legislature could have been what made him palatable to the strikers. When they met with Keeble at his office, they restated their demand for the majority of shop revenues along with calling for higher prices and denouncing the practice of hiring itinerant barbers in shops where journeymen worked steadily. Their demands represented a collective bid for a more respectable and secure income at the expense of boss barbers. Keeble made a counteroffer of 50 percent of the receipts, showing that shop owners recognized the power of the Union. The strikers flatly refused his offer and instructed Keeble to forward their demands to Nashville's barbershop proprietors. The resolution of the strike apparently went unrecorded, but it foreshadowed more division and strife among black barbers.[40]

The journeymen barbers of Nashville had their counterparts elsewhere. Since labor organizing among black barbers hardly fit white editors' definition of compelling news, the few notices that appeared in print more than likely were only the tip of an iceberg of protest. In Omaha journeymen went on strike in 1887, and the following year black barbers gathered in Greenville, South Carolina, to form the State Barbers' Union for "mutual benefit, the regulation of prices, and the elevation of the trade." When W. E. B. DuBois conducted his famous study of Philadelphia's African American community in 1899, he noted that the city's black barbers had formed their own union. He also noted that disaffection among journeymen had lessened the trade's appeal to young African American men. DuBois reported that, according to his surveys, "Today one would have to look a long time among young and aspiring Negroes to find one who would willingly become a barber—it smacks perhaps a little too much of domestic service, and is a thing to fall back upon but not to aspire to."[41]

The declining interest in barbering, while possibly fanned by discontented journeymen, almost certainly reflected the strident criticisms of barbers by black activists who sought to integrate barbershops. Even though black protests against segregated barbershops accomplished little, black barbers were probably unnerved at times by their brethren's willingness to confront them in public and bring lawsuits against them. Black leaders who had gathered at a meeting of the National Equal Rights League just four months after the surrender of Confederate forces in 1865 singled out black barbers for condemnation. The delegates maintained that those who discriminated against members of their own race degraded African Americans in the eyes of white Americans. Most black barbershop owners felt that they had little choice but to hold on to their white customers, which would be unlikely if they integrated their shops. Several tried opening "equal rights" barbershops, only to meet with failure. In Philadelphia, a handful of black-owned barbershops did manage to serve an integrated clientele, but white prejudice forced the overwhelming majority of black barbers to serve one race exclusively. The option of serving black men seemed poor business to most. When one black barber in Chattanooga refused to serve a group of black men, they asked him "if their money was not as good as a white man's?" Concerned that their presence would drive away white customers, the barber answered, "Yes, just as good, but there is not enough of it!"[42]

Black leaders throughout the nation, smarting from exclusion by their fellow African Americans's barbershops, continued to protest and lobby against this segregation for the rest of the nineteenth century. The Civil Rights Act passed by Congress in 1875 appeared to threaten segregated barbershops by guaranteeing equal access to public accommodations, which made white barbershop customers anxious and black men hopeful. In a letter that *Harper's Weekly* deemed worthy to print, the act's sponsor, Benjamin Butler, reassured a friend that the legislation did not entitle black men to patronize barbershops that served white men. "A barber," he explained, "has a right to shave whom he pleases." Many black men disagreed with Butler and tested the law. One group demanded shaves in a Nashville area barbershop; when refused service, these activists learned that the federal law had depressing limitations, so they attempted to force integration with direct action, confronting back barbers in their shops. Some, like black newspaper editor Horace Cayton, discovered that black barbers made no exceptions for prominent men like himself. When Cayton confronted Seattle barbershop owner John Cragwell, the barber had the editor arrested and fined for disorderly conduct. Although taking such actions against men who shared their standing in the black community may have been uncomfortable or painful for the shop owners, it only made sense to them. Black barbers distinguished between their role as businessmen and their role as community leaders, reasoning that unless they operated segregated barbershops they would lack the standing to serve their community. For example, even though George Knox edited the black newspaper in Indianapolis and so presumably had a comprehensive view of the community, he would not admit black customers to his barbershop.[43]

Black men denied service in parts of the country where African Americans had political influence often sought redress from elected officials, and in some cases succeeded in changing the law. After being ejected from a black-run barbershop, Harvard law student William Harris testified before the Massachusetts legislature on the need to desegregate all places that served the public. The legislators, persuaded of the justice of Harris's case, revised the state's antidiscrimination law accordingly and specifically mentioned barbershops. Similarly, the city council of Washington, D.C., expanded the city's antidiscrimination ordinance to include barbershops. Michigan legislators specifically prohibited discrimination in barbershops in the state's first civil rights law, although numerous complaints revealed that black as well as white barbers continued to operate segregated businesses.[44]

Convinced that the survival of their businesses and hence their middle-class status was at stake, black barbers thwarted antidiscrimination laws with ingenuity and the help of sympathetic judges. Some barbershop proprietors in the District of Columbia made black customers wait unduly long for service and posted exorbitant prices, such as "Haircut $30, Shampoo $40" with an addendum below in small print promising "a liberal reduction . . . to our regular customers." When one African American sued a black barber in Seattle for refusing to shave him, the court dismissed the suit after the barber claimed that he had denied the man service on account of his unsavory reputation. When black men in the District of Columbia won lawsuits against local barbershops, they received only token damages, which in turn led black barbers there to be more assertive of their right to refuse service to African Americans. One of the city's barbershop owners went so far as to take out an advertisement in the *Washington Bee*, a black newspaper:

> Preston's Pension Office Barbershop, first class in every particular.
> *Devoted Strictly to White Trade.*
> The rumor that this shop has been serving
> any colored trade is false in every particular.[45]

Their success at preventing integration within their shops earned black barbers the contempt of some leading members of the African American community. Many black newspapers branded them as traitors to the race. "It may be from a spirit of selfish indifference, or an uncalled for dependence upon the white man," speculated one black editor, "yet the fact is that as a rule this class of people [barbers] have no interest in the race's advancement." When counseling his readers to file lawsuits against businesses violating antidiscrimination laws, another editor repeatedly urged people to sue black barbers first. This animus toward black barbers reflected, in part, a concern that their businesses legitimized segregation. At least one white editor confirmed this argument by citing the refusal of black barbers to serve African Americans as a justification for segregation. According to the editor, businessmen, regardless of their color, turned away certain people simply because "the best paying class of customers can be retained only by excluding those who for any reason are objectionable to their fastidious notions."[46]

The difference between the issues and, more significantly, the tone of the controversies over black barbers in the antebellum and Reconstruction periods reveals fundamental changes in black society. Before the Civil War, black leaders focused less on the role of barbers in maintaining segregation and more on how they exemplified the degradation of African Americans forced to work in menial jobs. Black barbers seemed to infuriate their antebellum critics because they appeared to have traded their racial pride for a good livelihood, which explains the recurring charge that barbers had surrendered their manhood, when in fact they served as the breadwinners within their households and beyond. At the time, the same black leaders who criticized barbers were often struggling to earn a decent living in spite of their many talents. They expressed the frustration of an elite largely unable to acquire the material basis for a middle-class standard of living. During Reconstruction, with African Americans serving as representatives in the halls of Congress, the opportunities for the black elite seemed limitless. More importantly, a small but expanding group of African Americans of both sexes attended colleges, entered the professions, and served in voluntary organizations, accomplishments that even many white Americans recognized as the credentials for inclusion in a true middle class. These new members of the black middle class fiercely guarded their recently won status, and segregation rebuked their self-image as nothing else did. Hence, they attacked black barbers even though it was a commonplace that integrated or black-only shops would fail. From the point of view of the black elite, black barbers acted contrary to the interests of their class more than of their race. Only a tiny minority of African Americans possessed the wherewithal to patronize middle-class establishments, while the majority remained stuck in menial jobs that placed them at the beck and call of white employers.[47]

In accommodating the prejudices of their white customers, black barbers were displaying their own conception of self-interest and class identity.

In the North, just when it appeared that the march of black barbers toward progress would surmount all obstacles, race relations changed abruptly and placed the barbers in an untenable situation. White prejudice and residential segregation grew along with the black populations of northern cities, creating ghettos and threatening the political and civil rights of black barbers. In quest of the votes of newly arrived immigrants and of whites in the South, white Republican leaders downgraded their commitment to African Americans. The retreat from black civil rights and political participation began at the top of the Republican Party. President McKinley, one of George Myers's clients, used the spirit of sectional reconciliation fostered by the Spanish-American War as an occasion to court white southern voters, traveling to Atlanta, where he donned a Confederate gray badge and volunteered to have the federal government maintain the graves of dead rebels. Politically active black barbers also had to contend with the rise of corrupt ghetto bosses, who furnished poor black migrants with aid and alcohol in return for their votes. Once Sammy Williams and Gil Ball had established their political machines in Philadelphia's black wards, for example, Isaiah Wears lost the control he had had over the few offices and patronage jobs that Republican leaders were still willing to share.[48] In a critical convergence of circumstances, northern black barbers lost their political influence, their white friends abandoned them, and the African American community began to question their leadership because they were perpetuating assimilation even after the rise of Jim Crow.

Some northern black barbers risked alienating themselves from their communities by opposing the creation of separate black institutions to improve the conditions of poor migrants. To George Myers, who remembered the fight to secure the passage of civil rights legislation in northern states, calls for separate black organizations and self-help within the community were an unacceptable surrender to prejudice. Myers publicly opposed establishing a black YMCA in Cleveland, using his influence to arrange coverage sympathetic to his views in a local black newspaper, which cautioned readers that a black Y would lead to segregated schools. In addition, Myers discouraged his friend Booker T. Washington from helping Y supporters raise money from white philanthropists, telling him that African Americans in the city did not need or want the separate institution. He also frustrated Jane Edna Hunter's efforts to create the Phillis Wheatley home, a settlement house for young black women. When Hunter contacted Washington seeking help with her fundraising, he wrote to Myers for information about her. Myers replied that Hunter merely sought to make a name for herself and lacked "standing among the better class of our women." Again he told his powerful friend that the project was unnecessary, and once more, Washington declined to assist the effort. On the other hand, Myers did support Washington's program creating separate black institutions in the South. He believed, though, that the progress toward integration in the North made separatism there inadvisable. Explaining his views to Washington in a 1914 letter, Myers wrote, "Segregation here [in Cleveland] of any kind to me is a step backward." He also refused to join Washington's organization, the National Negro Business League, because he opposed the idea of African Americans creating a group economy. In a 1916 editorial, Myers encouraged young men to pursue business careers but warned them against trying "to make color an asset. . . . Don't be a colored business man. Don't be a colored professional man. It's an admission of inferiority." Instead, he advised, they should seek white as well as black customers, which would make them feel like "a man among men."[49] Given his success competing against white barbers, Myers thought that black businessmen who limited themselves to serving black customers were abandoning the playing field before the game had started. His critics might have replied that he had abandoned black customers. Perhaps Myers felt abandoned himself, for his call to young men was also an invitation to join him in a lonely outpost.

Myers also made some perceptive observations about the pitfalls of separatism. Myers feared that black appeals to racial solidarity would justify white backsliding on civil rights, which turned out to be a valid point largely overlooked by advocates of black nationalism. Although his lifestyle generally sheltered him from racism, he harbored no illusions about the continued existence of white prejudice. Myers used his influence to fight discrimination, convincing the *Cleveland Plain Dealer* to stop using the terms *negress* and *darkey.* He also lined up influential whites behind an effort to prevent the racist film *The Birth of a Nation* from being shown in Cleveland. Ultimately, however, Myers's dependence on white customers limited his capacity for fighting discrimination. After the management of the Hollenden Hotel, where he leased space for his barbershop, told him that once he left, white barbers would replace his black staff, he decided to forgo retirement. Unwilling to cause thirty employees to lose their jobs, he worked until the day he died, suffering a heart attack during his lunch break.[50]

The hopes that Emancipation and Reconstruction had inspired in black barbers, while not dashed entirely, remained unfulfilled as their access to political power waned. For the most part, forces beyond their control thwarted their ambitions, but they contributed to their own downfall as well. Northern barbers may have experienced the greatest disappointment, because many had grasped the promise of the middle-class dream only to have it slip away in the latter years of their life. Yet, the vision of assimilation promoted by George Myers and Isaiah Wears had always required turning a blind eye to the prejudices of their white customers and political allies; moreover, they seemed at times to advocate the doctrine of personal initiative as an excuse for not addressing the needs of the black masses. Similarly, black barbers from the lower South won election to some of the highest offices before stumbling, tripped up by treacherous political allies and, more importantly, the half-heartedness of their acceptance of freedmen. These handicaps developed out of the tension between their class interests and their racial identity. Even if the political arena had remained sunny for them, barbers faced conflicts with members of their own class over their policy of segregation and with the working-class employees of their first-class barbershops. In the upper South, although few black barbers won prominent roles in the Republican Party, their experience in the Reconstruction shakedown was more positive. Although white violence deprived them of their political rights, they managed to sustain their ties to the African American community that had been established during the antebellum period. Their unambiguous identification with their race and their emphasis on self-help would allow black barbers in the region to win support for their opinions about racial uplift in late-nineteenth-century America.

CHAPTER SIX

From Barbershops to Boardrooms

Worth more than $100,000, owner of Durham's leading first-class barbershop, and personal barber to Washington Duke, the founder of the American Tobacco Company, John Merrick possessed unsurpassed credentials as a successful black barber. Yet, during the 1890s, he moved away from serving whites. Merrick instead seized the economic opportunities presented by the growing urban black population, first by opening a string of barbershops that served African Americans and later by establishing the North Carolina Mutual Life Insurance Company. Because the company that he founded grew into the largest black-owned corporation in the world, Merrick attracted the notice of W. E. B. DuBois, who argued that Merrick provided the link between two important traditions within the African American community: the successful lone proprietor and the custom of mutual aid. Pointing to Merrick's involvement with fraternal orders and to the charitable aspects of the North Carolina Mutual Insurance Company, DuBois concluded that the barber had merged business with benevolence.[1] While the esteemed black scholar overlooked the African American tradition of barbering and its dedication to community uplift, he did document an important change among black barbers during the 1890s.

The onslaught of Jim Crow placed black barbers and consumers in a quandary. While black-owned businesses lost their white customers, white-owned firms such as the Prudential Insurance Company charged African Americans unfair rates or refused to serve them altogether. The first-class barbershop, already imperiled by growing conflicts between owners and journeymen barbers, in the 1880s for the first time faced the prospect of losing white customers. In the North, white barbers exploited the public's newly acquired anxieties about germs and zeal for public health reform. They lobbied states to enact licensing laws that would have allowed officials of the barbers' union to determine who worked in barbershops. Northern black barbers spent their last bit of political capital to defeat this movement only to see their white customers reject them as racial attitudes hardened throughout the region. In the South, white supremacy fanned racial hatred, leading white mobs to terrorize the African American community, a situation that made black barbers think twice about serving white men. Southern black barbers acknowledged that Jim Crow would change their lives, but they refused to surrender their ambitions for themselves and their community. Instead, they recognized that a new day had arrived.

In 1925, two decades after DuBois had lauded the accomplishments of black barber John Merrick, another distinguished black scholar, E. Franklin Frazier, wrote an essay about Merrick's hometown, Durham, North Carolina, for an anthology that celebrated the spirit of what its editor, Alain Locke, called the "New Negro." Frazier explained to his readers that, although the tobacco manufacturing center lacked the "color and creative life" of the more famous African American community in Harlem, "the Negro is at last developing a middle class, and its main center is in Durham." In describing the enterprising African Americans of this southern city, Frazier could have been writing the history of black barbers. "We find them," he wrote, "beginning their careers without much formal education and practicing the old-fashioned virtues of the old middle class." Comparing the black businessmen of Durham to Benjamin Franklin, he chronicled their rise through hard work to become "colored capitalists." He then illustrated his remarks by relating the details of Merrick's career. By focusing on the "business psychology" and respectability of Merrick and his counterparts, Frazier, a sociologist, documented the awakening of the black petite bourgeoisie, now conscious of its identity through an awareness of its members' shared class interests.[2]

Black barbers such as Merrick were indeed the men of the hour in the southern black community. With everything they had achieved placed at risk by the white backlash, they acted decisively to protect their interests. Urbanization aided their cause by providing them with a wage-earning black population that could patronize barbershops that served black clients and could support other black-owned enterprises. By founding corporations that met vital needs, the South's leading black barbers helped set their communities on a path toward an economic self-sufficiency that flourished until the Great Depression. Only a few of these entrepreneurs left their barbershops for corporate boardrooms, as Merrick did, but the actions of the rest bequeathed an even greater legacy. By establishing the black neighborhood barbershop and making it a central institution in the

Harlem Barber Shop in Oxford, North Carolina, 1939. W. M. Mallory not only focused on serving black customers but he emphasized his identification with the nation's leading African American community through the name of his shop. (Photograph by Marion Post Wolcott, November 1939; courtesy of the Library of Congress, Prints and Photographs Division, LC-USF34-052700-D, Washington, D.C.)

lives of black men, they adapted the earlier tradition of the knights of the razor and fitted it into the African American community. These achievements elevated the standing of black barbers within their race. After patiently suffering the barbs hurled at them by black professionals for nearly a century, black barbers found themselves honored by the African American community, as their ideas about respectability and self-help became the watchwords of the day.

By the middle of the nineteenth century, German immigrants had supplanted African Americans throughout the nation at the lower end of the barbering trade, serving poorer customers. However, after twenty years, the now second-generation immigrant barbers still had failed to win over the affluent white men whom black barbers served. Instead, they provided a relatively mundane service and attracted customers with their low prices, making them vulnerable to impoverished newcomers willing to charge even less than they did. To earn a decent living, most worked long hours, seven days a week. In the late nineteenth century, things went from bad to worse for these white barbers because of several developments. A new wave of immigration beginning in the 1880s brought large numbers of Italians, and barbering was the skill Italians were most likely to bring with them to America. Then, in 1893, A. B. Moler established the first of what became a national chain of barbering schools, which flooded the market with even more barbers, lowering prices and standards of skill. Hotels, with their first-class barbershops, siphoned off many affluent customers and refused to cooperate with efforts to give barbers Sundays off work. White native-born barbers, mostly second-generation immigrants, looked to unionization for relief, and it was provided by the Journeymen Barbers' International Union of America (JBIUA), established in 1886.[3]

The JBIUA flourished because it addressed the problems of its members. By 1900, the union had secured the passage of Sunday closing laws in a number of states, including Massachusetts, Pennsylvania, and Tennessee. The union also appealed to organized labor for help in controlling the journeymen's workplace. At the 1897 convention of the American Federation of Labor, the JBIUA president implored members of other unions not to patronize barbershops charging 5 cents or less for a shave and 15 cents or less for a haircut. Carefully regulating which barbershops qualified to display a union card proved an effective strategy, and the JBIUA flourished in areas where other tradesmen had been organized, because union men supported their brothers. When possible, the JBIUA engaged in collective bargaining with the proprietors of barbershops, negotiating a guaranteed salary, minimum prices, Sundays off, and limits on the number of apprentices in each shop.

Still, for JBIUA members to escape the cycle of low wages, underemployment, and failed shops, they needed to attract more affluent customers. Accordingly, JBIUA leaders insisted on the need to organize black barbers, who served these prized elite customers. They made strides toward the principle of including black barbers during the first two decades of the organization, with the hope of placing barbers serving the more lucrative market under a union contract. At the 1898 national convention in Memphis, the delegates resolved to make "a most strenuous effort" to organize black barbers, and by 1903, black barbers made up 10 percent of the union's membership. In a 1902 article, the editor of the union journal boasted about the organization's commitment to black barbers. He drew attention to the growing number of African Americans within the union and pointed out that a black barber had won election as first vice-president of the JBIUA in 1893. Continuing with his theme of black representation in leadership position, he declared that "we have not had a convention in ten years where there was not from one to ten colored delegates." Black barbers also held positions of union leadership at the local level. For example, James Gayle was secretary of Seattle's local and Bill Taylor served as chaplain of Grand Rapids' local. The JBIUA policy of "equality for all skilled members of the craft, irrespective of class, creed, or color" did not, however, extend to challenging segregation in the South. Instead, the union organized southern black barbers into separate locals, and it openly condemned segregation only in the North, where its national leaders demanded integrated local chapters.[4]

The concessions that JBIUA leaders made to the prejudices of white southerners established a pattern of sacrificing their principles to expediency. Their relatively enlightened attitude on race, at a time when most unions barred African Americans, ran into trouble immediately. In 1902, an American Federation of Labor official sought to exclude a JBIUA local from the Louisville trades council because it had black members. In the same year the trades council of Dennison, Texas, also opposed admitting a black JBIUA local, the council members explaining their opposition by invoking the horrors of social equality. If the council ever held a dance, "the colored delegates would demand admission . . . a privilege [that] would not be accorded them by whites." Dennison's black barbers could expect little help from their white union brothers, who had protested against the national union's recognition of the black barbers' local. In Washington, D.C., JBIUA leaders deferred to local white members, allowing them to decide whether black barbers there could organize their own local. An abrupt change of union policy in Detroit signaled that the resolve of national leaders had crumbled. Although the Detroit local had been integrated when first established in 1889, it reemerged after a period of dormancy in 1909 as a segregated body. National leaders also acquiesced to the exclusion of Asian barbers from Pacific Coast chapters in the same year.[5]

The inability of the JBIUA to overcome prejudice in the union movement and within its own ranks caused black barbers to dismiss the usefulness of the union. Although some black barbers, inspired by the union leaders' vision of solidarity, might have been willing to overlook the hostility they encountered in local trades councils and a few JBIUA locals, they would have found it difficult to ignore the racism of their white union brothers. For example, one white JBIUA member expressed disbelief that a black member of his local had violated union rules, considering how, in his opinion, the black man was "lucky enough to have himself taken up" by the union. Even sympathetic white members unwittingly made objectionable comments, revealing the extent to which prejudice shaped their point of view.

In a eulogy for a black JBIUA member, a white member praised the deceased barber for being "honest and white" in his dealings with people. The members of the dead man's local, furthermore, averred that their black comrade had "had a whiter heart and nobler ideas that many a white man to whom we pay the greatest respect." Not surprisingly, black barbers fairly soon lost any enthusiasm for the JBIUA. At its peak, the number of black JBIUA members—1,000 in 1903—constituted only 5 percent of the black men in the trade. Because the color line still divided the trade, black barbers turned their backs on the JBIUA and instead, as had been their tradition, relied on each other to protect their livelihood. One group of southern black barbers even went on strike to maintain an all-black workplace. According to the strikers, they considered it "unprofessional to work beside white competitors." First-class barbershop owner George Myers spoke for many black barbers when he called white union barbers prejudiced and maintained that they sought to "drive the colored barbers from the business. They have tried it by organization and discrimination and [they] failed."[6] When the JBIUA proposed a law in 1902 to license barbers in Ohio, Myers concluded that the union had merely shifted its efforts to the political arena.

The leaders of the JBIUA promoted licensing to gain a competitive advantage for their members by getting the public to associate scientific hygiene with union barbers. To an extent, the JBIUA acted to limit the damage caused by new findings about health threats in barbershops. In the 1880s, a Parisian doctor named Remlinger had generated a furor on both sides of the Atlantic over his microscopic examination of his barber's alum sticks (used to stop bleeding from razor nicks), which revealed the existence of more than 68,000 disease-producing germs. On a regular basis thereafter, American medical journals and health departments published warnings about contagious illnesses transmitted by barbers through their razors, brushes, and other tools of the trade. In the union's journal, JBIUA leaders coached members on how to promote licensing and sanitation. A union barbershop, according to the journal's editor, offered the public a "guarantee of cleanliness, workmanship, and protection against infection." Through licensing laws that favored dues-paying members, JBIUA leaders aimed to elevate a union card into a "valuable trade asset" by making it synonymous with hygienic conditions.

The union's lobbying for licensing began in 1896 and met with early success when Minnesota enacted the nation's first barber-licensing law just one year later. Missouri, Michigan, Nebraska, and Oregon followed suit in 1899, and fifteen other states, including California, Connecticut, Georgia, Kentucky, and Texas, had enacted laws to license barbers by 1914. As legislative victories piled up, JBIUA leaders became convinced that union barbers had distinguished themselves as possessors of unique credentials for hygienic service. One union official thought the licensing campaign had been so successful that it would disarm opponents of collective bargaining. "Even the enemies of trade unionism," he noted gleefully, would "scarcely carry their devotion to scabbery to the point where they are willing to be inoculated with disease germs."

By talking about how licensing would defeat the union's adversaries, this official also hinted at the exclusionary aspects of the JBIUA campaign to safeguard public health. Licensing reduced the competition that union barbers faced from Italian immigrants and African Americans. By claiming the mantle of scientific hygiene, union barbers not only allayed the fear of customers, who were just learning about the germ theory of disease, but also distinguished themselves from their main rivals, Italian barbers, who were associated in the public's mind with disease. Moreover, concerns were raised that barbershop customers found alarming. The U.S. Commissioner General of Immigration warned that unless "proper precautions" were taken to screen newcomers for disease, Americans might become "hairless." At the same time, the union barbers' growing reputation for knowledge of hygiene helped them win upscale customers away from black barbers. One black barber, Wendell Dabney, recalled how the issue of sanitation provided an opening for white barbers. "Finally," he remembered, "white men came into the barber business. The Negro barbers laughed. More white men came—less laughing. The white man brought business methods. He stood for the ridicule and kept working quiet, easy, like the Boll Weevil in a crop of cotton. He gave new names to old things. Sanitary and sterilized became his great words, the open sesame for the coming generation. . . . The inevitable happened. Old customers died and then came their sons 'who knew not Joseph.'"[7] In an age that was becoming fascinated with science and revered expertise, the JBIUA established a professional reputation for white union barbers that made the genteel rituals of deference and conviviality offered by black barbers seem archaic.

The long-term benefit of the licensing campaign for the JBIUA—elevating the status of union barbers in the eyes of the public—took years if not decades to come to fruition, but it furnished immediate benefits to union members by threatening to cut off the supply of apprentices to black barbers. The barbers' bill that Ohio legislators debated in 1902 illustrates how state regulation could be made to serve the interests of the JBIUA. Written by JBIUA secretary William Klapetzy, the proposed legislation was a boldfaced grab for union influence over the barbering trade. The key provision of the bill required that all Ohio barbers obtain a license from a board of examiners. Although the governor would appoint the board of examiners, who would have sweeping authority over the trade, the proposed bill granted the JBIUA the right to nominate one of the examiners. The examiners would use their judgment to determine whether applicants for a license possessed a "good moral character," would issue regulations as they deemed necessary, and could revoke the licenses of barbers who failed to conform to the board's directives. Since the board's decisions could not be appealed, the examiners would have had the last word concerning whether a barber could remain in the trade. The proposed legislation, because it required apprentices to obtain a license, also gave the examiners control over who became a barber. To George Myers and other black barbershop owners in Ohio, the board's control over apprentices would have given the union the means to exclude African Americans from the trade and thus deprive black barbershops of new employees. Myers was not alone in perceiving this threat; similar opposition was voiced by white barbershop owners to license law proposals in New York and Massachusetts.[8]

Had the union-sponsored legislation in Ohio become law, the union would have greatly expanded its control of the trade; however, a coalition of black barbershop owners and politicians led by Myers put up a determined fight. Myers's political influence suited him ideally for leading the opposition to licensing, and by showing that black barbers could take on the JBIUA, his efforts were significant. Myers's political network paid off in the eleven-year battle against licensing, as leading black businessmen, politicians, and journalists came to his aid. Among his allies, two black barbershop owners emerged as the leading figures. Fountain Lewis, proprietor of Cincinnati's leading barbershop, coordinated fundraising and petition drives among black barbers, while Henry Eubanks, owner of the Kenard House barbershop in Cleveland and a member of the Ohio legislature, spearheaded opposition to licensing in the statehouse. Two black legislators, Jere Brown and George Hayes, canvassed Republicans and delivered impassioned speeches against regulating barbers. To raise public awareness of the issue, Ralph Tyler, personal secretary to the publisher of the *Columbus Dispatch*, wrote editorials and letters to the editor that blasted state regulation.[9] These men successfully implemented Myers's strategy of depicting the proposed license laws as a test case for whether Republicans would defend the interests of black voters.

Myers, Ohio's most influential spokesman for African Americans within the Republican Party, made the barber bill into a litmus test for Republican lawmakers and implied that black voters would abandon the party if they failed to defeat the legislation. In letters to Republican officeholders, Myers outlined his argument against state regulation of barbers. Support for the union's bill, he explained to one legislator, involved more than choosing sides in a dispute among barbers.

As he saw it, the JBIUA asked the Republicans to act against their "most faithful and loyal allies, the colored voters." He asked another legislator, "Can the Republican Party of Ohio afford to be party to any such a scheme, which practically means a reenactment of the Black Laws that were wiped from the statute books of Ohio by a Republican legislature?"[10]

Myers campaigned statewide, driving home the potential injustice against African Americans. In letters to the Cincinnati and Columbus newspapers, he attacked the proponents of regulation as guilty of discrimination and publicized statements of support from leading Republicans who had answered his letters. His friend Ralph Tyler at the *Columbus Dispatch* reiterated Myers's claims of discrimination against black barbers in an article emblazoned with the headline "Colored Men Aroused Against . . . Barber Bill Which They Say Would Drive Colored Barbers Out of Business." According to Representative George Hayes, the article caused many Republican members of the General Assembly to pledge that they would not support the bill if it hurt colored voters, demonstrating the effectiveness of Myers's strategy. Hayes also submitted petitions opposing licensing and arranged for black barbers to lodge protests with the committee deliberating the bill. In a tactical move, Hayes pledged to keep the legislation bottled up in committee until the session ended.[11] The efforts of Myers and his allies met with success, for the barber licensing bill was defeated.

Attesting to Myers's political acumen and influence, supporters as well as opponents of licensing acknowledged that his efforts had been decisive. Ralph Tyler told Myers, "You can take all the credit for the defeat yourself. While others have done something, it was you who took up the cudgel." The editor of the JBIUA journal, unfamiliar with his nemesis, vaguely credited black barbers in Cleveland, where Myers lived, with solidifying opposition to the bill. Senator Mark Hanna asked for the barber's help with black voters in the fourteenth district as payback for having helped Myers defeat the bill. Myers's influence with Senator Hanna, his mentor, can be seen in letters they exchanged after licensing was defeated.[12]

Representative Hayes, however, advised that "something should be done to regulate the barber business," prompting Myers to go on the offensive. Myers and his allies moved to co-opt the issue of public health with their own barber bill, which inherently questioned the credibility of the JBIUA. Sponsored by Representative Eubanks in 1904, the bill treated sanitation as a distinct issue with no bearing on the expertise of barbers. The 1904 legislation omitted any provisions for creating a board of examiners or for licensing barbers; instead, it gave the Ohio Board of Health a mandate to issue sanitary regulations for barbershops and to monitor compliance. When barbers violated these regulations, county courts would be authorized to mete out penalties. Effectively, the bill allowed Myers and other foes of licensing to contest the premise that only greater union control of barbering would safeguard the public. They argued that the JBIUA had exceeded its authority in a bid to control the trade, because only public health officials had the expertise to ensure sanitation in barbershops. As one black barber said in favor of the bill, the new proposal "gave no combination control of our businesses and places our businesses under proper sanitary regulations by the recognized authority of the State Board of Health."[13] The bill's alternative sanitation proposals made union calls for licensing reforms in the name of public health ring hollow.

The same year, the JBIUA countered the black barbers' proposal by introducing a revised barber bill that ceded more authority to public health officials in the hope of restoring their credibility with Ohio legislators. Although the JBIUA-sponsored bill called for the creation of a board of examiners made up entirely of barbers, the JBIUA would not have the right to nominate an examiner and the board would have to act in concert with state health officials. For instance, the State Board of Health would have to approve the sanitation regulations issued by the barber examiners. The JBIUA proposal also gave barbers more rights to due process, leaving out subjective criteria such as establishing good moral character for licensing and allowing barbers to appeal board decisions to the governor or the attorney general.[14] In sum, the bill addressed many of the objections raised by opponents of licensing, but these concessions appeared to substantiate Myers's argument that the issue of public health disguised an effort to control the trade and oust black barbers from the market that served white men.

Myers and his allies lost no time in denouncing the JBIUA's revised bill as a Trojan horse disguising an attack on the interests of black voters. Dismissing the union's attempts at compromise as merely expedient, one black barber declared in a letter to Myers, "I recognize [the proposed law] as the Journeymen Barbers' International Union bill, and if it should pass into law, this organization will control [the] situation in Ohio. For this reason alone, we should endeavor to kill the bill." Representatives Hayes and Eubanks spoke against the JBIUA bill. To convince their Republican colleagues that the JBIUA was still attempting to discriminate against African Americans, they said that the union intended to file charges of incompetence against competent black barbers and "with the aid of apostates and false witnesses establish the trumped-up charges." Invoking the support of the African American community, Hayes and Eubanks warned legislators that 47,000 black voters wanted the bill defeated—and it was.[15]

The scenario of two black legislators defending black barbers on the floor of the Ohio General Assembly embodies the political influence that Myers and other barbershop proprietors could exert to defend their interests. By successfully portraying a threat to black barbershop owners as an assault on the rights of all African Americans, Myers convinced Republican legislators that they risked losing the black vote unless they opposed the regulation of barbers. This strategy defeated JBIUA-sponsored barber bills in 1902, 1904, 1910, and 1913; and Ohio barbers remained free from state regulation until 1933, long after Myers's death. Yet, this strategy had a weakness, for it depended on Myers's being recognized as a spokesman for the African American community, and the tepid support he received from black journeyman barbers revealed cracks in the foundation of his influence. During the lobbying campaign, wealthy black barbers grew concerned when their less prosperous counterparts passed resolutions of support but failed to donate funds to assist the effort. The black journalist Ralph Tyler also doubted the commitment of the rank and file when black barbers in Cincinnati failed to circulate a petition that he had given them. Commenting on their inaction, Tyler displayed a contempt that revealed class tensions: "Like the proverbial darkey, they won't move—simply trusting to Providence." Representative Hayes, responding to a white legislator's claim that black barbers in his district supported licensing, also expressed little confidence in ordinary African Americans, saying that the barbers did not appreciate the danger that licensing represented for them.[16] Because the struggle to retain white customers had estranged barbershop owners such as Myers from many of their workers and much of the larger African American community, they faced a situation in which they could become the victims of their own success.

The proprietors of first-class barbershops had little time to ponder their dilemma, however, since white barbers continued to challenge their dominance of the market serving affluent white men. White barbers in Tennessee sponsored bills to regulate the trade in 1903 and 1905, though without getting their proposals enacted into law. In Kentucky, the state courts actually rolled back the cause of licensing by declaring the state board of barbers' examiners unconstitutional; but twenty other state legislatures by 1914 had created regulatory agencies that, black barbers complained, excluded them from the lucrative business of serving white customers. Although JBIUA leaders encountered setbacks in their licensing campaign, they had raised the cost of remaining competitive by winning public acceptance for new standards of hygiene in barbershops. Even in states without license laws, black barbers found that they had to invest heavily in equipment to meet new standards for hygiene. George Myers, for example, spent the then-princely sum of $306 for a custom-made sterilizer, noteworthy for being the first to use electric rather than gas heat. When Myers placed the order with the Koken Barber Supply, he expressed his aim of surpassing his competition. The Koken representative assured him that the device would be "a newer and finer machine than the one at Statler's," his rival. Photographs of black-owned barbershops from this period demonstrate how important the proprietors thought sanitation equipment was to their businesses, for sterilizers and sinks appear prominently in the foreground of the pictures while employees and customers inhabit the background.[17] The public's new concern with hygiene added yet one more requirement for retaining white customers. The expensive equipment, the stresses of union organization, and the demands of licensing laws all contributed to a progressive loss of white customers by black barbershops.

A speech by a black barber, J. M. Hazelwood, at a National Negro Business League convention illustrated the challenges facing black barbers at the turn of the century. Booker T. Washington found the speech so insightful that he reproduced it in his 1907 book, *The Negro in Business*. Acknowledging that white men were making inroads on the trade, Hazelwood, himself a barber, held his peers responsible: "[They] have not kept pace with the times but are content with methods and customs of twenty-five years ago." The discerning white customer, he explained, preferred "modern and scientific" barbershops. To illustrate what he meant, Hazelwood described his flagship establishment, a state-of-the-art facility equipped with the latest appliances at a cost of over $6,000. His business attracted a stream of white customers who appreciated a "clean and well-kept shop; neat, polite, and tidy workmen; tools sterilized and in good order; pure and wholesome drugs, toilet articles, clean linens, and pleasant inviting surroundings." In Hazelwood's opinion, black barbers could "hold the ground we are losing and reclaim what we have lost" if they remained up to date.[18]

Hazelwood had correctly identified the trends within barbering, yet he failed to grasp how unions and white supremacy would transform his profession. The first-class barbershops that black barbers had created in white neighborhoods had begun to decline in the 1880s. Black barbers' decline within the trade by 1900 fit patterns established almost a half-century before. Overall, they fared worse in the North and better in the lower South. Boston and Charleston provide a study in contrasts. While black men monopolized the trade in Charleston in 1900, making up 97 percent of all barbers, they barely maintained a presence in Boston, constituting only 5 percent of the city's barbers. This decline in Boston, starting from less than dizzying heights than the percentages in the lower South, nevertheless had significant consequences for the city's African American community.

If black men had been able to hold onto their share of the trade, there would have been 350 black barbers in the city rather than 106, a change that would have provided one out of every twenty members of the working black population with an alternative to unskilled jobs. Black barbers in the Midwest suffered along with their counterparts in northeastern cities. In spite of remaining a larger presence in Cleveland and Detroit than in Boston and Philadelphia, black barbers saw

TABLE 9
Percentage of Barbers Who Were African American, 1870–1900

Region	City	1870 (%)	1880 (%)	1890 (%)	1900 (%)
North	Boston	17	14	11	5
	Cleveland	43	n.a.	15	16
	Detroit	55	n.a.	24	22
	New York (Manhattan)	n.a.	n.a.	10	10
	Philadelphia	31	10	14	11
Upper South	Louisville	n.a.	n.a.	28	n.a.
	Richmond	n.a.	93	89	83
Lower South	Atlanta	n.a.	n.a.	21[a]	n.a.
	Birmingham	n.a.	100	80	68
	Charleston	92	96	n.a.	97
	Mobile	66	74	60	62
	Montgomery	n.a.	n.a.	94[a]	n.a.
	New Orleans	37	30	30	26
	Savannah	43	82	n.a.	n.a.

Sources: Elizabeth Hafkin Pleck, *Black Migration and Poverty: Boston, 1865–1900* (New York: Academic Press, 1979), 145–46; Kenneth L. Kusmer, *A Ghetto Takes Shape: Black Cleveland, 1870–1930* (Urbana: University of Illinois Press, 1976), 76; David M. Katzman, *Before the Ghetto: Black Detroit in the Nineteenth Century* (Urbana: University of Illinois Press, 1973), 116; George Edmund Haynes, *The Negro at Work in New York City* (1912; reprint, New York: Arno Press, 1968), 71; Theodore Hershberg, "Mulattoes and Blacks: Intra-Group Color Differences and Social Stratification in Nineteenth-Century Philadelphia," unpublished paper cited in Pleck, 145; Howard N. Rabinowitz, *Race Relations in the Urban South, 1865–1890* (New York: Oxford University Press, 1978), 78; Paul B. Worthman, "Working-Class Mobility in Birmingham, Alabama, 1880–1914," in *Anonymous Americans: Explorations in Nineteenth-Century Social History,* edited by Tamara K. Hareven (Englewood Cliffs, N.J.: Prentice-Hall, 1971), 178–79; Bernard E. Powers, Jr., *Black Charlestonians: A Social History, 1822–1885* (Fayetteville: University of Arkansas Press, 1994), 270–76; George C. Wright, *Life Behind a Veil: Blacks in Louisville, Kentucky, 1865–1930* (Baton Rouge: Louisiana State University Press, 1985), 82; John W. Blassingame, *Black New Orleans, 1860–1880* (Chicago: University of Chicago Press, 1973), 230–35; idem., "Before the Ghetto: The Making of the Black Community in Savannah, Georgia, 1865–1880," *Journal of Social History* 6 (Summer 1973), 465–67; Herbert G. Gutman, *The Black Family in Slavery and Freedom, 1750–1925* (New York: Pantheon, 1976), 481. Percentage of black barbers in Mobile computed from U.S. manuscript census schedules, 1870–1900, Records of the Bureau of the Census, Record Group 29, National Archives, Washington, D.C.

[a]Figure is for 1891.

their portion of the trade in the two Midwest cities drop by more than half between 1870 and 1900. Black barbers in the lower South remained more competitive with white barbers, yet in every city within the region for which data is available they lost some ground, except in Charleston.[19] Black men composed 21 percent of all barbers and hairdressers nationally in 1890, but by 1930 their proportion of the trade had dropped to 9 percent.

Given the setbacks most black barbers encountered, those who did retain most of their white customers stood out as exceptional. Black barbers preserved some degree of competitiveness for white customers in two ways. In a few southern cities, they constituted the majority of all barbers, and so received the white custom by default. The continued presence of large black populations and persistence of old habits explained this preponderance somewhat. In Savannah and Montgomery, for example, a majority of the residents were African American, and white residents of those cities would have been accustomed to being served by African Americans. Black barbers in certain southern cities also benefited from a tradition of black artisans reaching back to the eighteenth century. In Charleston, Mobile, and Richmond, a combination of slaves and free African Americans had supplied anywhere between one-tenth and one-third of all skilled workers on the eve of the Civil War. In the latter half of the nineteenth century, skilled black workers continued to flourish in those cities.

Reliance on tradition, however, gave black barbers few incentives to keep up with the times, which left them vulnerable to innovative white barbers. According to a survey of black businesses in the 1890s, not one black barber in Richmond or Montgomery had invested at least $500 in his barbershop, and only one in Mobile had spent that much. Charleston, home to approximately 150 black barbers in 1900, had only six barbershops with $500 or more invested in the business. Yet, nationwide, sparing no expense to provide the best and most up-to-date service had proven the best way to retain white customers. In Cleveland, a city where fewer than one in five barbers was black, black barbershop proprietors invested more money collectively than did black barbers in any other city in the United States.[20] Being prepared to offer the best service to a large body of customers presented a less remediable challenge than installing new equipment. These first-class shop owners had to keep large staffs of barbers at a time when turnover among journeymen was high and a declining number of young black men were entering the trade. As a result, whether black barbers held on to white customers because they lived in the South or through investment in modern equipment, they faced problems that, in the long run, would become nearly insurmountable.

Because black barbers had designed their businesses specifically for coping with prejudice and were equipped to deal with a hostile racial climate, the deterioration of race relations at the end of the nineteenth century did not necessarily undermine their first-class barbershops. Their success had always depended on accommodating the bigotry of their white customers, who enjoyed the ritual of a razor-wielding black man cautiously scraping their throats precisely because it affirmed their feeling of racial superiority. Moreover, the passage of segregation laws in the 1890s merely sanctioned time-honored custom, for black barbers had long refused service to African Americans. Yet, in the struggle over licensing, black barbers discovered new subtleties in racial prejudice.

Even though JBIUA leaders never labeled black men as unsanitary, and indeed displayed a surprising amount of racial tolerance, they alarmed white customers about the illnesses that might be lurking in barbershops. Since white physicians in the late nineteenth century routinely branded African Americans as disease carriers, the JBIUA public health campaign surely triggered associations between blackness and illness. Barbershop proprietors such as George Myers could ward off their customers' prejudices by displaying the latest in sterilization equipment, but most barbers could not afford the investment.[21] Consequently, the JBIUA drove a wedge between black barbers and their white customers without making race an overt issue in the licensing debate. Black barbers, despite a long record of exploiting white prejudices to keep their white clientele, had few ways to influence the larger American discourse about race.

As the antipathy that white southerners had customarily felt toward African Americans grew into rage during the 1890s, deteriorating race relations led barbers to weigh the advantages and disadvantages of serving white customers. In Atlanta, months of race baiting by gubernatorial candidates and lurid newspaper accounts of black men raping white women prepared the way for an unprecedented wave of violence against the city's African American community. On September 22, 1906, at eight o'clock in the evening, a riot began. A white man climbed on a platform at a downtown intersection, held aloft a special edition of the newspaper devoted to the latest alleged assault by black men on white women, and demanded of the assembled white crowd: "Are white men going to stand for this?" Yelling "No! Save our women!" and "Kill the niggers!" the crowd broke up into roving mobs intent on attacking black people.[22]

One mob reached the Peachtree Street barbershop of Alonzo Herndon, the city's leading black barber, where they smashed the plate-glass windows and shot four of the black barbers inside. The future NAACP leader Walter White happened to be passing by with his father and saw what happened. Decades later,

White recalled the scene with horror. He saw "a lame bootblack from Herndon's barbershop pathetically trying to outrun a mob of whites." Little more than a hundred yards away, "the chase ended. We saw clubs and fists descending to the accompaniment of savage shouting and beating." Suddenly, the mob noticed another black man and ran off in hot pursuit. White and his father were left staring at the victim: "the body with the withered foot lay dead in a pool of blood on the street." In the aftermath of the riot, Alonzo Herndon and his wife contemplated moving away from the region. They did send their son to a school in Philadelphia for a short time. Rather than giving up on Atlanta, though, Herndon turned his attention from barbering to a small insurance company that he had bought the year before for $140.[23] His decision to remain in the South and provide much-needed life insurance to African Americans resulted in the creation of one of America's foremost black-owned corporations, Atlanta Life Insurance Company. Few black barbers possessed the financial resources of Alonzo Herndon, so they lacked the option of responding to white violence by going into another line of business. Instead, they simply had to decide whether to remain in central business districts serving white men or to relocate to black neighborhoods and serve African Americans.

In Mobile, where two incidents signaled that race relations had changed very much for the worse, black barbers moved as a group from their prime location downtown to a segregated black neighborhood up along Jefferson Davis Avenue which became the commercial district for African Americans, boasting a hotel, several restaurants, and a theater as well as barbershops. The first clash occurred in 1904 at the heart of the city's commercial district. On the Fourth of July, a white mob expelled African Americans from Bienville Square, a park adjacent to such leading institutions as Southern Bank, the Customs House, and the offices of the Mobile and Ohio Railroad. City officials, despite complaints from black leaders, took no action, implicitly endorsing the segregation of public space. Then, two years later, a white mob on the city's outskirts lynched two young black men accused of rape. A local black insurance company executive, Christopher Johnson, reported to Booker T. Washington that African Americans in Mobile had lost "much of the energy and pride we used to have for the South."[24]

Racial violence underscored how badly race relations had deteriorated. In response to the deterioration, many black barbers switched to serving black customers. Half as many black barbers operated shops downtown in 1900 as in 1880. During the same period, only one more white-owned barbershop opened, which suggests that white competition did not play a large role in the decision of black barbershop owners to move. The Davis Avenue enclave offered a promising mar-

TABLE 10
Distribution of Black-Owned Barbershops in Mobile, 1870–1910

Location	1870	1880	1900	1910
Downtown	8	13	7	15
Davis Avenue Area	0	1	6	23
Elsewhere	1	0	2	19

Sources: Mobile city directories and Sanborn Fire Insurance maps.

ket, and the impressive growth of barbershops there suggests that many barbers took advantage of the opportunity. Black barbers had lucrative white clients who remained loyal, however, and the African American community possessed a limited buying power. The shift from white to black customers took a generation or more, as younger whites increasingly shunned black barbers and as black neighborhoods grew in size and wealth.[25]

Edgar Harney and Andrew Jackson, for instance, continued to serve white customers downtown while they simultaneously operated barbershops for black customers along Davis Avenue. Through 1904, the two men had jointly operated Mobile's leading barbershop at the Battle House Hotel. A fire closed the hotel in that year of the Bienville Square incident, and when it reopened, the managers replaced Harney and Jackson with white barbers. The two dissolved their partnership, and each opened his own barbershop in the central city. In addition, Jackson built a new brick building in the Davis Avenue neighborhood expressly for the purpose of offering first-class service to black customers. Edgar Harney also bought into a funeral home serving the African American community, an investment opportunity that became available after its previous owner left Mobile in disgust over the worsening race relations.[26]

Barbering continued in the Harney family, and cordial relations apparently existed between white Mobilians and those black barbers who continued to serve them. James Hall, the grandson of Edgar Harney, worked as a barber serving whites in Mobile during the late 1920s and early 1930s; he recalled a friendly, albeit formal, atmosphere in the Tuttle and Bell Barbershop on St. Francis Street. Reflecting on his experience, Hall said that his employers stressed preserving an upscale atmosphere, and he remembered "watching his Ps and Qs as the barbers rolled out the carpet for the customers." For their part, the white men who patronized the barbershop, according to Hall, seemed to like the tradition of receiving fine service from a black man. Their tips were certainly good. Yet, Hall noted that no young white men came to the barbershop and that few young black men sought to enter the trade serving white men. What had seemed proper to one generation failed to appeal to the next. Without elaborating, Hall added that he had not liked working in the barbershop. He left Mobile to live in New Orleans in 1933, and when he moved back in 1939, the owners had retired and closed their shop.[27]

As the trade became more racially segregated, black barbers in Mobile increasingly plied their razors on Davis Avenue. Other proprietors of downtown barbershops pursued a black clientele after the turn of the century, although some left the central city entirely. By 1910, the number of black barbers on Davis Avenue surpassed the number downtown, and the neighborhood remained their stronghold until legal segregation ended in the 1960s. The new barbershops resembled their old ones downtown in several ways. Jackson advertised that his New Era Shaving Parlor on Davis Avenue was "the most modern sanitary barber shop in the city." The barber informed the readers of the *Negro Business Guide* that his shop occupied a large brick building "built for its accommodations," which included "four chairs, electric fans, and Hot and Cold Baths." Moreover, Jackson pledged that he employed the "most experienced and courteous barbers," who provided black customers with "Stylish Hair Cutting, Smooth Shaving and Electric Massages." Jackson also continued to retail products such as hair tonic, hair oils, and face creams. Yet, in a departure from earlier advertisements, Jackson recommended himself to his customers as a "Church man and fraternal order man."[28] The accommodations and services offered in the better black-owned barbershops remained the same, but the social character of the institution had changed.

Within black neighborhoods, people learned as much about a man by finding out which barbershop he patronized as which church he attended or which lodge he had joined. For example, the Abrams' Tonsorial Parlor of Mobile, established in 1904 and still in operation in 1997, acquired a reputation for catering to the "sporting crowd." When a black man came to the Abrams's shop, he could get a drink or play the numbers in addition to getting a shave. The more respectable, churchgoing members of Mobile's African American community gave Abrams's barbershop a wide berth. As James Hall recalled, his mother would probably have forbidden him to go to Abrams's if he had asked her about it, and she did tell him to use the barbershop patronized by the family's minister. More than wholesome and hurtful amusements separated barbershops, however. According to community historian Henry Williams, Sr., barbershops were divided into those where people spoke out against racism and others where more conservative customers avoided such topics. White people never criticized black gatherings at barbershops, so they provided a unique forum for black men to speak their minds. Whether debating the Brownsville incident during the Spanish-American War or the prospects for migrating North during World War I, barbershops like the one run by the Abrams brothers disseminated information and provided a training ground for black politicians.[29] Behind the veil of segregation, southern black barbers felt safer and found new satisfaction from their work as they helped the African American community in a new way.

It was in response to the unmet needs of the growing urban black population that John Merrick and Alonzo Herndon took the initiative to establish modern insurance companies. Although both men supported traditional charities in their respective communities, they came to realize that the mutual aid networks that had helped them get started were becoming inadequate for a changing community. Merrick's early career provides a case study in the ability of black barbers to nurture their own. Viewing the barbershop as a refuge from the exhausting labor of his job as a brick mason, Merrick began working as a bootblack at a shop in Raleigh, North Carolina. He quickly won the confidence of the barbers, who initiated him into the mysteries of the tonsorial trade. Along with one of his fellow knights of the razor, John Wright, Merrick became the favorite barber of the prominent Duke family (who endowed Duke University) and textile mill owner Julian Carr, who frequently traveled to Raleigh from Durham for personal services, like barbering and lawyering. Carr successfully prevailed upon Wright to relocate to Durham and open a barbershop there. Following his friend, Merrick worked as an assistant for six months before Wright sold him a half-interest in the shop. Merrick, in turn, helped Wright move to the North by buying his share of the business in 1892.[30] Less is known about Herndon's early beginnings, but his life also bore the hallmarks of the black barbers' tradition of helping fellow knights of the razor. Born a slave, as was Merrick, after emancipation Herndon labored as a farmhand in rural Georgia until he discovered that he could make a living cutting the hair of his coworkers. In search of greater profits, he switched to white customers and relocated to Atlanta in 1883 at the age of twenty-five. He found a job there in the Marietta Street barbershop owned by Dougherty Hutchins. What Herndon learned from that venerable black barber, who had operated a shop since before the Civil War, is a matter of speculation, but he somehow figured out how to smooth off the rough edges of his country upbringing and gain a following among the white customers. Hutchins gave his young employee the chance at entrepreneurship when he sold him a half-share of the business. Subsequently, both Merrick and Herndon enjoyed phenomenal success, Merrick owning nine barbershops at one point and Herndon employing fifty barbers.[31]

Personal wealth, at least on the scale that black businessmen could acquire it in the nineteenth century, proved inadequate to the mission of racial uplift that Merrick and Herndon set for themselves. Having relied on the African American tradition of barbering and on white patrons to realize his goals in business, Merrick applied the lessons of his tonsorial career to helping others in the African American community. His way of operating in his charitable work reveals continuities between his activities at his barbershops and in his charitable work. He parlayed his friendship with Washington Duke into a sizeable financial gift that made a black hospital in Durham possible. Serving with him on the hospital board of directors, in addition to black doctors and educators, were Duke's chauffer and head maid, which probably galled the white businessman. The hospital cornerstone bore an inscription expressing the thanks of white Durham to African Americans for their "fidelity and faithfulness . . . To the Mothers and Daughters of the Confederacy." Although his success resulted in large part from his reputation among whites for congeniality, Merrick paid a terrible price for securing white help. He was no Uncle Tom. His black contemporaries remembered that he could, with "great poise, tip his hat to the white man and, at the same time, call him a son-of-a-bitch under his breath."[32]

Until a better means of providing for the black community was found, charity and white patronage were the best help available. An apocryphal story about how Merrick came up with the idea to start his insurance company underscores this. As was the practice, a destitute member of the African American community came to the business of the wealthiest black man in town, Merrick's barbershop, to ask for money. While Merrick passed the hat around, Washington Duke suggested beginning an insurance company to forestall such visits. The story, according to Merrick's contemporaries, had no basis in fact, but the need was real and the idea sound, wherever it originated. When African Americans moved to Durham to find work in the Duke tobacco factories and the Carr textile mills, they traded the security of farming for the promise of wages. A widow could no longer make up for the death of her husband by taking his place in the fields. At the same time, churches with poor members found it increasingly difficult to collect alms for burying paupers. Merrick had already begun looking for the solution to this problem in the 1880s. He first worked as an agent selling insurance for the True Reformers, a black fraternal insurance organization, and then in 1883 cofounded another insurance society, the Royal Knights of King David.[33] For many newcomers to Durham, these groups provided no help, because the individuals lacked the means or the social standing to become members of a fraternal order. Black migrants to the cities required a new type of mutual aid organization, one they could afford and rely on to be solvent when they faced a personal crisis.

Just as Merrick came to realize the need for innovation in his charitable work, the 1898 Wilmington race riot led him to challenge existing ideals about racial uplift. The riot was the culmination of a vicious campaign by North Carolina Democrats to oust Republicans and Populists from the offices they had won in the 1896 election. Led by a congressman, a white mob burned down the offices of Wilmington's black newspaper, killed at least eleven African Americans, and forced the city's black assemblymen to resign their offices. Racial violence touched Merrick's community directly when a white mob lynched a black man for living with a white woman. The mob left his body hanging alongside the road between Chapel Hill and Durham as a chilling warning to any who would dare challenge white supremacy.[34]

In his only known public address, Merrick discussed the Wilmington riot, expressing bitterness that the African American community had pursued politics instead of business. Merrick denounced the riot in no uncertain terms as "a disgrace and a sin," before dwelling on the missed opportunities that he thought might have prevented innocent blood from flowing in the streets. "Our good men and lots of our best men," he observed, pursued elected office, lost interest in business, and ended up having no choice but to stay in politics "for protection" from hostile Democrats determined to prevent them from earning a living otherwise. As a result, black achievements in the economic realm paled beside those in the political realm. "Had the Negroes of Wilmington owned half of the city," he argued, "there wouldn't anything happened to compare with what they did." Given his extensive business holdings and the absence of mob violence in Durham, Merrick could have been reflecting on his personal experience. He saw politics as a dead end for African Americans, predicting that after "the way the Democratic party took us this fall by the heels and beat the life out of the Republican Party," Republican officials would "tell us to stand aside."[35]

At one point in his speech, Merrick expressed frustration with those who failed to grasp the potential of economic self-help. He criticized Bishop Henry Turner and other black leaders who urged African Americans to emigrate to Africa in the wake of disfranchisement. He thought the bishop should remain in the United States and tell his followers "the importance of economy and accumulation." By invoking the values of enterprising men, Merrick revealed his ideological heritage as a barber. Changing white opinion was less important to him than acquiring the material basis for claiming the mantle of respectability through business ownership. Finishing his statement on the importance of acquiring wealth, he said: "That is what makes people representative, is having something to represent." Merrick concluded by admitting that even he was surprised to be writing speeches about racial uplift, given that he had remained out of the public eye when possible, but he also asserted his right to lead the race during this troubled time. In Merrick's mind, his adherence to respectability had been vindicated. He attempted to preempt his critics by saying, "Now don't the writers of the race jump on the writer [Merrick] and try to solve my problem. Mine is solved." He meant the problem of escaping the constraints of racism. Explaining himself in terms that related to his work as a barber, he said, "I solved [my problem] by learning to be courteous to those that courtesy was due, working and trying to save and properly appropriate what I made." To underscore that he did not act from selfish motives, he signed the published version of his speech, "Yours for the betterment of the race, John Merrick."[36] The very next year, Merrick acted on his determination to make the African American community more independent from whites, when he organized the North Carolina Mutual Life Insurance Company and became the company's president.[37]

Although white violence clearly influenced Merrick and Herndon, each of whom went into the insurance business following race riots, they had other considerations in mind as well. Their decisions display a sense of stewardship that came with their wealth. Long before they had any reason to expect a return on their investment, both men repeatedly dipped into their personal savings to ensure the survival of their insurance companies. An unexpected number of claims only a year after the North Carolina Mutual started presented Merrick with an opportunity to show just how committed he was to the company. Of the six company founders, only Merrick and Dr. Aaron Moore were willing to invest more money to cover losses. Merrick, having invested only $50 up to that point, could easily have cut his losses and walked away. Instead, he deepened his commitment to the company and its policyholders.[38]

Herndon faced a similar choice but did not have the luxury of a year to mull over whether to commit significant resources. In 1905, the New York state legislature conducted a well-publicized series of hearings known as the Armstrong Investigation that exposed the shaky financial foundations of many insurance companies. Georgia joined the host of states that consequently passed new insurance regulations and required a $5,000 bond from insurance societies. For the two black ministers operating the Atlanta Benevolent Protection Association, raising this sum was impossible, so they looked for a potential purchaser within the African American community. They approached Herndon, Atlanta's leading black businessman, who bought the organization and deposited the full $5,000 bond with state officials within thirteen days, months before the new state law required. When the decisions of Merrick and Herndon are examined in the context of their other activities, it seems apparent that they turned to the black consumer market out of hope rather than fear. Both men continued to serve whites in their barbershops despite, in Herndon's case, knowledge that white rivals had used racial conflict as a subterfuge in an attempt to destroy his shop.[39]

Their personal generosity lent credibility to both men's public statements about the benefits of economic cooperation. In a speech at Tuskegee University, Herndon urged African Americans to pull together: "My aim has been for several years to get . . . our people together to cooperate in business. . . . If we wish to do anything of importance in a business way, we must have the cooperation of other people." Relating the logic of cooperation to his own company, John Merrick told African Americans that when they bought a policy from North Carolina Mutual they bought "double protection"; they insured their families against misfortune, and they provided white-collar jobs to black men and women. Contemplating the future, he added, "I hope that my children and yours will be in a better condition and will have this company to point to with pride."[40] The impact of deteriorating race relations had evidently left Merrick and Herndon committed to building a group economy, yet this commitment also reflected an awareness of the growing inadequacy of traditional forms of mutual aid and a realization that only businessmen possessed the capital to establish modern self-help organizations.

A combination of pragmatism and ideology led southern black barbers to join the movement that promoted the growth of businesses serving African Americans. To capture the white market, the owners of first-class barbershops occupied prominent locations downtown, which made them targets for white mobs. Mob violence, in turn, served as a cover for white barbers to destroy their black competitors. Among African Americans in Atlanta, it was widely believed that white barbers had led the attack on Alonzo Herndon's barbershop. The drive for segregation threatened to encompass whites-only barbershops. In 1926, the Atlanta City Council passed an ordinance that prohibited black barbers from serving white customers, and although Herndon directed a successful repeal effort, a precedent had been set that threatened the very existence of first-class black barbershops downtown. At the same time, segregation created an African American market of unprecedented size. Residential segregation ordinances funneled the growing number of black migrants from the countryside into black enclaves, and white discrimination often made it hard for African Americans to obtain the services they needed. For example, in the 1880s, Prudential Insurance began selling to black customers policies that offered one-third smaller benefits than white customers received for the same cost, and when northeastern states enacted laws prohibiting racial discrimination in insurance, the company all but ceased writing policies for African Americans.[41] The growing risks of staying in white business districts and the improving prospects in black neighborhoods made serving black customers the most sensible business plan for black barbers. It carried the additional benefit of polishing up the tarnished image of barbers within the African American community.

Late-nineteenth-century black leaders on all sides of the ideological spectrum agreed on the importance of business to their race. Perhaps the most notable endorsement came from the faculty of Atlanta University, which gave black entrepreneurs its imprimatur with a conference in 1899 devoted to African Americans in business. As the keynote speaker, Professor John Hope set the tone of the distinguished gathering with his paper "The Meaning of Business." Hope argued that black-owned companies would provide jobs for black workers displaced by white competitors and would start the African American community down the road toward accumulating the wealth needed to overcome poverty. Beyond meeting pressing needs, Hope maintained, business would lift the race by helping it enter the main current of American life. "The age in which we are living," he contended, "is an economic one. . . . For the sake of self-preservation and for the sake of grasping the meaning of the civilization in which we live, we must to a large extent adopt the life and use the methods of this people [white Anglo-Saxons] with whom we are associated. Business seems to be not simply the raw material of Anglo-Saxon civilization . . . but almost the civilization itself." Hope was enunciating a point that barbers had grasped a half-century earlier. From this premise, Hope drew conclusions that surely made his audience, full of academics and other professionals, squirm. He praised black men for becoming teachers, preachers, and physicians, but he also observed that none of these occupations paid enough money to develop the potential of the African American community fully. Breaking with the tradition of black leaders who had assigned the highest status to professionals, Hope extolled the virtues of black businessmen. "No field," he insisted, called for "trained minds and creative genius to a greater extent than does business." More importantly, businessmen laid the material foundation for racial uplift and therefore deserved the highest regard. Hope concluded his talk by lifting even humble businessmen to the firmament. "Were I a vendor of peanuts or an owner of a mill," he asserted, "I should feel that I, along with preachers and teachers and the rest of the saints, was doing God's service in the cause of the elevation of my people."[42] For black barbers, long accustomed to being vilified for demeaning the race and for refusing to serve African Americans, Hope's message promised redemption.

Predictably, the leading black barbers helped spearhead the effort to promote a group economy. One favored tactic for marketing black businesses was holding industrial fairs that spotlighted black economic contributions to society. In Tennessee, the former state legislator and a barbershop proprietor Sampson Keeble served as treasurer for the Colored Agricultural and Mechanical Association. John Merrick also supported public exhibitions as president of the North Carolina Industrial Association. In 1900, Booker T. Washington organized the National Negro Business League, which quickly took the lead nationally in encouraging African Americans to enter the ranks of business people. Merrick and Alonzo Herndon were among the three hundred businessmen from thirty-four states at the league's first meeting. While Herndon and Merrick agreed with Washington up to a point, their support for economic empowerment did not bind them to black leader's strategy of accommodation. The two men had prospered in a society dedicated to their oppression, so they viewed white people with a jaundiced eye and were not afraid to demand their rights. Alonzo Herndon took a public stand against disfranchisement following the Atlanta riot by signing a petition to the Georgia legislature.[43] In Herndon's independence, it is possible to discern the confidence of a black middle class that had finally come into its own.

Conclusion

Black barbers such as Caesar Hope, James Thomas, George Myers, Alonzo Herndon, and John Merrick could feel proud of what they had accomplished. From their origins in the colonial period, black barbers had exploited their skill and their knowledge of the white psyche to gain their freedom and to achieve a level of success in business that remained unsurpassed by other black men until the twentieth century. Their prosperity not only let them reach the elusive goals of nineteenth-century manhood but also gave them the means to help elevate other black men, through the fraternal order of knights of the razor and other mutual aid organizations. Having reached their own accommodation with the white power structure, barbers had a tenuous grasp on independence during a century of American history that consigned most black men to slavery, peonage, sporadic employment, or no job at all.

Black barbers understood that membership in the lower middle class, even if it was obtained by bowing to and scraping at pale faces, furnished them the self-esteem that came with the prestigious mantle of business ownership. Although this strategy for racial uplift mirrored that of black professionals like Frederick Douglass in that the barbers appropriated dominant ideologies for their own ends, they also accepted the need to wear the mask desired by white customers. Thus, they also employed the subterfuge that characterized the uplift strategy of the black masses, a behavior that came naturally to barbers, since they worked with their hands in personal service, as did most African Americans who had escaped the toil of the fields. Black barbers did more, however, than constantly shift their balance to keep one foot in each camp. They expressed a positive self-image, through their conception of respectability, that offered the African American community a vision of pride and self-help.

Although united in their struggle for dignity and success, black barbers followed different paths depending on where they lived. The lower South, except for major New South entrepots such as Atlanta, presented black barbers with a society polarized by race in which they had to choose between affluent but repressive white allies and oppressed but united black masses. With the election of Joseph Rainey to the U.S. Congress during Reconstruction, barbers in the region glimpsed their potential, only to have the privilege they had gained through close ties to whites jeopardize their newfound ties to the African American community. Northern barbers soared like Icarus in the late antebellum and postwar periods, only to plummet at the end of the nineteenth century. Through their involvement with the abolition movement and their early shift to an exclusively black clientele, many northern barbers appear to have sidestepped the conflicts of interest that came with serving white men. However, the false promise of the Republican Party to keep faith with African Americans led northern barbers to embrace a strategy of assimilation that left them isolated and with no legacy to bequeath to future generations.

Only in the upper South did black barbers fully realize the liberating potential of membership in a fraternity of knights of the razor. Because the circumstances of the region promoted the value of enterprise and identification with the black masses, the fraternity of black barbers living along the Mason-Dixon Line acquired a vitality that let them surmount one obstacle after another. They also maintained their priorities and values when they migrated to other parts of the nation. Black barbers in the upper South negotiated the tensions between their class and their racial identity during Reconstruction. Finally, they had the courage of their convictions and reinvented the traditions of African American barbering to serve their own community when white supremacy and urbanization presented them with new challenges and opportunities.

John Merrick blazed the path for this new direction, and a sense of his legacy can be gleaned from the speeches given when a Liberty Ship was named for him. On July 11, 1943, North Carolina governor J. Melville Broughton spoke at the launching ceremonies of the SS *John Merrick* at a shipyard in Wilmington. History weighed on the governor's mind. Somewhat uncomfortably, he acknowledged that "blood [had] flowed freely in the streets of this city" fifty-five years earlier in the Wilmington race riot. The riots that had just occurred in Detroit and other cities had caused him to recall this disquieting memory along with "the fact that delicate situations between the races exist in certain places in North Carolina." Although the governor chose to scold intemperate newspapers for exacerbating race problems in his state instead of addressing the relevant issues directly, he did examine Merrick's life in detail, as befit the occasion. His praise for the black barber's "achievements and philosophy" segued into a discussion of lessons "for this troubled time." According to the governor, Merrick exemplified "harmonious cooperation and mutual respect" between the races because he accepted the social order as he had found it and took advantage of the opportunity that society had offered to achieve success in business. Merrick, the governor continued, had prospered even though the state had failed to offer him the chance to attend public schools, a deficiency that he said North Carolina had remedied with state-supported education through the college level for African Americans and the recent equalization of black teacher pay. "Thus," he concluded, "John Merrick's faith in North Carolina has been justified."[1]

If Merrick's spirit witnessed the ceremony from on high, he must have been pleased. His life, which had begun in slavery, received a distinguished tribute from the highest official in the state, a white man. He would also have smiled approvingly when the governor quoted C. C. Spaulding, Merrick's successor as president of the insurance company that he had founded, who echoed Merrick's ideas about racial uplift. "The Negro is proud of his race," Spaulding had proclaimed. "He wants . . . to improve himself and make fuller use of his opportunities for development." In a phrase that captured Merrick's belief that enterprise could fulfill the destiny of his people, Spaulding said, "We are waking up and are learning to do big business and to become bigger people." Merrick's innate skepticism would also have put the governor's words in context. After all, he had started his insurance company in the wake of the riot that the governor mentioned, and the recent settlement with school teachers had been executed in response to a ruling handed down by the U.S. Supreme Court. Yet, the enduring success of his bank and insurance company had forced the white elite to recognize his accomplishments in a bid to quell racial dissent. The governor had to concede that the greatest advances made by African Americans in his state had been made according to the plans of a black rather than a white man. The governor's speech also included shrill warnings that civil rights for African Americans would lead to the creation of a "mongrel race," and to that Merrick would simply have tipped his hat to the politician and under his breath called him a son of a bitch.[2]

Notes

ACKNOWLEDGMENTS

1. Mark Brown, *Barbershop*, screenplay, State Street Productions, 52.

INTRODUCTION

1. Henry A. Murray, *Lands of the Slave and the Free: Cuba, the United States, and Canada* (n.p.: John W. Parker & Son, 1855), 19; Stephen Miller, "Recollection of New-bern Fifty Years Ago," 56, unpublished manuscript, 1872, typescript copy in Search Room, Archives, Division of Archives and History, Raleigh, N.C.

2. W. Jeffrey Bolster, *Black Jacks: African American Seamen in the Age of Sail* (Cambridge: Harvard University Press, 1997).

3. James Baldwin, "Many Thousands Gone," in his *Notes of a Native Son* (Boston: Beacon Press, 1955), 28; W. E. B. DuBois, *The Souls of Black Folk by W. E. B. DuBois*, ed. David W. Blight and Robert Gooding-Williams (New York: Bedford Books, 1997), 38.

4. Nathan Irving Huggins introduced the corollary to double consciousness in his *Harlem Renaissance* (New York: Oxford University Press, 1971), 244–45.

5. I am indebted to Leslie Harris, who raised but did not pursue the argument that antebellum black barbers "potentially exemplified an alternative model of independent manhood" in her *In the Shadow of Slavery: African Americans in New York City, 1626–1863* (Chicago: University of Chicago Press, 2003), 234.

6. Patrick Rael, *Black Identity and Black Protest in the Antebellum North* (Chapel Hill: University of North Carolina Press, 2002), 8–10.

7. See the Guide to Further Reading for a review of historical research on black barbers.

8. Kevin K. Gaines, *Uplifting the Race: Black Leadership, Politics, and Culture in the Twentieth Century* (Chapel Hill: University of North Carolina Press, 1996); Joanne Pope Melish, *Disowning Slavery: Gradual Emancipation and Race in New England, 1780–1860* (Ithaca: Cornell University Press, 1998); Rael, *Black Identity and Black Protest.* Gail Bederman offers this type of analysis of Ida B. Wells in her *Manliness and Civilization: A Cultural History of Gender and Race in the United States, 1880–1917* (Chicago: University of Chicago Press, 1995).

9. For this framework for understanding the duality of black barbers' lives I am indebted to Earl Lewis, *In Their Own Interests: Race, Class, and Power in Twentieth-Century Norfolk, Virginia* (Berkeley: University of California Press, 1991), 5–7.

CHAPTER 1: THE ORIGINS OF BLACK BARBERS

1. York County (Virginia) Orders, Wills, and Inventories Book 19, 1740–1746, p. 209; William Waller Hening, ed., *The Statutes at Large, being a collection of all the laws of Virginia, from the first sesssion of the Legislature in the year 1619*, vol. 10 (1819; reprint, Charlottesville: University Press of Virginia, 1969). The county, municipal, and tax records cited for Caesar Hope are on microfilm at the Library of Virginia, Richmond, Virginia. I am indebted to Michael Nichols for sharing his research on Caesar Hope with me. Nichols, "Caesar Hope: 'The Famous Barber of York,' 1733–1810" (unpublished paper). The research for this chapter was greatly aided by the publication of *Runaway Slave Advertisements: A Documentary History from the 1730s to 1790*, comp. Lathan A. Windley, 4 vols. (Westport, Conn.: Greenwood Press, 1983). In subsequent notes, the advertisements will be cited as follows: slave owner's name, date published, newspaper title, and then, in parentheses, the references to the Windley volumes. For an example of a runaway slave barber from Africa, see Charles Atkins, June 20, 1780, *Royal South Carolina Gazette* (Windley, vol. 3, 707–8).

2. Ira Berlin, "From Creole to African: Atlantic Creoles and the Origins of African-American Society in Mainland North America," *William and Mary Quarterly*, 3rd ser., 53 (April 1996): 251–88; and Berlin, *Many Thousands Gone: The First Two Centuries of Slavery in North America* (Cambridge, Mass.: Belknap Press, 1998). Philip Morgan, "Three Planters and Their Slaves: Perspectives on Slavery in Virginia, South Carolina, and Jamaica, 1750–1790," in *Race and Family in the Colonial South*, ed. Winthrop D. Jordan and Sheila L. Skemp (Jackson: University Press of Mississippi, 1987).

3. Sylvia R. Frey, *Water from the Rock: Black Resistance in a Revolutionary Age* (Princeton: Princeton University Press, 1991); Berlin, *Many Thousands Gone*, 245, 246–48, 262–63, 269–71, 273–75, 311–32, 317–18, 337.

4. Gerald Mullin, *Flight and Rebellion: Slave Resistance in Eighteenth-Century Virginia* (New York: Oxford University Press, 1972); 73–78; Philip D. Morgan, *Slave Counterpoint: Black Culture in the Eighteenth-Century Chesapeake and Lowcountry* (Chapel Hill: University of North Carolina Press, 1998), 244–46; Richard L. Bushman, *The Refinement of America: Persons, Houses, Cities* (New York: Vintage Books, 1993).

5. Frey, *Water from the Rock*.

6. *Virginia Gazette*, Sept. 26, 1745, Oct. 31, 1745, and Mar. 27, 1746; George Washington quoted in Mullin, *Flight and Rebellion*, 73; York County Wills and Inventories, book 21, 1760–1771, 419–20, 434–35.

7. Thomas Jefferson, *Jefferson's Memorandum Books; Accounts, with Legal Records and Miscellany, 1767–1826*, ed. James A. Bear, Jr., and Lucia C. Stanton, vol. 1, *The Papers of Thomas Jefferson*, 2nd ser. (Princeton: Princeton University Press, 1997).

8. Bushman, *Refinement of America*, 3–29, 32–33, 55, 63; Benjamin Franklin, *The Autobiography of Benjamin Franklin*, ed. R. Jackson Wilson (New York: Modern Library, 1981), 101; Bernard Bailyn, *Voyagers to the West: A Passage in the Peopling of America on the Eve of the Revolution* (New York: Knopf, 1986), 151, 153.

9. Richard Corson, *Fashions in Hair: The First Five Thousand Years*, 3rd ed. (London: Peter Owen, 1971), 159, 169, 290–91.

10. William Prynne, *The Unlovlinesse of Lovelockes*, no. 825 of *The English Experience: Its Record in Early Printed Books Published in Facsimile* (1628; reprint, Norwood, NJ: Walter J. Johnson, Inc., 1976), 4; Charles DeZemler, *Once Over Lightly: The Story of Man and His Hair* (New York: privately printed, 1939), 70–73; Corson, *Fashions in Hair*, 215–16, 270–71 (quote).

11. Dominique di Giovanni Burchiello, a barber of fifteenth-century Florence, won such renown for his poetry that his portrait hung in the Medici gallery. In France, the acclaim for Jacques Jasmin as a poet induced the government to award him a pension, and the public erected a monument to him after his death. Richard Wright Proctor, *The Barber's Shop*, rev. ed. (1883; reprint, Detroit: Singing Tree Press, 1971), 8–9, 12; DeZemler, *Once Over Lightly*, 10–12, 61. Corson, *Fashions in Hair*, 136, 171; William Andrews, *At the Sign of the Barber's Pole: Studies in Hirsute History* (1904; reprint, Detroit: Singing Tree Press, 1969), 8.

12. Bushman, *Refinement of America*, xiv, 25–26, 209; Prynne, *The Unlovlinesse of Lovelockes*, 5; Proctor, *The Barber's Shop*, 22; Andrews, *At the Sign of the Barber's Pole*, 53–57.

13. Corson, *Fashions in Hair*, 261; Pierre Augustin Caron de Beaumarchias, *The Figaro Plays: The Barber of Seville, The Marriage of Figaro, The Guilty Mother: Three Plays by Beaumarchais*, trans. Graham Anderson (1993; reprint, London: Oberon Books, 1997), *Marriage of Figaro*, act 1, sc. 4, p. 107.

14. Beaumarchias, *Marriage of Figaro*, act 5, sc. 3, p. 226.

15. Edward M'Crady, Oct. 24–Nov. 7, 1776, Robert Raper, Mar. 18, 1779, *South Carolina and American General Gazette* (Windley, vol. 3, 489, 552–53); Robert Darnall, Oct. 20, 1763, *Maryland Gazette* (Windley, vol. 2, 51); William Roane, Aug. 17, 1769, Gabriel Jones, June 18, 1774, James Mercer, Mar. 19, 1772, Hamilton Ballantine, May 22, 1779, *Virginia Gazette* (Windley, vol. 1, 72, 111, 149–50, 202); Charles Yates, Sept. 20, 1783, *Virginia Gazette and Weekly Advertiser* (Windley, vol. 1, 219–20.

16. Gabriel Jones, June 30, 1774, Hamilton Ballantine, May 22, 1779, *Virginia Gazette*, Charles Yates, Sept. 20, 1783, *Virginia Gazette and Weekly Advertiser* (Windley, vol. 1, 149, 202, 220); Henry Laurens to John Laurens, May 29, 1778, in David R. Chesnutt et al., eds., *The Papers of Henry Laurens* (Columbia: University of South Carolina Press, 1992), vol. 13, 365.

17. Philip Vickers Fithian, *Journal and Letters of Philip Vickers Fithian, 1773–1774: A Plantation Tutor of the Old Dominion*, ed. Hunter Dickinson Farish (Williamsburg: Colonial Williamsburg, 1943), 250.

18. Scipio quoted in Morgan, *Slave Counterpoint*, 460; Robert Darnall, Oct. 20, 1763, *Maryland Gazette* (Windley, vol. 2, 51); Benjamin Guerrard, Aug. 30, 1774, *South Carolina Gazette and Country Journal* (Windley, vol. 3, 696). In an advertisement for

runaway slave barber Titus, Charles Atkins described Titus as customarily tying a red and white handkerchief around his head. Charles Atkins, Sept. 30–Oct. 7, 1774, *South Carolina and American General Gazette* (Windley, vol. 3, 459).

19. Landon Carter, *The Diary of Colonel Landon Carter of Sabine Hall, 1752–1778*, ed. Jack P. Greene (Charlottesville: University Press of Virginia, 1965), vol. 1, 254, 417, 505, vol. 2, 596, 667, 797 (quote), 829, 903, 946; Morgan, *Slave Counterpoint*, 312, 324, 356.

20. Carter, *Diary*, vol. 1, 289–90, vol. 2, 996–97.

21. Slaves formed an identity in the New World that incorporated African ethnicity and European culture. Michael A. Gomez, *Exchanging Our Country Marks: The Transformation of African Identities in the Colonial and Antebellum South* (Chapel Hill: University of North Carolina Press, 1998), especially 8–11. Allan D. Austin, *African Muslims in Antebellum America: Transatlantic Stories and Spiritual Struggles* (New York,: Routledge, 1997); Gwendolyn Midlo Hall, *Africans in Colonial Louisiana: The Development of Afro-Creole Culture in the Eighteenth Century* (Baton Rouge: Louisiana State University Press, 1992); and Hall, *Slavery and African Ethnicities in the Americas: Restoring the Links* (Chapel Hill: University of North Carolina Press, 2005); Douglas B. Chambers, *Murder at Montpelier: Igbo Africans in Virginia* (Jackson: University Press of Mississippi, 2005).

22. Carter, *Diary*, vol. 1, 372–73.

23. Darlene Clark Hine, "Rape and the Inner Lives of Black Women in the Middle West: Preliminary Thoughts on the Culture of Dissemblance," in *Unequal Sisters: A Multicultural Reader in U.S. Women's History*, ed. Ellen DuBois and Vicki L. Ruiz (New York: Routledge, 1990); song lyrics quoted in Lawrence W. Levine, *Black Culture and Black Consciousness: Afro-American Folk Thought from Slavery to Freedom* (New York: Oxford University Press, 1977), xiii. The following analyze the relationship between Carter and Nassau in the context of patriarchy: Morgan, "Three Planters and Their Slaves"; Rhys Isaac, *Landon Carter's Uneasy Kingdom: Revolution and Rebellion on a Virginia Plantation* (New York: Oxford University Press, 2004).

24. Carter, *Diary*, vol. 2, 953, 1111.

25. Landon Carter, Mar. 3, 1768, *Virginia Gazette*, cited in Mullin, *Flight and Rebellion*, 78; Carter, *Diary*, 778.

26. Carter, *Diary*, vol. 2, 940–41.

27. For a discussion of how Carter's religious views informed the way he understood slavery, see Isaac, *Landon Carter's Uneasy Kingdom*, 72. Nassau had run away before, in 1773. Carter, *Diary*, vol. 1, 492 (quote), vol. 2, 1128, 1144–45. Philip Morgan based his determination that Nassau returned or was captured on finding the slave listed in the inventory of Carter's estate. See Morgan, *Slave Counterpoint*, 357, n. 73.

28. Philip Morgan, examining slave inventories of large plantations in the rural South Carolina Lowcountry, found that waiting men comprised one percent or less of the slaves on average. Morgan, *Slave Counterpoint*, 210. Out of the 1,138 men whom Gerald Mullin found listed in runaway slave advertisements in Virginia newspapers between 1736 and 1801, 359 were listed as skilled slaves. Mullin, *Flight and Rebellion*, 94–95. James Mercer, Mar. 19, 1772, *Virginia Gazette* (Windley, vol. 1, 111); letter from

James Mercer to John Francis Mercer, Mar. 3, 1787, and article by Austin Brockenbrough, *Virginia Independent Chronicle*, Mar. 4, 1780, both quoted in Mullin, 76. Wellins Calcott, Sept. 28–Oct. 5, 1772, *South Carolina and American General Gazette* (Windley, vol. 3, 450).

29. Mullin, *Flight and Rebellion*, 100–102.

30. Alexander G. Strachan, Apr. 2, 1779.

31. Gabriel Jones, June 30, 1774, *Virginia Gazette* (Windley, vol. 1, 149–50, 200); Wellins Calcott, Sept. 28–Oct. 5, 1772, *South Carolina and American General Gazette* (Windley, vol. 3, 450). For other examples of runaway waiting men with extensive wardrobes, see William Roane, Aug. 17, 1769, and Hamilton Ballantine, May 22, 1779, *Virginia Gazette* (Windley, vol. 1, 72, 202).

32. Allan Kulikoff, *Tobacco and Slaves: The Development of Southern Cultures in the Chesapeake, 1680–1800* (Chapel Hill: University of North Carolina Press, 1986), 276–77, 399; Morgan, *Slave Counterpoint*, 210.

33. Charles Yates, Sept. 20, 1783, *Virginia Gazette and Weekly Advertiser* (Windley, vol. 1, 219–20); Richard-Park Stobo, Feb. 16, 1760, and Robert Hume, Oct. 21–28, 1732, *South Carolina Gazette* (Windley, vol. 3, 3–4, 181); John Jouet, Oct. 10, 1777, *Virginia Gazette* (Windley, vol. 1, 186–87).

34. York County Order Book 4, 1774–1784, 95, *Virginia Gazette* (Pinkney), Nov. 23, Dec. 9, 1775.

35. Bertram Wyatt-Brown, "The Mask of Obedience: Male Slave Psychology in the Old South," *American Historical Review* 93 (Dec. 1988): 1237–38; Petition of Susanna Riddell, Oct. 29, 1779, York County Legislative Petitions, box 1, Library of Virginia; Hening, ed., *The Statutes at Large of Virginia*, vol. 10, 211.

36. Bushman, *Refinement of America*, 47–48; "Ledger" of an unidentified barber, 1790–1794, continued as Joshua Saltonstall's ledger, 1803–1806, Manuscript Department, Historical Society of Pennsylvania, Philadelphia; Royall Tyler, "The Bay Boy," in *The Prose of Royall Tyler*, ed. Marius B. Peladeau (Montpelier, Vt.: Vermont Historical Society, 1972), 50–53; *The Progress of Dulness*, part 2, lines 332 and 208 in John Trumbull, *The Satiric Poems of John Trumbull: The Progress of Dulness and M'Fingal*, ed. Edwin T. Bowden (Austin: University of Texas Press, 1962).

37. Gordon S. Wood, *The Creation of the American Republic, 1776–1787* (Chapel Hill: University of North Carolina Press, 1969), 107–18; Edmund S. Morgan, "The Puritan Ethic and the American Revolution," *William and Mary Quarterly*, 3rd ser., 24 (1967): 3–43; Rhys Isaac, *The Transformation of Virginia, 1740–1790* (Chapel Hill: University of North Carolina Press, 1982), 172–80, 243–72, quote on 251. Emory G. Evans, "Planter Indebtedness and the Coming of the American Revolution," *William and Mary Quarterly*, 3rd ser., 19 (1962): 511–33.

38. Kathy Peiss, *Hope in a Jar: The Making of America's Beauty Culture* (New York: Henry Holt, 1998), 22–23; Franklin quoted in Ronald W. Clark, *Benjamin Franklin: An Autobiography* (New York: Random House, 1983), 313.

39. For a discussion of the anti-luxury literature written after the Revolution, see Neil Harris, *The Artist in American Society*, 28–33, quote on 31, and Kenneth Silverman, *A Cultural History of the American Revolution*, 504–17; *Philadelphia Aurora*,

Feb. 15, 1796, quoted in Stuart M. Blumin, *The Emergence of the Middle Class: Social Experience in the American City, 1760–1900* (New York: Cambridge University Press, 1989), 18; Governor Treadwell (Connecticut) (1802) and Timothy Dwight, "Greenfield Hill" (1794), both quoted in Bushman, *Refinement of America*, 193–94, 196.

40. Bushman, *Refinement of America*, xvii–xix, 197, 263–64, 406–9; John Adams to James Warren, July 4, 1786, and "An Essay on American Genius," *New Haven Gazette and Connecticut Magazine*, Feb. 1, 1787, both quoted in Merrill Jenson, *The New Nation: A History of the United States during the Confederation, 1781–1789* (New York: Knopf, 1950), 91, 190.

41. David R. Roediger, *Wages of Whiteness: Race and the Making of the American Working Class* (New York: Verso, 1991), 43–47; Bruce Laurie, *Artisans into Workers: Labor in Nineteenth-Century America* (New York: Hill & Wang, 1989), 15–46; Alexis de Tocqueville, *Democracy in America*, and Thomas C. Gratten, *Civilized America* (1859), both quoted in Daniel E. Sutherland, *Americans and Their Servants: Domestic Service in the United States from 1800–1920* (Baton Rouge: Lousiana State University Press, 1981), 5, 122–23; John M. Todd, *A Sketch of the Life of John M. Todd (Sixty Years in a Barber Shop) and Reminiscences of His Customers* (Portland, Me.: William W. Roberts, 1906), 168–69.

42. Although Bailyn notes that barbers and hairdressers numbered among the immigrants in these groups, he fails to give specific numbers of individuals. Bailyn, *Voyagers to the West*, 211; Todd, *Life of John M. Todd*, 168–69.

43. Todd began his career in 1844. Todd, *Life of John M. Todd*, vii, 7, 22, 27, 38, 47, 95–96. According to the oral history of white barbers, the existence of slave barbers led to a decline in the prestige of the trade. Mic Hunter, *The American Barbershop: A Close Look at a Disappearing Place* (Mount Horeb, Wisc.: Face to Face Books, 1996), 107. On the conflation of servants in general with slaves, see Roediger, *Wages of Whiteness*, 47–50.

44. Ira Berlin, "Time, Space, and the Evolution of Afro-American Society in British Mainland North America," *American Historical Review* 85 (Feb. 1980): 44–78.

45. Gary Nash, *Forging Freedom: The Formation of Philadelphia's Black Community, 1720–1840* (Cambridge: Harvard University Press, 1988), 146–54; Shane White, *Somewhat More Independent: The End of Slavery in New York City, 1770–1810* (Athens: University of Georgia Press, 1991), 157–158; Graham Russell Hodges, *Root and Branch: African Americans in New York and East Jersey, 1613–1863* (Chapel Hill: University of North Carolina Press, 1999), 232.

46. Fithian, *Journal and Letters*, 178.

47. York County Order Book 4, 1774–1784, 242; York County Deed Book 6, 1777–1791; Williamsburg Census, 1782; Williamsburg Personal Property Tax Lists, 1783–1784; Richmond City Personal Property Tax Lists, 1787–1807; Richmond City Land Tax Lists, 1792–1817; Henrico County Deed Book 7, 1803–1806; Richmond City Will Book 1, 1810–1816, 165; Richmond City Hustings Wills Book 4, 1824–1828, 400–401.

48. James Sidbury, *Ploughshares into Swords: Race, Rebellion, and Identity in Gabriel's Virginia, 1730–1810* (New York: Cambridge University Press, 1997), 160–76, and

"Slave Artisans in Richmond, Virginia, 1780–1810," in *American Artisans: Crafting Social Identity, 1750–1850*, ed. Howard B. Rock, Paul A. Gilje, and Robert Asher (Baltimore: Johns Hopkins University Press, 1995), 58–59, 214 n. 16.

49. Loren Schweninger, "John Carruthers Stanly and the Anomaly of Black Slaveowning," *North Carolina Historical Review* 68 (Apr. 1990): 161–92.

50. Schweninger, "John Carruthers Stanly," 165, 167, 186, 187, 189.

51. Juliet E. K. Walker, *The History of Black Business in America: Capitalism, Race, Entrepreneurship* (New York: Twayne Publishers, 1998), 44; European tourist quoted in Hodges, *Root and Branch*, 203; Berlin, *Many Thousands Gone*, 243; Quaid was 60 in 1850, and Cord was 80 in 1860. Entries for John Quaid and John Cord, Philadelphia, Pa., U.S. Census, 1850, microfilm of the manuscript census returns, roll 817, p. 370, roll 1155, p. 267, Record Group 29, National Archives, Washington, D.C.

52. Hodges, *Root and Branch*, 177.

53. *Echoes of a Belle* quoted in Hannah Farnham Sawyer Lee, *Memoir of Pierre Toussaint, Born a Slave in St. Domingo* 2nd ed. (1854; reprint, Westport, Conn.: Negro Universities Press, 1970) (also in a more recent reprint: Sunbury, Pa.: Western Hemisphere Cultural Society, 1992, with same paging), 21, 37; Jack Curry, "Church Hopes Grave Will Yield a Black Saint," *New York Times*, Aug. 11, 1990, late edition.

54. Lee, *Memoir of Pierre Toussaint*, 27–28.

55. Ibid., 57, 77.

56. Ibid., 56.

57. Ibid., 21–23.

58. White, *Somewhat More Independent*, 49–50, 106–11, 144. Lee, *Memoir of Pierre Toussaint*, 27 (quote), 30–31, 63.

59. Lee, *Memoir of Pierre Toussaint*, 23–25.

60. Ibid., 25–28 (quote on 28), 33, 35, 56.

61. Ibid., 30, 43, 70–72 (quote).

62. Lee, *Memoir of Pierre Toussaint*, 38–43; Herbert S. Klein, *Slavery in the Americas: A Comparative Study of Virginia and Cuba* (Chicago: University of Chicago Press, 1967), 158; correspondence between Pierre Toussaint and A. Berard, Pierre Toussaint Papers, 1793–1853, Rare Books and Manuscripts Division, New York Public Library, New York, New York.

CHAPTER 2: BECOMING KNIGHTS OF THE RAZOR

1. James Thomas, *From Tennessee Slave to St. Louis Entrepreneur: The Autobiography of James Thomas*, ed. Loren Schweninger (Columbia: University of Missouri Press, 1984), 2, 7, 197.

2. Two years after Foster had purchased James on Sally's behalf, his law partner, Francis Fogg, conducted the negotiations that allowed Sally to buy her own freedom. Thomas, *Autobiography*, 29–30, 60.

3. Thomas, *Autobiography*, 30; Loren Schweninger, *James T. Rapier and Reconstruction* (Chicago: University of Chicago Press, 1978), 1–4; John Hope Franklin and Loren Schweninger, *In Search of the Promised Land: A Slave Family in the Old South*

(New York: Oxford University Press, 2006), 11–14, 16–18. Herbert Gutman provides a chapter-length survey of slave surnames that demonstrates that the process of passing on an old master's surname to indicate family ties among slaves was widespread and went back to colonial times. See his *The Black Family in Slavery and Freedom, 1790–1925* (New York: Vintage Books, 1976), 230–56.

4. Thomas, *Autobiography*, 4, 28–29, 32; John Rapier, Sr., to Henry Thomas, Feb. 28, 1843, Rapier Family Papers, Moorland-Spingarn Research Center, Howard University, Washington, D.C. (hereafter Rapier Family Papers);

5. Franklin and Schweninger, *In Search of the Promised Land*, 35–36.

6. The Clamorgans served as role models for another trio of brothers, the Robinsons. Francis Robinson moved to St. Louis in 1848 and is listed in the 1851 city directory as a barber. By 1857, Francis had taken over the barbershop at Barnum's Hotel, and three years later he took his brother William into the business. The third brother, Robert, joined them in the barbershop not long afterwards. Cyprian Clamorgan, *The Colored Aristocracy of St. Louis by Cyprian Clamorgan*, ed. Julie Winch (Columbia: University of Missouri Press, 1999), 22–29, 95.

7. Letter from William Johnson to Mrs. James Miller, Oct. 4, 1837, quoted in William Johnson, *William Johnson's Natchez: The Ante-Bellum Diary of a Free Negro*, ed. William Ransom Hogan and Edwin Adams Davis (1951; reprint, Baton Rouge: Louisiana State University Press, 1993), 45; see also pp. 16–20.

8. Ibid., 19–20.

9. When Johnson took one of the Bills hunting, along with his close friend Robert McCary, on November 24, 1836; and on the way home, the apprentice lost the birds Johnson had shot. Johnson, *Diary of a Free Negro*, 88, 99, 148, 152, 153, 169, 241.

10. Adams County (Mississippi) Will Books, Book 2, 81–83, quoted in Johnson, *Diary of a Free Negro*, 28; see also pp. 126, 135, 316, 394–95.

11. Letter from Rachel Winston to William Johnson, June 27, 1837, quoted in Johnson, *Diary of a Free Negro*, 29 n. 42; see also pp. 44 n. 66, 576; Edwin Adams Davis and William Ransom Hogan, *The Barber of Natchez* (1954; reprint, Baton Rouge: Louisiana State University Press, 1973), 58–59. On the growing opposition to manumission, see Ira Berlin, *Slaves Without Masters: The Free Negro in the Antebellum South* (New York: Vintage Books, 1976), 367–68, and Charles S. Sydnor, *Slavery in Mississippi* (1931; reprint, Gloucester, Mass.: P. Smith, 1965), 203–39.

12. Berlin, *Slaves Without Masters*, 226–227; John Hope Franklin, *The Free Negro in North Carolina, 1790–1860* (1943; reprint, New York: W. W. Norton, 1971), 122–30.

13. Christopher Phillips, *Freedom's Port: The African American Community of Baltimore, 1790–1860* (Urbana: University of Illinois Press, 1997), 158–59.

14. Franklin, *The Free Negro in North Carolina*, 126, 128; Loren Schweninger, "John Carruthers Stanly and the Anomaly of Black Slaveowning," *North Carolina Historical Review* 68 (Apr. 1990): 172; Davis and Hogan, *The Barber of Natchez*, 55.

15. Bettye Jane Gardner, "Free Blacks in Baltimore, 1800–1860" (Ph.D. diss., George Washington University, 1974), 161, 187; Phillips, *Freedom's Port*, 158–59. Clamorgan included biographical sketches of Norton Reynolds, Jr., James Williams, Thomas Gunnell, and George Carey. The term *journeyman* denotes an individual who has

completed an apprenticeship but works for a master artisan. Clamorgan, *Colored Aristocracy*, 62.

16. James Oliver Horton, *Free People of Color: Inside the African American Community* (Washington, D.C.: Smithsonian Institution Press, 1993), 35; entry for John Robinson, Boston, Massachusetts Census of Population, National Archives Microfilm Publication, roll 521, p. 858, Seventh Census of the United States, 1860, Records of the Bureau of the Census, Record Group 29, National Archives, Washington, D.C. (hereafter name, city, state, U.S. Census, date, roll no., page no.); Clamorgan, *Colored Aristocracy*, 53, 81–82, 102–3.

17. Johnson paid Sterns $25 per month plus board, which was twice what he paid William Nix, the protégé whom he helped secure a barbershop of his own. Davis and Hogan, *The Barber of Natchez*, 60; William Johnson, *William Johnson's Natchez: The Ante-Bellum Diary of a Free Negro*, ed. William Ransom Hogan and Edwin Adams Davis (1951; reprint, Port Washington, N.Y.: Kennikat Press, 1968), vol. 1, 287, n. 2, 401, vol. 2, 485–86, 782.

18. Johnson, *Diary of a Free Negro* (1993 reprint), 79; Bayard R. Hall, *Frank Freeman's Barber Shop; A Tale* (New York: Charles Scribner, 1852), 320–21.

19. Clamorgan, *Colored Aristocracy*, 53, 57, 62.

20. Thomas, *Autobiography*, 73–74.

21. Ibid., 4, 84.

22. Ibid., 2, 8, 83–84; Adby, *Journal of a Residence and Tour*, vol. 3, 185, quoted in Leon Litwack, *North of Slavery: The Negro in the Free States, 1790–1860* (Chicago: University of Chicago Press, 1961), 157.

23. Berlin, *Slaves Without Masters*, 234–35; Robert Barnwell Rhett, "Address to the People of Beaufort and Colleton Districts Upon the Subject of Abolition" (1838), quoted in Stephanie McCurry, "The Two Faces of Republicanism: Gender and Pro-Slavery Politics in Antebellum South Carolina," *Journal of American History* (Mar. 1992): 1261; Thomas, *Autobiography*, 89–90.

24. P. T. Barnum, *The Life of P. T. Barnum* (London: Sampson Low, Son, & Co., 1855), 203–4. For a similar anecdote, see Mark Twain, "About Barbers," *Sketches; New and Old* (New York: Harper & Brothers, 1903).

25. Barnum once toured the nation promoting Vivalla, a black singer and dancer named James Sandford. When Sandford "abruptly left me," Barnum took his place. "Being determined not to disappoint the audience, I blacked myself thoroughly, and sung the songs advertised. . . . It was decidedly a 'hard push,' but the audience supposed the singer was Sandford, and, to my surprise, my singing was applauded, and in two of the songs I was encored." Barnum had special insights into how white Americans wanted to view African Americans because he had established himself as a showman by displaying a black slave woman named Joice Heth, who he claimed had been the nursemaid for the infant George Washington. Benjamin Reiss, *The Showman and the Slave: Race, Death, and Memory in Barnum's America* (Cambridge, Mass.: Harvard University Press, 2001), 168–69.

26. Karen Haltunnen, *Confidence Men and Painted Women: A Study of Middle-Class Culture in America, 1830–1870* (New Haven: Yale University Press, 1982).

27. Herman Melville, *The Confidence Man: His Masquerade*, vol. 10, *The Writings of Herman Melville* (Chicago: Northwestern University Press, 1984), 226, 232.

28. Incidentally, Oily was white. *Harper's New Monthly Magazine* (Nov. 1855): 854–55, quoted in Tom Quirk, *Melville's Confidence Man: From Knave to Knight* (Columbia: University of Missouri Press, 1982), 141, 164–66 n. 24. Similar depictions of barbers can be found in D. Corcoran, "The Danger of Diddling a Barber," in his *Pickings from the Portfolio of the Reporter of the New Orleans Picayune* (Philadelphia: Carey & Hart, 1846). Used as a verb, *to barber* referred to one thief stealing from another thief. Eric Partridge, ed., *A Dictionary of the Underworld* (New York: Macmillan, 1950).

29. George M. Fredrickson, *Black Image in the White Mind: The Debate on Afro-American Character and Destiny, 1817–1914* (New York: Harper Torchbooks, 1972), 97–129; and Reginald Horseman, *Race and Manifest Destiny: The Origins of American Racial Anglo-Saxonism* (Cambridge, Mass.: Harvard University Press, 1981), 158–86. James Freeman Clarke, *Slavery in the United States: A Sermon Delivered on Thanksgiving Day, 1842* (Boston, 1843), 24.

30. When delivering this positive assessment of his protagonist, Hall acknowledged the insistence on innate black inferiority maintained by the biological school of thought on race: "[In] spite of certain philosophers and ethnologists, Frank—Negro Frank—was better in all respects than some white men." Hall, *Frank Freeman's Barber Shop*, 40.

31. Ibid., 62–63, 249–51, 307–9, 338–39.

32. Hannah Farnham Sawyer Lee, *Memoir of Pierre Toussaint: Born a Slave in St. Domingo* (1854; reprint, Westport, Conn.: Negro Universities Press, 1970), 119–22. Lee reproduced Toussaint's obituaries in an appendix.

33. Lee, *Memoir of Pierre Toussaint* , 83–84, 120; Clamorgan, *Colored Aristocracy*, 59.

34. *Fay's Mobile Directory for 1837* (Mobile, Ala.: H. M. McGuire and T. C. Fay, 1837), v. Katherine Grier developed the concept of the commercial parlor in her *Culture and Comfort: People, Parlors, and Upholstery, 1850–1930* (Washington, D.C.: Smithsonian Institution Press, 1997), 22–59, especially 29–31, 61–63; Daniel Boorstin, Jr., *The Americans: National Experience* (New York: Random House, 1965), 137; Doris Elizabeth King, "The First-Class Hotel and the Age of the Common Man," *Journal of Southern History* 23 (May 1957): 173–88. According to Carolyn Brucken, "the experience of luxury within the hotel was based on a definition of luxury as the emotional pleasure that accompanied the desire for goods. The luxury hotel, as part of this redefinition of luxury, encouraged vicarious consumption based on pleasure, experience, and novelty." See her "Consuming Luxury: Hotels and the Rise of Middle-Class Public Space, 1825–1860" (Ph.D. diss., George Washington University, 1997), 168.

35. Hall, *Frank Freeman's Barber Shop*, 320; Robert Lacour-Gayet, *Everyday Life in the United States before the Civil War, 1830–1860*, trans. Mary Ilford (New York: Frederick Ungar Publishing, 1969), 37.

36. Grier, *Culture and Comfort*, 44. For examples of an advertisement for a shaving saloon, see: Clamorgan, *Colored Aristocracy*, 40; and Rapier Family Papers, Series-D cards, box 84-2, file 108. Barber's chairs were the precursor of today's ubiquitous over-

stuffed recliners. Grier, *Culture and Comfort*, 47; Edgar Winfield Martin, *Standard of Living in 1860* (Chicago: University of Chicago Press, 1942), 219.

37. For example, Frank Parrish, a black barber working in Nashville, advertised socks, collars, and suspenders. Apr. 23, 1836, *Nashville Republican* (final quote also appeared in this ad). Jacob White also carried products geared toward nineteenth-century standards of beauty, such as white lead and bear oil. John C. White, Sr., B & R, 1839–1841, American Negro Historical Society Collection, reel 5, frames 12, 103, 117, 153, Historical Society of Pennsylvania, Philadelphia. In fact, the desire to appear genteel played a greater role in getting Americans to bathe than did concerns about health. Richard L. Bushman and Claudia L. Bushman, "The Early History of Cleanliness in America," *Journal of American History* 74 (Mar. 1988): 1219–22, 1225.

38. Grier, *Culture and Comfort*, 61–63; For the concepts of genteel performance and the laws of tact, along with the significance of parlors to the emerging middle class, I am indebted to Haltunnen in *Confidence Men*, 92–111.

39. For an overview of the barbershop gossip retailed at Johnson's Natchez establishment, see Davis and Hogan, *Barber of Natchez*, 118–28. Thomas, *Autobiography*, 75.

40. Berlin, *Slaves Without Masters*, 255–56; Phillips, *Freedom's Port*, 99, 158–59. The author calculated the number of stand-alone barbershops from lists compiled out of the manuscript census returns and John W. Woods, *Woods' Baltimore City Directory* (Baltimore: John W. Woods, 1860).

41. The author identified Auter and Eddy as prosperous barbers in the manuscript census returns, looked up the addresses of their businesses in the Philadelphia city directory, and then found the neighboring businesses through the *Philadelphia Shopping Guide*, which listed establishments by their location on the street. Auter owned $3,000 worth of real estate, and Eddy's property was valued at $2,000. Entries for James Auter and Joshua Eddy, Philadelphia, Pa., U.S. Census, 1860, roll 1157, p. 122, and roll 1155, p. 370; William H. Boyd, *Boyd's Philadelphia City Business Directory, 1859–60* (Philadelphia: Joseph Monier, 1859), 181–82; *The Philadelphia Shopping Guide and Housekeeper's Companion* (Philadelphia: S. E. Cohen, 1859), 1–5, 12; Whittington B. Johnson, *The Promising Years, 1750–1830: The Emergence of Black Labor and Business* (New York: Garland Publishing, 1993), 183.

42. Thomas, *Autobiography*, 121.

43. Quoted in Lee, *Memoir of Pierre Toussaint*, 96–98; John H. Rapier, Sr., to John H. Rapier, Jr., Mar. 17, 1857, Florence, Alabama, Rapier Family Papers.

44. Bertram Wyatt-Brown, "The Mask of Obedience: Male Slave Psychology in the Old South," *American Historical Review* 93 (Dec. 1988): 1245–46. Frederick Douglass, *Narrative of the Life of Frederick Douglass, an American Slave, Written by Himself*, ed. William L. Andrews and William S. McFeely (New York: W. W. Norton, 1997), 21–22; Arlie Russell Hochschild, *The Managed Heart: The Commercialization of Human Feeling* (Berkeley: University of California Press, 1983): 7, 132–36.

45. Clamorgan, *Colored Aristocracy*, 58. For an overview of animal trickster tales and how they informed African American culture during slavery, see Lawrence W. Levine, *Black Culture and Black Consciousness: Afro-American Folk Thought from Slavery to Freedom* (New York: Oxford University Press, 1977), 102–33.

46. Herman Melville, "Benito Cereno" in his *The Piazza Tales*, vol. 10 of *The Works of Herman Melville* (New York: Russell & Russell, 1963), 70, 73.

47. Ibid., 120, 121. For the entire shaving scene, see pp. 117–26.

48. Ibid., 122.

49. Clamorgan, *Colored Aristocracy*, 52.

CHAPTER 3: CAUGHT BETWEEN REGIONAL ORIGINS AND THE BARBER'S TRADE

1. *Weekly Anglo-African*, Aug. 20, 1859, 3; Leroy Graham, *Baltimore: The Nineteenth-Century Black Capital* (Lanham, Md.: University Press of America, 1982), 203, 254–55; Christopher Phillips, *Freedom's Port: The African American Community of Baltimore* (Urbana: University of Illinois Press, 1997), 174, 280 note 50.

2. Ira Berlin, "The Structure of the Free Negro Caste in the Antebellum United States," *Journal of Social History* 9 (Spring 1976): 297–318.

3. Quoted in Leslie M. Harris, *In the Shadow of Slavery: African Americans in New York City, 1626–1863* (Chicago: University of Chicago Press, 2003), 80.

4. Berlin, "Structure of the Free Negro Caste," 298, 301; Frederick Douglass, *Narrative of the Life of Frederick Douglass, an American Slave, Written by Himself*, ed. William L. Andrews and William S. McFeely (New York: W. W. Norton, 1997), 74: Benjamin C. Bacon, *Statistics of the Colored People of Philadelphia* (Philadelphia: T. Ellwood Chapman, 18 56), 15: "Memorial of the People of Color of the City of Philadelphia and Its Vicinity to the Honorable the Senate and House of Representatives of the Commonwealth of Pennsylvania," Jan. 1832, quoted in Gary Nash, *Forging Freedom: The Formation of Philadelphia's Black Community, 1720–1840* (Cambridge: Harvard University Press, 1988), 253: Theodore Hershberg et al., "A Tale of Three Cities: Blacks, Immigrants, and Opportunity in Philadelphia, 1850–1880, 1930, 1970," in *Philadelphia: Work, Space, Family, and Group Experience in the Nineteenth Century*, ed. Theodore Hershberg et al. (New York: Oxford University Press, 1981), 470: For evidence on the decline of northern black artisans in a range of cities, see Leonard Curry, *The Free Black in Urban America, 1800–1850* (Chicago: University of Chicago Press, 1981), 15–36, 258–66. Employment statistics taken from the secondary literature should be viewed as approximate, because historians' definitions of a trade as skilled or artisanal have varied. For example, Leonard Curry excludes barbers from totals of black artisans. *Register of Trades of the Colored People in the City of Philadelphia and Districts* (Philadelphia: Merrihew & Gunn, 1838), 3, 6–7; *U.S. Census Office, Seventh Census of the United States, 1850. Population, Slave, and Manufacturing Schedules*, Philadelphia (hereafter city, state, U.S. Census, date, roll no., page no.); Robert Ernst, "The Economic Status of New York City Negroes, 1850–1863," *Negro History Bulletin* 12 (Mar. 1949): 139.

5. For Richard Allen, see Nash, *Forging Freedom*, 113, 117, 119, 126–27, 192–99. For Prince Hall, see James Oliver Horton, *Free People of Color: Inside the African American Community* (Washington, D.C.: Smithsonian Institution Press, 1993), 42–43. Peter P. Hinks, *To Awaken My Brethren: David Walker and the Problem of Antebellum Slave*

Resistance (University Park, : Pennsylvania State University Press, 1997), 78; Peter C. Ripley, ed., *The Black Abolitionist Papers* (Chapel Hill: University of North Carolina Press, 1985), vol. 3, 305.

6. The barbershops attacked by the antiabolitionists were located in New York City and Pittsburgh. Paul Gilje, *Road to Mobocracy: Popular Disorder in New York City, 1763–1834* (Chapel Hill: University of North Carolina Press, 1988), 166; Dorothy Sterling, *Making of an African-American: Martin Robinson Delany, 1812–1885* (Garden City, N.J.: Doubleday, 1971), 44; Julie Winch, *Philadelphia's Black Elite: Activism, Accommodation, and the Struggle for Autonomy, 1787–1848* (Philadelphia: Temple University Press, 1988), 127, 146–48; *Colored American*, Sept. 22, 1838.

7. James Oliver Horton and Lois E. Horton, *Black Bostonians: Family Life and Community Struggle in the Antebellum North* (New York: Holmes & Meier, 1979), 32–33, 36–37, 142 n. 48.

8. Joseph Wilson, *Sketches of the Higher Classes of Colored Society in Philadelphia. By a Southerner* (Philadelphia, Merrihew & Thompson, 1841), 80–81; Harry C. Silcox, "Philadelphia Negro Educator: Jacob C. White, Jr., 1837–1902," *Pennsylvania Magazine of History and Biography* 97 (Jan. 1973): 75–98.

9. Frederick Douglass, *My Bondage and My Freedom*, quoted in Phillips, *Freedom's Port*, 200–201. In addition, see Frank Towers, "Job Busting at Baltimore Shipyards: Racial Violence in the Civil War–Era South," *Journal of Southern History* 66 (May 2000): 221–56.

10. Ira Berlin, *Slaves Without Masters: The Free Negro in the Antebellum South* (New York: Vintage Books, 1976), 218–21, 228–32, 234–41; Curry, *The Free Black in Urban America*, 260; M. Ray Della, "The Problem of Negro Labor in the 1850s," *Maryland Historical Magazine* 66 (Spring 1971): 28; Matchett, *Baltimore Directory for 1827*, cited in Phillips, *Freedom's Port*, 111; John W. Woods, *Woods' Baltimore City Directory* (1860), cited in Della, "The Problem of Negro Labor in the 1850s," 28. Phillips and Della both note that city directories failed to list all free African Americans. To get a more complete listing of the free black population and their occupations, researchers must rely on the U.S. censuses, as Ira Berlin did for his statistics on free black employment in Richmond and Charleston. Leonard Curry compared data on free black male occupations from city directories and the censuses and discovered two weaknesses in statistics compiled from city directories. First, the degree of correlation between data in city directory and in the census varies from city to city. Second, even in cities where there is a high degree of correlation among the data generally, there may not be for the percentage of black men listed in specific occupational categories. Curry, *The Free Black in Urban America*, 263–64.

11. To free African Americans in Maryland and North Carolina, this legislative assault marked a departure from relatively benign race relations. John Hope Franklin points out that the North Carolina Legislature had acted with restraint after earlier slave revolts, such as the one led by Denmark Vesey in 1822. Elsewhere in the South, placing new restrictions on free African Americans after slave insurrections followed established custom. Phillips, *Freedom's Port*, 32–34, 182–83, 200, 215–18, 292 n. 23; John Hope Franklin, *The Free Negro in North Carolina, 1790–1860* (1943; re-

print, New York: W. W. Norton, 1971), 59–62; Berlin, *Slaves Without Masters*, 188--89, 202–4.

12. Phillips, *Freedom's Port*, 155–59.

13. Ibid., 159–60; Bettye Jane Gardner, "Free Blacks in Baltimore, 1800–1860" (Ph.D. diss., George Washington University, 1974), 96–97; Charles G. Steffen, *The Mechanics of Baltimore: Workers and Politics in the Age of Revolution, 1763–1812* (Urbana: University of Illinois Press, 1984).

14. Phillips, *Freedom's Port*, 174–75.

15. Loren Schweninger, *Black Property Owners in the South, 1750–1915* (Urbana: University of Illinois Press, 1990), 121. The barbers who went out West were Albert White and Gabriel Helms. Cyprian Clamorgan, *The Colored Aristocracy of St. Louis by Cyprian Clamorgan*, ed. Julie Winch (Columbia: University of Missouri Press, 1999), 46, 49, 52, 54, 82, 93–94; James Thomas, *From Tennessee Slave to St. Louis Entrepreneur: The Autobiography of James Thomas*, ed. Loren Schweninger (Columbia: University of Missouri Press, 1984), 91.

16. Clamorgan, *Colored Aristocracy*, 52, 54.

17. Berlin, "Structure of the Free Black Caste."

18. Curry, *The Free Black in Urban America*, 260; Berlin, *Slaves Without Masters*, 221, 237. Although both historians collected their data from the manuscript census, Berlin found a larger number of black artisans because he counted more occupations, such as barbering, as skilled trades: Berlin, *Slaves Without Masters*, 222; Ira Berlin and Herbert G. Gutman, "Natives and Immigrants, Free Men and Slaves: Urban Workingmen in the Antebellum American South," *American Historical Review* 88 (Dec. 1983), 1188. The free black barbers in Mobile were Charles Harris and John Raymon. U.S. Census, 1860, Mobile, Ala., roll 233, p. 723.

19. An 1867 letter from fourteen black barbers in Mobile to an official of the Freedmen's Bureau, protesting the licensing fees they had to pay, revealed the presence of slave barbers before the Civil War. "Before the war," they explained, "[we] never paid any license or ever was required to do so on account of us being recognized as property." Cited in Peter Kolchin, *First Freedom: The Responses of Alabama's Blacks to Emancipation and Reconstruction* (Westport, Conn.: Greenwood Press, 1972), 133. Two is a conservative estimate of the number of skilled slaves; it is restricted to the number of slave men owned by artisans. As subsequent discussion of Mobile's slave barbers will show, it is likely that slave owners who were not artisans owned slave artisans who hired themselves out. Berlin and Gutman, "Natives and Immigrants," 1186; T. C. Fay, *Mobile Directory or Stranger's Guide for 1839*, cited in Harriet E. Amos, *Cotton City: Urban Development in Antebellum Mobile* (Tuscaloosa: University of Alabama Press, 1985), 91.

20. Richard C. Wade, *Slavery in the Cities: The South, 1820–1860* (New York: Oxford University Press, 1964), 38–43; Amos, *Cotton City*, 89; Paulette Horton, *Avenue: The Place, the People, the Memories* (Mobile, Ala.: Horton, Inc., 1991), 165; Larry Koger, *Black Slaveowners: Free Black Slave Masters in South Carolina, 1790–1860* (Jefferson, N.C.: McFarland, 1985), 153; Alabama Slaves Schedules, Mobile, Ala., U.S. Census, 1860, p. 6.

21. Christopher Morris, "An Event in Community Organization: The Mississippi Insurrection Scare of 1835," *Journal of Social History* 22 (Autumn 1988): 93–111.

22. William Johnson, *William Johnson's Natchez: The Antebellum Diary of a Free Negro*, ed. William Ransom Hogan and Edwin Adams Davis (1951; reprint, Baton Rouge: Louisiana State University Press, 1993), 341–42, 345–46 (quote on 346), 348.

23. Berlin, *Slaves Without Masters*, 137, table 8, 273–77.

24. Loren Schweninger, "John Carruthers Stanly and the Anomaly of Black Slaveowning," *North Carolina Historical Review* 68 (Apr. 1990), 171, 186–87; Johnson, *Diary*, vol. 1, 28, 53, 63.

25. Between 1815 and 1836, the value of farmland in Craven Country dropped by one-third. Schweninger, "John Carruthers Stanly," 169–70, 173–75, 182. The editors of Johnson's diary assert that he felt owning farmland to be the "key to happiness." Johnson, *Diary of a Free Negro*, 32, 35–39, 55, 641, 643.

26. Schweninger, "John Carruthers Stanly," 177–78; Johnson, *Diary of a Free Negro*, 34–35. Michael Johnson and James Roark make a similar argument to explain why free African Americans in the lower South became slave owners. See their "Strategies of Survival: Free Negro Families and the Problems of Slavery," in *In Joy and in Sorrow: Women, Family, and Marriage in the Victorian South, 1830–1900*, ed. Carol Bleser (New York: Oxford University Press, 1992).

27. Koger, *Black Slaveowners*, 90–91, 151–53; Johnson, *Diary of Free Negro*, 26, 29, 277, 771, 782, 784. After Charles gained his freedom in 1851, Johnson had another slave, named Jim, take his place at the Under-the-Hill barbershop.

28. Edwin Adams Davis and William Ransom Hogan, *The Barber of Natchez* (1954; reprint, Baton Rouge: Louisiana State University Press, 1973), 243, 244–46.

29. Johnson, *Diary of a Free Negro*, 259.

30. Ibid., 90–91, 134, 137, 347, 469–70.

31. Horton, *Free People of Color*, 28; entry for John J. Smith, Boston, Massachusetts Census of Population, 1860 (National Archives Microfilm Publication, roll 521), 85; Floyd J. Miller, *The Search for Black Nationality: Black Emigration and Colonization, 1787–1863* (Urbana: University of Illinois Press, 1975), 94; *Directory of Pittsburgh and Vicinity for 1859–1860* (Pittsburgh: George H. Thurston, 1859), 288; *Weekly Afro-American*, Mar. 10, 1860; entry for John Vashon, Pittsburgh, Pa., U.S. Census, 1860, p. 32; various entries, Philadelphia, Pa., U.S. Census, 1860, pp. 71, 72, 84, 87, 94, 122, 149, 207, 268, 523, 537, 711, 715, 757. George Baptiste provides another example of a migrant black barber from the upper South. After working as a personal servant in Virginia, Baptiste moved to Madison, Indiana, in 1838, then to Detroit, where he became one of the city's wealthiest barbers. David M. Katzman, *Before the Ghetto: Black Detroit in the Nineteenth Century* (Urbana: University of Illinois Press, 1973), 14; and Emma Lou Thornbrough, *The Negro in Indiana before 1900*: A Study of a Minority (1957; reprint, Bloomington: Indiana University Press, 1993), 42.

32. Various entries, Philadelphia, Pa., U.S. Census, 1860, reel 1157, pp. 71, 72, 84, 87, 94, 122, 149, 207, 268, 523, 537, 711, 715, 757; *Philadelphia Evening Bulletin*, Sept. 26, 1882.

33. Thomas, *Autobiography*, 2, 4, 8, 90–91; John H. Rapier, Sr., to John H. Rapier, Jr., Oct. 27, 1856, and June 18, 1858, Rapier Family Papers Moorland-Spingarn Research Center, Howard University, Washington D.C.

CHAPTER 4: SELF-IMPROVEMENT AND SELF-LOATHING BEFORE THE WAR

1. John H. Rapier, Sr., to John H. Rapier, Jr., Mar. 17, 1857, Florence, Ala., Rapier Family Papers 84-1, Moorland-Spingarn Research Center, Howard University, Washington, D.C. (Hereafter Rapier Family Papers.)

2. *Report of the Proceedings of the Colored National Convention, Held at Cleveland, Ohio, on Wednesday, September 6, 1848* (Rochester, N.Y.: printed by John Dick, at the North Star Office, 1848), 19, reprinted in *Minutes of the Proceedings of the National Negro Conventions, 1830–1864*, ed. Howard Holman Bell (New York: Arno Press, 1969). This somewhat lengthy citation is necessary because the Arno Press edition lacks a cumulative pagination, so the page numbers refer to those printed in the original proceedings. (Hereafter Bell, *Negro Conventions*, year, page.)

3. Philip S. Foner and George E. Walker, eds., *Proceedings of the Black State Conventions, 1840–1865* (Philadelphia: Temple University Press, 1979), vol. 1, 277.

4. Bell, *Negro Conventions*, 1843, 32.

5. George M. Fredrickson, *Black Image in the White Mind: The Debate on Afro-American Character and Destiny, 1817–1914* (New York: Harper Torchbooks, 1972), 2.

6. William H. Pease, "Antislavery Ambivalence: Immediatism, Expediency, Race," *American Quarterly* 17 (Winter 1965): 682–95.

7. Some confusion exists over the date of the riot. Richard Wade writes that it occurred on August 22, but he cites as his source a newspaper article published on August 19. Wade, "The Negro in Cincinnati, 1800–1830," *Journal of Negro History* 39 (Jan. 1954): 55 n. 60; Frank U. Quillin, *The Color Line in Ohio: A History of Prejudice in a Typical Northern State* (1913; reprint, New York: Negro Universities Press, 1969), 22, 32; Carter G. Woodson, "The Negroes of Cincinnati Prior to the Civil War," *Journal of Negro History* 1 (Jan. 1916): 6–7.

8. Cincinnati Colonization Society quoted in Wade, "The Negro in Cincinnati," 54; *African Repository* 6 (Mar. 1830), 12; Henry Clay quoted in Fredrickson, *Black Image in the White Mind*, 15, 16–19. On racial discrimination in the North, see Leon F. Litwack, *The Negro in the Free States, 1790–1860* (Chicago: University of Chicago Press, 1961). Excerpts from articles in the *African Repository* and the speeches of Colonization Society leaders quoted in Lawrence J. Friedman, *Inventors of the Promised Land* (New York: Knopf, 1975), 209.

9. *Cincinnati Daily Gazette*, July 24, 1829, quoted in Wade, "The Negro in Cincinnati," 50.

10. *Cincinnati Daily Gazette*, July 24, 1829, Aug. 17, 1829, quoted in Wade, "The Negro in Cincinnati," 47, 50, 55, n. 60. The barbershops were located in New York City and Pittsburgh. Paul Gilje, *Road to Mobocracy: Popular Disorder in New York City, 1763–1834* (Chapel Hill: University of North Carolina Press, 1988), 153–58, 166; Emma

Jones Lapsansky, "'Since They Got Those Separate Churches': Afro-Americans and Racism in Jacksonian Philadelphia," *American Quarterly* 32 (Spring 1980): 64; Julie Winch, *Philadelphia's Black Elite: Activism, Accommodation, and the Struggle for Autonomy, 1787–1848* (Philadelphia: Temple University Press, 1988), 148–51; Dorothy Sterling, *The Making of an Afro-American: Martin Robinson Delany, 1812–1855* (Garden City, N.J.: Doubleday, 1971), 44.

11. *Cincinnati Daily Gazette*, Aug. 17, 1829, quoted in Wade, "The Negro in Cincinnati," 56–57; Lapsansky, "Since They Got Those Churches,"64–67; Eric Lott, *Love and Theft: Blackface Minstrelsy and the American Working Class* (New York: Oxford University Press, 1993), 131–35.

12. Bell, *Negro Conventions*, 1831, iv, 8.

13. Howard H. Bell, "The American Moral Reform Society, 1836–1841," *Journal of Negro Education* 27 (Winter 1958): 34–40; Bell, *Negro Conventions*, 1835, 31–32. *Constitution of the American Society of Free Persons of Color . . . Also Proceedings of the Convention . . .* 1831, reprinted in Bell, *Negro Conventions*, 1831, iv, 8–9; Winch, *Philadelphia's Black Elite*, 94. For biographical sketches of Burr, Butler, Cassey, Hinton, Niger, and White, and also James Barbadoes, mentioned later, see Peter C. Ripley, ed., *The Black Abolitionist Papers* (Chapel Hill: University of North Carolina Press, 1985), vol. 3, 89, 153, 195, 197, 306.

14. Bell, *Negro Conventions*, 1831, 4, 14.

15. Patrick Rael, *Black Identity and Black Protest in the Antebellum North* (Chapel Hill: University of North Carolina Press, 2002), 38–41.

16. Bell, *Negro Conventions*, 1831, 4; Floyd L. Miller, "'The Father of Black Nationalism': Another Contender," *Civil War History* 17 (Dec. 1971): 311; Lewis Woodson, published under the pseudonym Augustine, *Colored American*, Aug. 12, 1837; Rael, *Black Identity and Black Protest*, 197–203; Frederick Cooper, "Elevating the Race: The Social Thought of Black Leaders, 1827–1850," *American Quarterly* 24 (Dec. 1972): 621–22.

17. Miller, "Father of Black Nationalism," 310–12; Cyril E. Griffith, *The African Dream: Martin R. Delany and the Emergence of Pan-African Thought* (University Park: Pennsylvania State University Press, 1975), 2–3; Sterling, *Martin Robinson Delany*, 39, 43–44.

18. Lewis Woodson, *Liberator*, Jan. 12, 1833 and *National Inquirer*, Aug. 3, 1837.

19. Petition to the Honorable the Delegates of the People of Pennsylvania . . . *National Enquirer*, Mar. 1, 1838. For a biographical sketch of Frederick Hinton, see Ripley, *Black Abolitionist Papers*, vol. 3, 197.

20. *Colored American*, Dec. 2, 1837; Ripley, *Black Abolitionist Papers*.

21. Quoted in Floyd J. Miller, *The Search for Black Nationality: Black Emigration and Colonization, 1787–1863* (Urbana: University of Illinois Press, 1975), 98: Miller, "Father of Black Nationalism," 310–19. Frederick Hinton, also southern-born and a leader in the American Moral Reform Society, offered similar arguments. Hinton responded to William Whipper's proposal that the society cease acting as a race organization by arguing that the only viable option was to focus on self-improvement within the African American community because "the degree of respectability that

we enjoy has been wrested from the hands of oppressors." Fredrick Hinton to Samuel Cornish, Aug. 21, 1837, published in the *Colored American*, Sept. 7, 1837; Ripley, *Black Abolitionist Papers*, vol. 3, 197.

22. David Walker, *Appeal to the Colored Citizens of the World*, ed. Herbert Aptheker (New York: Humanities Press, 1965), 16, 29. According to Peter Hinks, Walker "had no time for quibbling over the viability of some marginalized niche an individual may have carved out for himself within the structure of exploitation." Hinks also noted that "questioning the man's character" probably alienated such individuals from listening to Walker's message. Peter P. Hinks, *To Awaken My Brethren: David Walker and the Problem of Antebellum Slave Resistance* (University Park: Pennsylvania State University Press, 1997), 252–53.

23. Anthony Rotundo has described this mid-nineteenth-century conception of masculinity as "self-made manhood" in his *American Manhood: Transformations in Masculinity from the Revolution to the Modern Era* (New York: Basic Books, 1993). George Fredrickson concluded that both white elected officials and the managers of black moral reform institutions were implying that free black men had fallen short of this ideal of manhood when they referred to African Americans as degraded, *Black Image in the White Mind*, 5. *Constitution of the American Society of Free Persons of Color, For Improving Their Condition in the United States . . .* , reprinted in Bell, *Negro Conventions*, 9, 11.

24. Stuart Blumin, *The Emergence of the Middle Class: Social Experience in the American City, 1790–1900* (New York: Cambridge University Press, 1989), 83–137.

25. Patrick Rael developed this estimate of the size of the black elite from 1850 and 1860 manuscript censuses in his *Black Identity and Black Protest*, 39; Hinks, *To Awaken My Brethren*, 67, 84; *Philadelphia Evening Bulletin*, Sept. 26, 1882.

26. Ira Berlin, *Slaves Without Masters: The Free Negro in the Antebellum South* (New York: Vintage Books, 1976), 190–91, 332–36; Barbara Jeanne Fields, *Slavery and Freedom on the Middle Ground: Maryland during the Nineteenth Century* (New Haven: Yale University Press, 1985), 36–37, 45–47; *Proceedings and Debates of the Constitutional Convention of 1835* (Raleigh, N.C., 1835), 67, quoted in John Hope Franklin, *The Free Negro in North Carolina, 1790–1860* (1943; reprint, New York: W. W. Norton, 1971), 111, 202–4.

27. Fredrickson, *Black Image in the White Mind*, 58–59; Berlin, *Slaves Without Masters*, 194–96; William Johnson, *William Johnson's Natchez: The Ante-Bellum Diary of a Free Negro*, ed. William Ransom Hogan and Edwin Adams Davis (1951; reprint, Port Washington, N.Y.: Kennikat Press, 1968), vol 1, 41, 53, 63; Harriet E. Amos, *Cotton City: Urban Development in Antebellum Mobile* (Tuscaloosa: University of Alabama Press, 1985), 100–101.

28. Michael Myers, ed., *Frederick Douglass: The Narrative and Selected Writings* (New York: Modern Library, 1984), 350; 1850 U.S. Census, manuscript census returns for New York City and the *New York State Census of 1855*, cited in Robert Ernst, "The Economic Status of New York City Negroes, 1850–1863," *Negro History Bulletin* 12 (Mar. 1949): 139, 143; James Oliver Horton and Lois E. Horton, *Black Bostonians: Family Life and Community Struggle in the Antebellum North* (New York: Holmes &

Meier, 1979), 78; Charles H. Wesley, *Negro Labor in the United States, 1850–1925* (1927; reprint, New York: Russell & Russell, 1967), 48.

29. 1860 U.S. Census, manuscript census returns for Richmond, cited in Berlin, *Slaves Without Masters*, 237; Richard C. Wade, *Slavery in the Cities: The South, 1820–1860* (New York: Oxford University Press, 1964), 18, 326. Both the high level of skill required for rice production and the prevalence of slave ownership among white (and black) artisans contributed to the tradition of employing African American artisans in Charleston. Ira Berlin and Herbert G. Gutman, "Natives and Immigrants, Free Men and Slaves: Urban Workingmen in the Antebellum American South," *American Historical Review* 88 (Dec. 1983), 1185.

30. Ira Berlin calculated the proportion of skilled workers that were free African Americans in 1860 from the manuscript census returns. After butchers, of whom 41% were free black men, the next highest concentration of free black tradesmen were tailors (38%) and carpenters (27%). Berlin found twenty free black men working as barbers in Charleston in 1860. Berlin, *Slaves Without Masters*, 237. Larry Koger found that seven out of Charleston's twenty-three free black barbers (26%) owned nineteen slaves among them in 1850. Larry Koger, *Black Slaveowners: Free Black Slave Masters in South Carolina, 1790–1860* (Jefferson, N.C.: McFarland, 1985), 153.

31. Determining whether barbers recorded in the census of 1850 appear also in the census of 1860 gauges their persistence in the trade. I made this determination using the manuscript returns of 1850 and 1860 for Baltimore and Philadelphia with the aid of the Statistical Package for the Social Sciences software.

32. Johnson, *Diary of a Free Negro*, vol. 1, 339.

33. James Thomas, *From Tennessee Slave to St. Louis Entrepreneur: The Autobiography of James Thomas*, ed. Loren Schweninger (Columbia: University of Missouri Press, 1984), 85–86. Antebellum Americans referred to Germans as "Dutchmen," which was how census takers often identified them.

34. John W. Woods, *Woods' Baltimore City Directory* (Baltimore: John W. Woods, 1860).

35. Loren Schweninger, *Black Property Owners in the South, 1790–1915* (Urbana: University of Illinois Press, 1990), 124; Cyprian Clamorgan, *The Colored Aristocracy of St. Louis by Cyprian Clamorgan*, ed. Julie Winch (Columbia: University of Missouri Press, 1999), 52; John H. Russell, *The Free Negro in Virginia, 1619–1865* (Baltimore: Johns Hopkins Press, 1913), 151; Luther Porter Jackson, *Free Negro Labor and Property Holding in Virginia, 1830–1860* (Chapel Hill: University of North Carolina Press, 1942), 98.

36. Schweninger, *Black Property Owners*, 71–72, 82, 124. In Mobile, Daniel Sterling and Joseph Sunter, both from Scotland, respectively owned $1,500 and $900 worth of real estate. Mobile, Ala., U.S. Census, 1860, roll 471, p. 733. The author confirmed the lack of property ownership among Mobile barbers through an examination of municipal tax lists and probate court records.

37. Computed from the manuscript returns of 1860 for Baltimore and Philadelphia with the aid of the Statistical Package for the Social Sciences software.

38. The ledgers of the almshouse have no page numbers; entries for patients are organized by the first letter of their surname. "Penn, Charles," admitted Feb. 13, 1849,

and "Peter, John," admitted Jan. 23, 1849, *Register of Males*, Almshouse, Guardians of the Poor, Record Group 35, Series 113, Reel 956466, City Archives, Philadelphia, Pa. (hereafter Philadelphia Almshouse). The ledgers of the county prison have a similar organization. "Russell, Barney," incarcerated June 14, 1827, County Prison, *Convict Description Docket, 1826–1830*, Philadelphia County, Pennsylvania, Record Group 38, Series 41, Reel 974090, City Archives, Philadelphia, Pa. (hereafter Philadelphia County Prison).

39. W. Jeffrey Bolster, *Black Jacks: African American Seamen in the Age of Sail* (Cambridge: Harvard University Press, 1997), 92–93 (quote on 93), 236. The prison clerks actually drew copies of tattoo designs. "Russell, Barney," incarcerated June 14, 1827, Philadelphia County Prison; "Brown, David," admitted Sept. 11, 1848, Philadelphia Almshouse.

40. John Hope Franklin and Loren Schweninger, *In Search of the Promised Land: A Slave Family in the Old South* (New York: Oxford University Press, 2006), 95–99. Jim Bearden and Linda Jean Butler, *Shadd: The Life and Times of Mary Shadd Cary* (Toronto: NC Press, 1977), 186. Thomas, *Autobiography*, 78–79.

41. John H. Rapier, Sr., to John H. Rapier, Jr., Feb. 14, 1859, and Mar. 17, 1857, Rapier Family Papers; Loren Schweninger, *James T. Rapier and Reconstruction* (Chicago: University of Chicago Press, 1978), 18, 20–22, 44–45, 106–7.

42. Thomas, *Autobiography*, 8–10, 150–53, 134–35, 139 n. 24; James P. Thomas to John H. Rapier, Jr., Oct. 30, 1856, Rapier Family Papers.

43. Thomas, *Autobiography*, 8–10, 150–53.

44. Thomas, *Autobiography*, 134, 139, 142; Feb. 12 and 27, 1857, Diary of John Rapier, Jr., 61, 66–67, Rapier Family Papers.

45. Leon Litwack, *North of Slavery: The Negro in the Free States, 1790–1860* (Chicago: University of Chicago Press, 1961), 100–103; Leslie Maria Harris, "Creating the African American Working Class: Black and White Workers, Abolitionists, and Reformers in New York City, 1785–1863" (Ph.D. diss., Stanford University, 1995), 171–72, 201–2, 204; Leslie M. Harris, *In the Shadow of Slavery: African Americans in New York City, 1626–1863* (Chicago: University of Chicago Press, 2003), ch. 7; Rael, *Black Identity and Black Protest*, 35–36, 191–93. The ferocity of Douglass's criticism of barbers seemed to go beyond matters of principle and merge into personal vendetta. Perhaps Douglass smarted from the jibes of Charles Redmond, a black barber and antislavery lecturer, about his slave origins. In an 1852 article in his newspaper, Douglass pointed out that Redmond repeatedly made such remarks: "In contrasting his position with that of Frederick Douglass, Redmond (for the hundredth time), 'thanked God that he, though a colored man, had never been a slave, nor was he the son of a slave.' He then contemplated a devastating counter-attack, asking, what would be thought of Frederick Douglass, if he should come before a public meeting (in which Mr. Redmond was taking part), and say, 'Mr. Chairman, I thank God, I am not a barber, nor the son of a barber.'" He concluded by saying that such remarks would be seen as an ad hominem attack. *Frederick Douglass' Paper*, May 20, 1852.

46. "Make Your Sons Mechanics and Farmers—Not Waiters, Porters, and Barbers," *Frederick Douglass' Paper*, Mar. 18, 1853.

47. Ibid. Douglass had already raised the issue twice before that month on March 4 and 11.

48. Delany quoted at 1848 convention in Rael, *Black Identity and Black Protest*, 35; Martin Delany, *The Condition, Elevation, Emigration, and Destiny of the Colored People of the United States* (1852; reprint, New York: Arno Press, 1968), 43; Harris, *In the Shadow of Slavery*, 234.

49. Henry Bradshaw Fearon, *Sketches of America: A Narrative of a Journey of Five Thousand Miles Through the Eastern and Western States* (1818; reprint, New York: Benjamin Blom, Inc., 1969), 58–60; Resolution of the 1852 Ohio Convention quoted in Litwack, *North of Slavery*, 181.

50. *Frederick Douglass' Paper*, Apr. 22, 1853; Ripley, *Black Abolitionist Papers*, vol. 3, 279–80.

51. *Frederick Douglass' Paper*, Apr. 22, 1853.

52. *Pennsylvania Freeman*, June 27, 1850; *Frederick Douglass' Paper*, Oct. 28, 1853; Report on the American League of Colored Voters, *Anti-Slavery Bugle*, July 27, 1856.

CHAPTER 5: DEFINING THE MEANING OF FREEDOM

1. James Thomas, *From Tennessee Slave to St. Louis Entrepreneur: The Autobiography of James Thomas*, ed. Loren Schweninger (Columbia: University of Missouri Press, 1984), 154, 155, 159.

2. For example, Eric Foner has noted that, during Reconstruction, the politics of the black middle class remained largely disconnected from the radicalism of freedmen in the countryside. He regarded the former's conciliatory attitude toward white Southerners and emphasis on self-improvement as a "secondary theme in black thought." Eric Foner, *Reconstruction: America's Unfinished Revolution, 1863–1877* (New York: Harper & Row, 1988), 100–102, 112–17, 546–47, quote on p. 546.

3. Thomas, *Autobiography*, 156–59, quotes on 156, 159.

4. Ibid., 157, 159.

5. John Rapier, Jr., to James Thomas, Oct. 17, 1861, Rapier-Thomas Papers, Moorland-Spingarn Research Center, Howard University, Washington, D.C. (hereafter Rapier Family Papers); Thomas, *Autobiography*, 164.

6. Cyprian Clamorgan, *The Colored Aristocracy of St. Louis by Cyprian Clamorgan*, ed. Julie Winch (Columbia: University of Missouri Press, 1999), 45–47.

7. Ibid., 47, 51, 52, 59.

8. Thomas, *Autobiography*, 158, 166–67, 178.

9. Clamorgan, *Colored Aristocracy*, 33; Thomas, *Autobiography*, 167–68.

10. Thomas, *Autobiography*, 169, 173.

11. Ibid., 173, 178.

12. James Oliver Horton and Lois E. Horton, *Black Bostonians: Family Life and Community Struggle in the Antebellum North* (New York: Holmes & Meier, 1979), 32–33, 36–37, 142 n. 48; Thomas Holt, *Black over White: Negro Political Leadership in South Carolina during Reconstruction*. (Urbana: University of Illinois Press, 1977), 11

n. 7, 21–22, 130; Maurine Christopher, *America's Black Congressmen* (New York: Thomas Y. Crowell, 1971), 98–99.

13. Christopher, *America's Black Congressmen*, 25–26; Holt, *Black over White*, 78.

14. Holt, *Black over White*, 17, 59–60.

15. Holt, *Black over White*, 229–41; David C. Rankin, "The Origins of Negro Leadership in New Orleans during Reconstruction," and Michael B. Chesson, "Richmond's Black Councilmen, 1871–96," both in *Southern Black Leaders of the Reconstruction Era*, ed. Howard N. Rabinowitz (Urbana: University of Illinois Press, 1982), 181–89, 198–99. The exceptional situation of South Carolina and Louisiana can be appreciated through comparison to Georgia. See Edmund L. Drago, *Black Politicians and Reconstruction in Georgia: A Splendid Failure* (Baton Rouge: Louisiana State University Press, 1982), 37–40. Eric Foner notes that a disproportionate number of local black leaders had artisan backgrounds; Foner, "Black Reconstruction Leaders at the Grass Roots," in *Black Leaders of the Nineteenth Century*, ed. Leon Litwack and August Meier (Urbana: University of Illinois Press, 1988).

16. *Athens Post*, June 16, 1866, quoted in Peter Kolchin, *First Freedom: The Responses of Alabama's Blacks to Emancipation and Reconstruction* (Westport, Conn.: Greenwood Press, 1972), 154; Sept. 23, 1869, quoted in Loren Schweninger, *James T. Rapier and Reconstruction* (Chicago: University of Chicago Press, 1978), 20, 44–45; *Nashville Union and American-Conservative*, Dec. 6, 1872, quoted in Alrutheus Taylor, *The Negro in Tennessee, 1865–1880* (Washington, D.C.: Associated Publishers, 1941), 160, 247–48, 250. Southern black barbers in politics who are not discussed in this chapter include Isham Sweat, a delegate to the North Carolina Colored Convention and a member of the state legislature; Hanson Hughes, another state legislator in North Carolina; Joseph Clouston, a city councilman in Memphis; Moses Bentley, the chair of the Republican County Committee in Atlanta; and Christopher Burke, deputy sheriff of Charleston. Foner, *Reconstruction*, 114; Robert C. Kenzer, *Enterprising Southerners: Black Economic Success in North Carolina, 1865–1915* (Charlottesville: University Press of Virginia, 1989), 90; Howard N. Rabinowitz, *Race Relations in the Urban South, 1865–1890* (New York: Oxford University Press, 1978), 89; Bernard E. Powers, Jr., *Black Charlestonians: A Social History, 1822–1885* (Fayetteville: University of Arkansas Press, 1994), 116.

17. Charles W. Chesnutt, "The March of Progress," *Century Magazine* 61 (Jan. 1901): 422–25, quote on 424.

18. Ibid., 424–25.

19. Harry C. Silcox, "Nineteenth-Century Philadelphia Black Militant: Octavius V. Catto," *Pennsylvania History* 44 (Jan. 1977): 72–73; and Silcox, "The Black 'Better Class' Political Dilemma: Philadelphia Prototype Isaiah C. Wears," *Pennsylvania Magazine of History and Biography* 113 (Jan. 1989): 50–51.

20. Peter C. Ripley, ed., *The Black Abolitionist Papers* (Chapel Hill: University of North Carolina Press, 1985), vol. 4, 318–19; Silcox, "Black 'Better Class' Political Dilemma," 46–47; George Freeman Bragg, Jr., "Isaiah C. Wears, Logician and Orator," in George F. Bragg, *Men of Maryland* (Baltimore: Church Advocate Press, 1914),

132–33. On the members of the Gilbert Lyceum, one of Wears's clubs, which included other black barbers, see Joseph Wilson, *Sketches of the Higher Classes of Colored Society in Philadelphia. By a Southerner* (Philadelphia: Merrihew & Thompson, 1841), 109–10; Isaiah Wears to the American Negro Historical Society, "In Memory of Robert Purvis," no date; and M. B. Lowry to Isaiah Wears, Mar. 12, 1869, Leon C. Gardiner Collection, box 9G, Department of Manuscripts, Historical Society of Pennsylvania, Philadelphia (hereafter Gardiner MSS).

21. Silcox, "The Black 'Better Class' Political Dilemma," 47–49; William Still, *Brief Narrative of the Streetcar Struggle,* 4–5, 10–11, pamphlet, Historical Society of Pennsylvania, Philadelphia; Philip S. Foner and George E. Walker, eds., *Proceedings of the Black National and State Conventions, 1865–1900* (Philadelphia: Temple University Press, 1986), vol. 1, 381–85, quotes on 385. Other black barbers whose activism changed focus include John Richards and George Baptiste of Detroit. In a gesture symbolic of the end of one era and the beginning of another, Baptiste posted the following sign on the front of his barbershop during the celebration for the ratification of the Fifteenth Amendment: "Notice to Stockholders, Office of the Underground Railway. This office is permanently closed. Hereafter stockholders will receive dividends according to their desserts." David M. Katzman, *Before the Ghetto: Black Detroit in the Nineteenth Century* (Urbana: University of Illinois Press, 1973), 3–4, 49–50, 85, 176–78, 180–81, 187.

22. George Myers to Charles Dick, Feb. 4, 1902, George A. Myers Collection, Ohio Historical Society, Columbus Ohio (hereafter Myers MSS); Ripley, *Black Abolitionist Papers*, vol. 4, 319; Katzman, *Before the Ghetto*, 178, 180; Kenneth L. Kusmer, *A Ghetto Takes Shape: Black Cleveland, 1870–1930* (Urbana: University of Illinois Press, 1976), 144.

23. Katzman, *Before the Ghetto,* 176, 194–95; Roger Lane, *Roots of Violence in Black Philadelphia, 1860–1900* (Cambridge: Harvard University Press, 1986), 116.

24. *Philadelphia Evening Bulletin,* Oct. 2, 1882; Silcox, "The Black 'Better Class' Political Dilemma," 58–62, 64 (quote from the *Philadelphia Press,* Nov. 15, 1881, on 60); James Mitchell to Isaiah Wears, no date, G. W. Gardiner to Isaiah Wears, Apr. 30, 1891, Charles Warwood to Isaiah Wears, Dec. 7, 1897, Gardiner MSS.

25. Bettye C. Thomas, "A Nineteenth Century Black Operated Shipyard, 1866–1884: Reflections on Its Inception and Ownership," *Journal of Negro History* 59 (Jan. 1974): 1–12.

26. George A. Myers and James Ford Rhodes, *The Barber and the Historian: The Correspondence of George A. Myers and James Ford Rhodes, 1910–1923,* ed. John A. Garraty (Columbus: Ohio Historical Society, 1956), xii, xv–xix, quotes are from Myers to Rhodes, Mar. 8, 1908, p. 101, and Myers to Rhodes, Feb. 16, 1923, 146; David A. Gerber, *Black Ohio and the Color Line, 1860–1915* (Urbana: University of Illinois Press, 1976), 345–60.

27. Silcox, "The Black 'Better Class' Dilemma," 64; Kusmer, *A Ghetto Takes Shape,* 57, 77, 122 (article from the *Cleveland Advocate,* June 15, 1918, quoted on 125); Gerber, *Black Ohio and the Color Line,* 54–55.

28. Kusmer, *A Ghetto Takes Shape*, 57, 76, 98, 126; George Myers to James Ford Rhodes, May 29, 1913, and Jan. 8, 1918, James Ford Rhodes to George Myers, Apr. 30, 1914, and Jan. 16, 1918, in Myers and Rhodes, *Correspondence*, 21, 30, 74–79.

29. Wears, "In Memory of Robert Purvis," 23 and 25.

30. Philadelphia *City Directory for 1874*. Articles of Agreement for Sale of Lands, Wears papers in the Gardiner MSS; Quintard Taylor, *In Search of the Racial Frontier: African Americans in the American West, 1528–1990* (New York: W. W. Norton, 1998), 202–3; Gerber, *Black Ohio and the Color Line*, 88–89; Katzman, *Before the Ghetto*, 131–32; Kusmer, *A Ghetto Takes Shape*, 145–46; Douglas Henry Daniels, *Pioneer Urbanites: A Social and Cultural History of Black San Francisco* (Philadelphia: Temple University Press, 1980), 74; Willard B. Gatewood, *Aristocrats of Color: The Black Elite, 1880–1920* (Bloomington: Indiana University Press, 1990), 191, 265. Still is quoted in Elizabeth Hafkin Pleck, *Black Migration and Poverty: Boston, 1865–1900* (New York: Academic Press, 1979), 98.

31. Foner and Walker, *Black National and State Conventions*, vol. 1, 49; *New York Times*, Aug. 6, 1865, quoting the *Petersburg Daily Index*, quoted in Leon E. Litwack, *Been in the Storm So Long: The Aftermath of Slavery* (New York: Alfred A. Knopf, 1979), 322: Rabinowitz, *Race Relations in the Urban South*, 85; John W. Blassingame, "Before the Ghetto: The Making of the Black Community in Savannah, Georgia, 1865–1880," *Journal of Social History* 6 (Summer 1973); 465–67; John W. Blassingame *Black New Orleans, 1860–1880* (Chicago: University of Chicago, 1973), 229–33; Powers, *Black Charlestonians*, 270–76; Pleck, *Black Migration and Poverty*, 145–46; Katzman, *Before the Ghetto*, 116; Kusmer, *A Ghetto Takes Shape*, 76; Taylor, *In Search of the Racial Frontier*, 203; Quintard Taylor, *The Forging of a Black Community: Seattle's Central District from 1870 through the Civil Rights Era* (Seattle: University of Washington Press, 1994), 28.

32. For descriptions of consumerism in the Gilded Age, see *The Gilded Age: A Tale of To-Day*, by Mark Twain and Charles Dudley Warner (1873; reprint, New York: Oxford University Press, 1996). Thorstein Veblen, *The Theory of the Leisure Classes: An Economic Study in the Evolution of Institutions* (New York: Macmillan, 1899); Jackson Lears, "Beyond Veblen: Rethinking Consuming Culture in America," in *Consuming Visions: Accumulation and the Display of Goods in America, 1880–1920*, ed. Simon J. Bronner (New York: W. W. Norton, 1989); William Leach, *Land of Desire: Merchants, Power, and the Rise of a New American Culture* (New York: Pantheon Books, 1993).

33. John Dittmer, *Black Georgia in the Progressive Era, 1900–1920* (Urbana: University of Illinois Press, 1977), 38; Myers and Rhodes, *Correspondence*, xvi–xvii.

34. Kusmer, *A Ghetto Takes Shape*, 76; Gerber, *Black Ohio and the Color Line*, 308; W. E. B. DuBois, *The Negro in Business; Report of a Social Study Made under the Direction of Atlanta University Together with the Proceedings of the Fourth Conference for the Study of Negro Problems, Held at Atlanta University, May 30–31, 1899* (reprint, New York: Arno Press, 1968), 37; Rabinowitz, *Race Relations in the Urban South*, 86; Taylor, *Forging a Black Community*, 28–30; George C. Wright, *Life Behind*

a Veil: Blacks in Louisville, Kentucky, 1865–1930 (Baton Rouge: Louisiana State University Press, 1985), 82, 94.

35. Frenise A. Logan, "Economic Status of the Town Negro in Post-Reconstruction North Carolina," *North Carolina Historical Review* 35 (Oct. 1958), 457; DuBois, *The Negro in Business*, 6–9, 16, 37–38.

36. Clamorgan, *Colored Aristocracy*, 53, 81; William Johnson, *William Johnson's Natchez: The Antebellum Diary of a Free Negro*, ed. William Ransom Hogan and Edwin Adams Davis (1951; reprint, Port Washington, N.Y.: Kennikat Press, 1968), 24–25; DuBois, *The Negro in Business*, 9.

37. Katzman, *Before the Ghetto*, 115–16; Roger Lane, *William Dorsey's Philadelphia and Ours: On the Past and Future of the Black City in America* (New York: Oxford University Press, 1991), 116; W. E. B. DuBois, *The Philadelphia Negro: A Social Study* (1899; reprint, Schocken Books, 1967), 133.

38. *Nashville Republican Banner*, Oct. 18, 1871, and *Atlanta Constitution*, Dec. 18, 1887, quoted in Rabinowitz, *Race Relations in the Urban South*, 86; *Philadelphia Evening Bulletin*, Sept. 26, 1882; Loren Schweninger, *Black Property Owners in the South, 1790–1915* (Urbana: University of Illinois Press, 1990), 156, 217, 299–300; Thomas, *Autobiography*, 12–13.

39. *St. Paul and Minneapolis Pioneer Press*, Jan. 20, 1884, 8; Wendell P. Dabney, *Cincinnati's Colored Citizens: Historical, Sociological, and Biographical* (1926; reprint, New York: Negro Universities Press, 1970), 184; Taylor, *In Search of the Racial Frontier*, 205; George Brown Tindall, *South Carolina Negroes, 1877–1900* (Baton Rouge: Louisiana State University Press, 1966), 129; DuBois, *The Philadelphia Negro*, 227; Gerber, *Black Ohio and the Color Line*, 176, 308.

40. Rabinowitz, *Race Relations in the Urban South*, 86, 229; Scott W. Hall, *The Journeyman Barber's International Union of America* (Baltimore: Johns Hopkins Press, 1936), 13; Taylor, *The Negro in Tennessee*, 147.

41. Taylor, *In Search of the Racial Frontier*, 205; Tindall, *South Carolina Negroes*, 129; DuBois, *The Philadelphia Negro*, 116.

42. Foner and Walker, *Black National and State Conventions*, vol. 1, 49; Gerber, *Black Ohio and the Color Line*, 81; Lane, *William Dorsey's Philadelphia*, 116; Nashville *Republican Banner*, June 17, 1874, quoted in Rabinowitz, *Race Relations in the Urban South*, 196. Katzman, *Before the Ghetto*, 98.

43. *Harper's Weekly*, Apr. 24, 1875, 336; Rabinowitz, *Race Relations in the Urban South*, 196; Taylor, *Forging of a Black Community*, 19, 29; Emma Lou Thornbrough, *The Negro in Indiana before 1900: A Study of a Minority* (1957; reprint, Bloomington: Indiana University Press, 1993), 264.

44. John Daniels, *In Freedom's Birthplace* (1914; reprint, New York: Arno Press, 1969), 95–96; Constance McLaughlin Green, *The Secret City: The History of Race Relations in the Nation's Capitol* (Princeton: Princeton University Press, 1967), 94, 109; Katzman, *Before the Ghetto*, 97–98.

45. *Washington Bee*, July 21, 1888, quoted in Green, *Secret City*, 125, see also pp. 109 and 166; Taylor, *Forging a Black Community*, 29.

46. For examples, see: *Indianapolis Freeman*, July 20, 1901, and Aug. 10, 1907, *New York Freeman*, Sept. 12, 1885, cited in Wright, *Life Behind a Veil*, 94; *People's Advocate*, July 5, 1879, Nov. 15 and 29, 1879, July 10, 1880, Aug. 6, 1881, cited in Green, *Secret City*, 122, 125–26.

47. Leslie Harris emphasizes the importance of considering the consistent underemployment of New York City's black elite when analyzing antebellum black reform. See Harris, *In the Shadow of Slavery: African Americans in New York City, 1626–1863* (Chicago: University of Chicago Press, 2003), 119–21.

48. Richard B. Sherman, *The Republican Party and Black America: From McKinley to Hoover, 1896–1933* (Charlottesville: University Press of Virginia, 1973), 7–8, 11–12, 21; Lane, *Roots of Violence*, passim; Silcox, "The Black 'Better Class' Dilemma," 53–64.

49. *Cleveland Advocate*, June 15, 1918, quoted in Kusmer, *A Ghetto Takes Shape*, 124; Gerber, *Black Ohio and the Color Line*, 454–57.

50. Kevin K. Gaines, *Uplifting the Race: Black Leadership, Politics, and Culture in the Twentieth Century* (Chapel Hill: University of North Carolina Press, 1996); George Myers to Booker T. Washington, July 20, 1914, quoted in Kusmer, *A Ghetto Takes Shape*, 124, 126; Gerber, *Black Ohio and the Color Line*, 456–57, 419; George Myers to James Ford Rhodes, Jan. 8, 1918, Myers and Rhodes, *Correspondence*, xxii–xxiii, 78.

CHAPTER 6: FROM BARBERSHOPS TO BOARDROOMS

1. W. E. B. DuBois, *Economic Cooperation among Negro Americans*, Atlanta University Publications, no. 12 (Atlanta, Ga.: Atlanta University Press, 1907), 10–11.

2. E. Franklin Frazier, "Durham: Capital of the Black Middle Class," in *The New Negro: An Interpretation*, ed. Alain Locke (New York: Albert & Charles Boni, 1925), 333–35, 338–40 (quotes on 333 and 340).

3. Scott W. Hall, *The Journeyman Barber's International Union of America* (Baltimore: Johns Hopkins Press, 1936), 13, 16, 44; *Journeyman Barber*, Sept. 1909, 352–56.

4. *Journeyman Barber*, Feb. 1902, 34; Mar. 1903, 57; Sept. 1909, 354–55; Quintard Taylor, *The Forging of a Black Community: Seattle's Central District from 1870 through the Civil Rights Era* (Seattle: University of Washington Press, 1994), 27; Lester C. Lamon, *Black Tennesseans, 1900–1930* (Knoxville: University of Tennessee Press, 1977), 141.

5. William H. Harris, *The Harder We Run: Black Workers since the Civil War* (New York: Oxford University Press, 1982), 40–50; W. E. Klapetzky to Samuel Gompers, Dec. 29, 1902, Frank Noschang to Samuel Gompers, July 25, 1902, Charles T. Williams to Dennison Labor Trades Council, July 22, 1902, W. E. Klapetzky to Frank Morrison, Nov. 4, 1901, all in Peter Albert, ed., *American Federation of Labor Records: The Samuel Gompers Era* (Microfilming Corporation of America, 1979) (hereafter *AFL Records*); David M. Katzman, *Before the Ghetto: Black Detroit in the Nineteenth Century* (Urbana: University of Illinois Press, 1973), 125; Hall, *Journeyman Barber's International Union*, 43–44; David A. Gerber, *Black Ohio and the Color Line, 1860–1915* (Urbana: University of Illinois Press, 1976), 72.

6. *Journeyman Barber*, Mar. 1902, 53–54. There were 19,942 black barbers in the United States in 1900. U.S. Bureau of the Census, *Special Reports, Supplementary Analysis and Derivative Tables, 12th Census of the United States: 1900* (Washington, D.C., 1906), 234; Quintard Taylor, *In Search of the Racial Frontier: African Americans in the American West, 1528–1990* (New York: W. W. Norton, 1998), 205; George Myers to Charles Dick, Feb. 4, 1902, George A. Myers Collection, Ohio Historical Society, Columbus (hereafter Myers MSS).

7. Hall, *Journeyman Barber's International Union*, 79; *Journeyman Barber*, Feb. 1902, 33 and 37, June 1917, 194; Wendell P. Dabney, *Cincinnati's Colored Citizens: Historical, Sociological, and Biographical* (1926; reprint, New York: Negro Universities Press, 1970), 184–85.

8. House Bill 100, 75th General Assembly of Ohio, *Printed Bills*, Legislative Services, State Archives, Ohio Historical Society, Columbus, (hereafter *Printed Bills*); *Journeyman Barber*, Feb. 1902, 33; Mar. 1902, 56; J. H. Jones et al. to George Myers, Mar. 6, 1913, Myers MSS; *Barber's Journal*, June 1905, 120. The Journeyman Barber's International Union of America succeeded at influencing licensing in other states. For example, John Young, a JBIUA member who also served in the Kentucky House, received credit for getting a licensing bill passed through that chamber of the legislature, and he later served as one of the state's examiners. See *Journeyman Barber*, Feb. 1902, 33; Jacob Fischer to Frank Morrison, Dec. 18, 1909, *AFL Records*.

9. Gerber, *Black Ohio and the Color Line*, 82, 323–33, 341, 349; Kenneth L. Kusmer, *A Ghetto Takes Shape: Black Cleveland, 1870–1930* (Urbana: University of Illinois Press, 1976), 121, 144.

10. George Myers to H. M. Daugherty, Feb. 17, 1902, Myers to J. B. Foraker, Feb. 11, 1902, Myers MSS. Myers wrote dozens of letter to leading Republicans, including both Ohio senators and the governor.

11. Jere Brown to George Myers, Mar. 17, 1902, Ralph Tyler to George Myers, Feb. 7, 1902, George Hayes to George Myers, Jan. 30, Feb. 26, Mar. 4, 1902, Myers MSS; Columbus *Dispatch*, Feb. 5, 1902, 5.

12. Ralph Tyler to George Myers, Mar. 25, 1902, Mark Hanna to George Myers, Mar. 31, 1902, Myers MSS; *Journeyman Barber*, Feb. 1902, 33.

13. George Hayes to George Myers, Jan. 30, Apr. 1, 1902, Myers MSS; House Bill 160, 76th General Assembly of Ohio, 1904, *Printed Bills*; B. F. Stewart to George Myers, 23 Feb. 1904, Myers MSS.

14. House Bill 100, 76th General Assembly of Ohio, 1904, *Printed Bills*.

15. B. F. Stewart to George Myers, Feb. 23, 1904, Myers MSS. For a discussion of the speeches that Hayes and Eubanks delivered to the legislature, see Ralph Tyler to George Myers, Mar. 8, 1904, Myers MSS.

16. Ralph Tyler to George Myers, Mar. 8, 1904, J. H. Jones et al. to George Myers, Mar. 6, 1913, Fountain Lewis to George Myers, Feb. 18, 1904, Ralph Tyler to George Myers, Feb. 7, 1902, George Hayes to George Myers, Jan. 30, 1902, Myers MSS. Amended Senate Bill 29, "An act to create a state board of barber examiners and to regulate the business of barbering," Ohio, *Legislative Acts Passed by the 90th General Assembly of Ohio*, vol. 115 (Columbus, 1933).

17. Lamon, *Black Tennesseans*, 141; Jacob Fischer to Frank Morrison, Dec. 18, 1909, *AFL Records*; Earl Lewis, *In Their Own Interests: Race, Class, and Power in Twentieth-Century Norfolk, Virginia* (Berkeley: University of California Press, 1991), 154; George F. Rogers to George Myers, Mar. 21, 1913, Myers MSS. For examples of such photographs, see the Wilson Collection, Historic Mobile Preservation Society, Mobile, Ala.

18. Booker T. Washington, *The Negro in Business* (1907; reprint, Chicago: Afro-Am Press, 1969), 251–55.

19. *Eleventh Census of the United States, 1890, Population*, part 2, 354–55; *Fifteenth Census of the United States, 1930, Population*, part 4, 33; Elizabeth Hafkin Pleck, *Black Migration and Poverty: Boston, 1865–1900* (New York: Academic Press, 1979), 146.

20. Loren Schweninger, *Black Property Owners in the South, 1790–1915* (Urbana: University of Illinois Press, 1990), 166–67; Ira Berlin and Herbert G. Gutman, "Natives and Immigrants, Free Men and Slaves: Urban Workingmen in the Antebellum American South," *American Historical Review* 88 (Dec. 1983): 1181–87; Herbert G. Gutman, *The Black Family in Slavery and Freedom, 1750–1925* (New York: Vintage Books, 1976), 480–81; Bernard E. Powers, Jr., *Black Charlestonians: A Social History, 1822–1885* (Fayetteville: University of Arkansas Press, 1994), 270–76; W. E. B. DuBois, ed., *The Negro in Business; Report of a Social Study Made under the Direction of Atlanta University Together with the Proceedings of the Fourth Conference for the Study of Negro Problems, Held at Atlanta University, May 30–31, 1899* (reprint, New York: Arno Press, 1968), 30, 33–35, 37.

21. For a case study that examines the association of African Americans with tuberculosis, see Tera W. Hunter, *To 'Joy My Freedom: Southern Black Women's Lives and Labors after the Civil War* (Cambridge: Harvard University Press, 1997), chap. 9. Another book that examines how racial ideas defined issues of black health is Keith Wailoo, *Dying in the City of the Blues: Sickle Cell Anemia and the Politics of Race and Health* (Chapel Hill: University of North Carolina Press, 2001).

22. Joel Williamson, *A Rage for Order: Black-White Relations in the American South since Emancipation* (New York: Oxford University Press, 1986), 141–48.

23. Alexa Benson Henderson, *Atlanta Life Insurance Company: Guardian of Black Economic Dignity* (Tuscaloosa: University of Alabama Press, 1990), 17, 24, 29; Walter White, *A Man Called White* (New York: Viking Press, 1948), 9.

24. David E. Alsobrook, "Mobile's Forgotten Progressive: A. N. Johnson, Editor and Entrepreneur," *Alabama Review* 33 (July 1979), 193–99 (quote from C. F. Johnson to Booker T. Washington, Nov. 1, 1906, on 198). In a piece of bitter irony, a Mobile archivist informed me that the year Alsobrook published this article—1979—documenting the 1906 lynchings, a black man was lynched on the outskirts of the city.

25. James Hall (grandson of Edgar Harney), interview with the author, Mobile, Ala., Aug. 13 and 14, 1997; Henry Williams, Sr., interview with the author, Mobile, Ala., Aug. 13, 1997.

26. Paulette Davis-Horton, *Davis Avenue: The Place, the People, the Memories* (Mobile, Ala.: Horton, Inc., 1991), 115, 166. Although Davis-Horton's book lacks the traditional scholarly apparatus of citations, her research was meticulous. Davis-

Horton kindly introduced the author to several local archivists, who in turn attested to the extensive research she had done at their repositories. In addition, she conceived of the book while working as a nurse providing home-based health care to the elderly. Realizing that her patients were guardians of the history of her community, she conducted at least one hundred oral history interviews. Hall interview; Alsobrook, "Mobile's Forgotten Progressive," 200.

27. Hall interview.

28. Davis-Horton, *Davis Avenue*, 165–72, Jackson's ad reproduced on 166.

29. Hall interview; Williams interview.

30. Robert M. Andrews, *John Merrick: A Biographical Sketch* (Durham, N.C.: Seeman Printery, 1920), 31–35; Walter B. Weare, *Black Business in the New South: A Social History of the North Carolina Mutual Life Insurance Company* (Urbana: University of Illinois Press, 1973), 51.

31. Henderson, *Atlanta Life Insurance Company*, 21–22.

32. For his part, Herndon saw first hand the lack of financial resources in the African American community to support charitable works, for example, in his involvement with the First Congregational Church. He admired the church's innovative pastor, Reverend Henry Hugh, whose outreach programs included one of the city's first health centers for African Americans, a home for girls, a gymnasium for boys, an employment bureau, and a prison mission. As the church's treasurer, Herndon became closely involved in its ministries and repeatedly covered financial shortfalls with his own donations. He maintained a few programs with his personal funds when the church discontinued many of its programs in the 1920s. Henderson, *Atlanta Life Insurance Company*, 40–41; Andrews, *John Merrick*, 46–50.

33. Robert Watson Winston, *It's a Far Cry* (New York: Henry Holt, 1937), 249; Weare, *Black Business in the New South*, 14–15, 32–33, 43–45.

34. The historian of the North Carolina Mutual Life Insurance Company credits the 1898 campaign of violence and coercion with shaping Merrick's decision to establish the company. Weare, *Black Business in the New South*, 20–22, quote on 23; Edward L. Ayers, *The Promise of the New South: Life after Reconstruction* (New York: Oxford University Press, 1992), 300–304; C. Vann Woodward, *Origins of the New South, 1877–1913* (Baton Rouge: Louisiana State University Press, 1951), 348–50.

35. Quoted in Andrews, *John Merrick*, 154–61, quotes on 158, 159, 160.

36. Ibid., 157, 161.

37. Ibid., 161.

38. *North Carolina Mutual* (company-sponsored newspaper), Nov. 1903, quoted in Weare, *Black Business in the New South*, 96.

39. *Atlanta Independent*, Dec. 20, 1913, quoted in Henderson, *Atlanta Life Insurance Company*, 35–39.

40. According to company historian Walter Weare, Merrick must have ventured more capital out of a belief that "to desert their policyholders was to discredit their people. For socially conscious black businessmen more was at stake than organizing an enterprise; they saw themselves organizing a people." Weare, *Black Business*, 48–49; Henderson, *Atlanta Life Insurance Company*, 16–19, 24.

41. Henderson, *Atlanta Life Insurance Company*, 24; Joel Williamson, *The Crucible of Race: Black-White Relations in the American South since Emancipation* (New York: Oxford University Press, 1984), 122–23.

42. On the widespread agreement about the need for economic self-help, see August Meier, *Negro Thought in America, 1880–1915: Racial Ideologies in the Age of Booker T. Washington* (Ann Arbor: University of Michigan Press, 1963), 42–58; and Louis R. Harlan, "Booker T. Washington and the National Negro Business League," in *Booker T. Washington in Perspective: Essays of Louis R. Harlan*, ed. Raymond Smock (Jackson: University Press of Mississippi, 1988); John Hope, "The Meaning of Business," in *The Proceedings of the Fourth Conference for the Study of Negro Problems, Held at Atlanta University, May 30–31, 1899*, reprinted in *The Atlanta University Publications* (New York: Arno Press, 1968), 56–60.

43. Alrutheus Taylor, *The Negro in Tennessee, 1865–1880* (Washington, D.C.: Associated Publishers, 1941), 157–58; Robert C. Kenzer, *Enterprising Southerners: Black Economic Success in North Carolina, 1865–1915* (Charlottesville: University Press of Virginia, 1989), 75–76; *Atlanta Independent*, Dec. 20, 1913, quoted in Henderson, *Atlanta Life Insurance Company*, 35–40; *North Carolina Mutual*, Nov. 1903, quoted in Weare, *Black Business in the New South*, 96.

CONCLUSION

1. "Address by Governor J. M. Broughton at the launching of the Liberty Ship *John Merrick . . . ,*" press release from the North Carolina Shipbuilding Company, July 12, 1943, "John Merrick: The Growth Years" file, C. C. Spaulding Papers, box 1, Special Collections, Perkins Library, Duke University, Durham, N.C.

2. Ibid.

Guide to Further Reading

White and black barbers have long been the subject of nostalgic books written for a popular audience. For lighthearted overviews, see Richard Wright Proctor, *The Barber's Shop*, rev. ed. (1883; reprint, Detroit: Singing Tree Press, 1971); William Andrews, *At the Sign of the Barber's Pole: Studies in Hirsute History* (1904; reprint, Detroit: Singing Tree Press, 1969); Richard Corson, *Fashions in Hair: The First Five Thousand Years*, 3rd ed. (London: Peter Owen, 1971); Vince Staten, *Do Bald Men Get Half-Price Haircuts? In Search of America's Great Barbershops* (New York: Simon & Schuster, 2001); and Craig Marberry, *Cuttin' Up: Wit and Wisdom from Black Barber Shops* (New York: Doubleday, 2005). Black-owned barbershops are examined as important forums for the present-day African American community in Melissa Victoria Harris-Lacewell, *Barbershops, Bibles, and BET: Everyday Talk and Black Political Thought* (Princeton: Princeton University Press, 2004).

To read what black barbers wrote themselves, see William Johnson, *William Johnson's Natchez: The Ante-Bellum Diary of a Free Negro*, ed. William Ransom Hogan and Edwin Adams Davis (1951; reprint, Baton Rouge: Louisiana State University Press, 1993); George Myers and James Ford Rhodes, *The Barber and the Historian: The Correspondence of George A. Myers and James Ford Rhodes, 1910–1923*, ed. John A. Garraty (Columbus: Ohio Historical Society, 1956); James Thomas, *From Tennessee Slave to St. Louis Entrepreneur: The Autobiography of James Thomas*, ed. Loren Schweninger (Columbia: University of Missouri Press, 1984); and Cyprian Clamorgan, *The Colored Aristocracy of St. Louis by Cyprian Clamorgan*, ed. Julie Winch (Columbia: University of Missouri Press, 1999).

Works by historians of free blacks and black property owners that pay significant attention to black barbers include Edwin Adams Davis and William Ransom Hogan, *The Barber of Natchez* (Baton Rouge: Louisiana State University Press, 1954); Luther Porter Jackson, *Free Negro Labor and Property Holding in Virginia, 1830–1860* (1942; reprint, New York: Antheneum, 1969); John H. Russell, *The Free Negro in Virginia, 1619–1865* (1913; reprint, New York: Negro Universities Press, 1969); Ira

Berlin, *Slaves Without Masters: The Free Negro in the Antebellum South* (New York: Vintage Books, 1976); Leonard P. Curry, *The Free Black in Urban America, 1800–1850: The Shadow of a Dream* (Chicago: University of Chicago Press, 1981); Leon Litwack, *North of Slavery: The Negro in the Free States, 1790–1860* (Chicago: University of Chicago Press, 1961); Loren Schweninger, *Black Property Owners in the South, 1790–1915* (Urbana: University of Illinois Press, 1990); and John Hope Franklin and Loren Schweninger, *In Search of the Promised Land: A Slave Family in the Old South* (New York: Oxford University Press, 2006). Two works that examine black barbers as slave owners are Loren Schweninger, "John Carruthers Stanly and the Anomaly of Black Slaveowning," *North Carolina Historical Review* 68 (Apr. 1990): 161–92; and Larry Koger, *Black Slaveowners: Free Black Slave Masters in South Carolina, 1790–1860* (Jefferson, N.C.: McFarland, 1985).

One reason the author began this study was to disprove assertions that African Americans lacked a tradition of success in business. For a discussion of how the negative views of black businessmen contributed to this negative assessment of black business, see Robert E. Weems, Jr., "Out of the Shadows: Business Enterprise and African American Historiography," *Business and Economic History* 26 (Fall 1997): 200–212. Notable works that have assisted a reappraisal of black business include Walter B. Weare, *Black Business in the New South: A Social History of the North Carolina Mutual Life Insurance Company* (1973; reprint, Durham, N.C.: Duke University Press, 1993); Juliet E. K. Walker, *Free Frank: A Black Pioneer on the Antebellum Frontier* (Lexington: University Press of Kentucky, 1983); Elsa Barkley Brown, "Womanist Consciousness: Maggie Lena Walker and the Independent Order of St. Luke," *Signs* 14 (Spring 1989): 610–33; Alexa Benson Henderson, *Atlanta Life Insurance Company: Guardian of Black Economic Dignity* (Tuscaloosa: University of Alabama Press, 1990); Richard A. Plater, *African American Entrepreneurship in Richmond, 1890–1940: The Story of R. C. Scott* (New York: Routledge, 1996); Robert E. Weems, Jr., *Black Business in the Black Metropolis: The Chicago Metropolitan Insurance Company, 1925–1985* (Bloomington: University of Indiana Press, 1996); Robert C. Kenzer, *Enterprising Southerners: Black Economic Success in North Carolina, 1865–1915* (Charlottesville: University Press of Virginia, 1997); Juliet E. K. Walker, *The History of Black Business in America: Capitalism, Race, Entrepreneurship* (New York: Macmillan Library Reference USA, 1998); and Kathy Peiss, *Hope in a Jar: The Making of America's Beauty Culture* (New York: Henry Holt, 1998).

Work and work culture defined a great deal of the lives of black barbers. Other studies that examine positive occupational identities of African Americans include Paul Gilje and Howard Rock, "'Sweep O! Sweep O!': African-American

Chimney Sweeps and Citizenship in the New Nation," *William and Mary Quarterly*, 3rd ser., 51 (July 1994): 507–19; Tera W. Hunter, *To 'Joy My Freedom: Southern Black Women's Lives and Labors after the Civil War* (Cambridge: Harvard University Press, 1997); W. Jeffrey Bolster, *Black Jacks: African American Seamen in the Age of Sail* (Cambridge: Harvard University Press, 1997); and Juliet A. Willett, *Permanent Waves: The Making of the American Beauty Shop* (New York: New York University Press, 2000). For overviews of the dismal employment opportunities for African Americans before the civil rights movement, see William H. Harris, *The Harder We Run: Black Workers since the Civil War* (New York: Oxford University Press, 1982); and Jacqueline Jones, *American Work: Four Centuries of Black and White Labor* (New York: W. W. Norton, 1998). Two fascinating books about the colonial period that link acculturation and work culture are Gerald Mullin, *Flight and Rebellion: Slave Resistance in Eighteenth-Century Virginia* (New York: Oxford University Press, 1972); and James Sidbury, *Ploughshares into Swords: Race, Rebellion, and Identity in Gabriel's Virginia, 1730–1810* (New York: Cambridge University Press, 1997).

Black barbers often disagreed with other prominent members of the African-American community, and a number of recent works provide historical context for these controversies. Some of these books focus on the development and pitfalls of ideas about racial uplift. For a perceptive discussion of respectability and its role in early black leadership strategies, see two articles by James Brewer Stewart, "The Emergence of Racial Modernity and the Rise of the White North, 1790–1848," *Journal of the Early Republic* 18 (Spring 1998): 186–93; "Modernizing 'Difference': The Political Meanings of Color in the Free States, 1776–1840," *Journal of the Early Republic* 19 (Winter 1999): 694–700. For the antebellum years, see Joanne Pope Melish, *Disowning Slavery: Gradual Emancipation and Race in New England, 1780–1860* (Ithaca: Cornell University Press, 1998); Patrick Rael, *Black Identity and Black Protest in the Antebellum North* (Chapel Hill: University of North Carolina Press, 2002); Leslie M. Harris, *In the Shadow of Slavery: African Americans in New York City, 1626–1863* (Chicago: University of Chicago Press, 2003). For the late nineteenth and early twentieth century, see August Meier, *Negro Thought in America, 1880–1915: Racial Ideologies in the Age of Booker T. Washington* (Ann Arbor: University of Michigan Press, 1963); and Kevin K. Gaines, *Uplifting the Race: Black Leadership, Politics, and Culture in the Twentieth Century* (Chapel Hill: University of North Carolina Press, 1996).

Disputes over class status within the African American community influenced the debate over racial uplift. For a persuasive argument that members of the lower middle class have a distinct identity, see Arno J. Mayer, "The Lower Middle Class as Historical Problem," *Journal of Modern History* 47 (Sept. 1975): 409–36. Scholars who place class at the center of their studies include Armstead Robinson, "'Plans Dat Comed from God': Institution Building and the Emergence of Black Leadership in Reconstruction Memphis," in *Toward a New South? Studies in Post–Civil War Southern Communities*, ed. Orville C. Burton and Robert C. McMath, Jr. (Westport, Conn.: Greenwood Press, 1982); Thomas Holt, *Black over White: Negro Political Leadership in South Carolina during Reconstruction* (Urbana: University of Illinois Press, 1977); Willard Gatewood, *Aristocrats of Color: The Black Elite, 1880–1920* (Bloomington: University of Indiana Press, 1990).

The goal of upholding black manhood often shaped the policies adopted by leaders and reveals much about black identity in the nineteenth century. For more research on black conceptions of masculinity, see James Oliver Horton and Lois E. Horton, "Violence, Protest, and Identity: Black Manhood in Antebellum America," in James Oliver Horton, *Free People of Color: Inside of the African American Community* (Washington, D.C.: Smithsonian Institution Press, 1993); Glenda Elizabeth Gilmore, *Gender and Jim Crow: Women and the Politics of White Supremacy in North Carolina, 1896–1920* (Chapel Hill: University of North Carolina Press, 1996); Maggie Montesinos Sale, *The Slumbering Volcano: American Slave Ship Revolts and the Production of Rebellious Masculinity* (Durham, N.C.: Duke University Press, 1997); Jane Dailey, *Before Jim Crow: The Politics of Race in Postemancipation Virginia* (Chapel Hill: University of North Carolina Press, 2000). For an insightful discussion of the different paradigms scholars have used to understand black masculinity as well as a nuanced interpretation of the intersection of gender and class, see Martin Summers, *The Black Middle Class and the Transformation of Masculinity, 1900–1930* (Chapel Hill: University of North Carolina Press, 2004), 12–14. Gail Bederman makes a powerful argument that studying the concept of manhood as understood in the late nineteenth century helps explain the deteriorating race relations of that era in *Manliness and Civilization: A Cultural History of Gender and Race in the United States, 1880–1917* (Chicago: University of Chicago Press, 1995).

Part of what makes the story of black barbers intrinsically interesting is the light it sheds on notions of race and the state of race relations from the colonial era to the early twentieth century. Although the books on these latter subjects would fill many shelves, good overviews include Winthrop Jordan, *White over Black: American Attitudes towards the Negro, 1550–1812* (Chapel Hill: University of North Carolina Press, 1968); George M. Fredrickson, *Black Image in the White Mind: The Debate on Afro-American Character and Destiny, 1817–1914* (New York: Harper Torchbooks, 1972); Joel Williamson, *The Crucible of Race: Black-White Relations in the American South since Emancipation* (New York: Oxford University Press, 1984); Ronald Takaki, *Iron Cages: Race and Culture in Nineteenth-Century America*, rev. ed. (New York: Oxford University Press, 2000).

Eighteenth and nineteenth-century black barbers depended on white guardians for protection, and these white friends viewed these relationships through the lense of patriarchy during the colonial period and of paternalism afterwards. On patriarchy, see Philip Morgan, "Three Planters and Their Slaves: Perspectives on Slavery in Virginia, South Carolina, and Jamaica, 1750–1790," in *Race and Family in the Colonial South*, ed. Winthrop D. Jordan and Shelia L. Skemp (Jackson: University Press of Mississippi, 1987); and Jeffrey Robert Young, *Domesticating Slavery: The Master Class in Georgia and South Carolina, 1670–1837* (Chapel Hill: University of North Carolina Press, 1999). The literature on paternalism is extensive, but the classic introduction is Eugene Genovese, *Roll, Jordan, Roll: The World the Slaves Made* (New York: Vintage Books, 1972). Slave owners embraced paternalism because of particular historical circumstances; Willie Lee Rose examined this context in "The Domestication of Domestic Slavery," in her *Slavery and Freedom*, ed. William W. Freehling (New York: Oxford University Press, 1982). For a critical view of slave-owner paternalism, see Clarence E. Walker, "Massa's New Clothes: A Critique of Eugene D. Genovese on Southern Society, Master-Slave Relations, and Slave Behavior," in his *Deromanticizing Black History: Critical Essays and Reappraisals* (Knoxville: University Press of Kentucky, 1991). An insightful study of the transition from paternalism under slavery to patronage in freedom in the post-Emancipation South is Peggy G. Hargis, "For the Love of Place: Paternalism and Patronage in the Georgia Lowcountry, 1865–1898," *Journal of Southern History* 70 (Nov. 2004): 825–64.

To a large extent, nineteenth-century black barbers' success was due to their understanding that white men needed black men as a reference point for their identity. For discussions of how republican ideology shaped this dynamic, see Roland Berthoff, "Conventional Mentality: Free Blacks, Women, and Business Corporations as Unequal Persons, 1820–1870," *Journal of American History* 76 (Dec. 1989): 753–84; David R. Roediger, *The Wages of Whiteness: Race and the Making of the American Working Class* (New York: Verso, 1991); and Stephanie McCurry, "The Two Faces of Republicanism: Gender and Pro-Slavery Politics in Antebellum South Carolina," *Journal of American History* (Mar. 1992): 1245–64. Eric Lott drew attention to how antebellum white men stole a piece of black culture in *Love and Theft: Blackface Minstrelsy and the American Working Class* (New York: Oxford University Press, 1993). Other studies of "whiteness" that touch on issues raised in this book include Noel Ignatiev, *How the Irish Became White*

(New York: Routledge, 1995); and Grace Elizabeth Hale, *Making Whiteness: The Culture of Segregation in the South, 1890–1940* (New York: Pantheon Books, 1998). For widely disparate assessments of these studies, see Eric Arnesen, "Whiteness and the Historians' Imagination," *International Labor and Working-Class History* 60 (Fall 2001), 3–32; and Peter Kolchin, "Whiteness Studies: The New History of Race in America," *Journal of American History* 89 (June 2002): 154–73.

The story of black barbers covers a broad swath of the African American experience. Fortunately, there are sophisticated and readable overviews of the historical periods covered in this book. See Ira Berlin, *Generations of Captivity: A History of African-American Slaves* (Cambridge: Belknap Press of the Harvard University Press, 2003); Eric Foner, *Reconstruction: America's Unfinished Revolution, 1863–1877* (New York: Harper & Row, 1988); Leon Litwack, *Trouble in Mind: Black Southerners in the Age of Jim Crow* (New York: Knopf, 1998).

Index